Fleet Admiral Halsey in 1945. Courtesy of the Naval Historical Center

ADMIRAL "BULL" HALSEY

THE LIFE AND WARS OF THE NAVY'S MOST CONTROVERSIAL COMMANDER

JOHN WUKOVITS

palgrave
macmillan

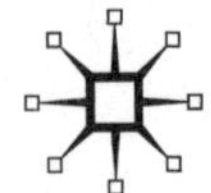

ADMIRAL "BULL" HALSEY

First published in 2010 by PALGRAVE MACMILLAN® in the US - a division of St. Martin's Press LLC, 175 Fifth Avenue, New York, NY 10010.

Where this book is distributed in the UK, Europe and the rest of the world, this is by Palgrave Macmillan, a division of Macmillan Publishers Limited, registered in England, company number 785998, of Houndmills, Basingstoke, Hampshire RG21 6XS.

Palgrave Macmillan is the global academic imprint of the above companies and has companies and representatives throughout the world.

ISBN: 978-0-230-60284-7

Wukovits, John F., 1944–
Admiral "Bull" Halsey : the life and wars of the navy's most controversial commander / John Wukovits.
p. cm.
ISBN 978-0-230-60284-7 (hardback)
1. Halsey, William Frederick, 1882–1959. 2. Admirals—United States—Biography. 3. United States. Navy—Biography. 4. World War, 1939–1945—Naval operations, American. 5. World War, 1939–1945—Campaigns—Pacific Area. I. Title.
E746.H3W855 2010
359.0092—dc22
[B]

2009050130

A catalogue record of the book is available from the British Library.

Design by Letra Libre

First edition: July 2010

10 9 8 7 6 5 4 3 2 1
Printed in the United States of America.

To my daughter, Karen,
a constant source of pride

TABLE OF CONTENTS

PREFACE

I was first exposed to Admiral William F. Halsey during my undergraduate career, when a professor asked us to read a book of our choosing on modern U.S. history. After scanning the list of acceptable titles, I selected Halsey's autobiography and settled in to read a fascinating account of the man and his wars.

Many historians have cast a spotlight on Halsey through the years, though they have focused primarily on Halsey's disasters—his actions during typhoons, and his tactical behavior during the 1944 Battle of Leyte Gulf. In concentrating on those aspects, however, historians allow Halsey's real or supposed faults to dwarf his other contributions for which, on their own, he merits significant admiration. During the war, Halsey was as much a home-front hero as any commander who served in the Pacific. One need only read the contemporary newspapers and magazines to observe Halsey's profound impact on his fellow countrymen. His popularity rivaled the adulation later received by astronauts and film stars.

Halsey is neither hero nor villain. He is a mixture of both, which in the final assessment only makes him human. When the scales are balanced, however, Halsey deserves recognition as one of the Pacific War's great figures, a man whose exploits deserve a place with Chester Nimitz, Douglas MacArthur, and other great military personalities.

One note about Halsey's two books is required. While it is tempting to draw material from the autobiography Halsey published in 1947, I have leaned heavily on the personal memoir he wrote in preparation for the autobiography. The almost 700 typewritten pages of reminiscences are often poorly crafted and sometimes confusing, but they offer a compelling glimpse into the admiral's thinking and what he considered crucial. The memoir has been overlooked for too long. Throughout this book I refer to the 1947 book as the autobiography and his unpublished reminiscences as his memoir.

Many individuals aided my efforts in conducting research for this biography. Archivists at the Library of Congress, the National Archives, the Chester Nimitz Library at the United States Naval Academy, and the Franklin D. Roosevelt Library helped smooth the path. William T. Barr and other members of the USS *Enterprise* Association offered reminiscences and photographs of a man they recall fondly. My agent, Jim Hornfischer, brought a unique combination of expertise as both a literary agent and a skilled author of World War II volumes. The constructive comments of Alessandra Bastagli, my editor at Palgrave Macmillan, as well as of Palgrave Macmillan editors Colleen Lawrie and Yasmin Mathew, improved the manuscript.

As always, I will never forget the wise advice and deep friendship of two men who helped my writing career move from its infancy. My adviser at the University of Notre Dame, Dr. Bernard Norling, and historian/biographer Tom Buell gave of themselves in many ways so that my dreams of writing a book could come true. I consider myself fortunate in knowing two such kindly, beautiful human beings. Sadly, both are now gone, but I will cherish their memories with each word I craft.

I also enjoyed the support of loved ones throughout the process. My three daughters, Amy, Julie, and Karen, never let me forget how proud they are of my efforts. The thought that my four grandchildren, Matthew, Megan, Emma, and Kaitlyn, might benefit from the example of individuals about whom I write keeps me eager to continue my endeavors. My older brother, Tom, a naval aviator during the Vietnam War, lent a supportive ear as well as the helpful comments that only one in the military can render. The memories of my parents, Tom and Grace, as well as of my younger brother, Fred, prod me to produce a worthy work. Terri Faitel, my fiancée, scrutinizes my manuscript with the same thoroughness for which she is known as a mathematics scholar of national repute. To all I give my deepest thanks.

John F. Wukovits
Trenton, Michigan
December 1, 2009

INTRODUCTION

"WHEN YOU WENT IN, THE JAPS WENT OUT"

Admiral William F. Halsey was no stranger to momentous occasions, but he could recall few in his forty-one-year career in the United States Navy that matched the emotion of standing on the bridge of his flagship, USS *Missouri,* then floating off the Japanese coast that August 15, 1945, afternoon. After almost four years of warfare against a skilled enemy, aircraft aboard Halsey's carriers remained still and guns lay silent. Victory, at last, had arrived.

Halsey, a commander filled with pride in his nation's efforts and his men's sacrifices, collected his thoughts in the moments before delivering a victory speech that would be broadcast to crews throughout his massive Third Fleet and to citizens in the United States. He now addressed a fleet that would have been unimaginable in the war's early days, when he had collected the remnants of a navy that had been savagely mauled at Pearl Harbor and raced Pacific waters stemming the enemy's advance. One of the few admirals who could claim that he commanded ships at sea on both the war's opening day and its last, Halsey spoke of his 1942 raids against enemy-held land, when "with nothing but indomitable courage and hope to support us, we left our mark on a cruel and treacherous enemy. We paved the way—we blazed the trail—for the overwhelming victories that have followed."

That afternoon, the admiral recounted his first visit, in late 1942, as commander in the South Pacific to the Marines on Guadalcanal, who, though exhausted from unrelenting combat against a merciless opponent, fought gallantly. "With little to start with, we bore the brunt of the Japanese easternmost offensive in the Solomon Islands. We stopped them dead in their tracks."

He described how his Third Fleet rose from the ashes of Pearl Harbor to become the mightiest conglomeration of sea power in history. Armed with that potent arsenal, Halsey pursued the Japanese Imperial Navy until its tattered survivors hid in harbors and bays, hoping to evade the guns and bombs and bullets that Halsey inevitably brought.

Pausing for a moment, Halsey, reflective of what had become a cornerstone trait of his command, spoke of the affection he felt for the men serving under him. "I am one of the oldest, if not the oldest, living naval officers actively engaged in any combat zone in the world," he said. "You shall always occupy a special and honored space in my mind and heart. We have been through this trying time together. We have shared the good, we have shared the bad. We are brothers—blooded by our active participation in combat operations in an unprecedented naval war."

Halsey did not want to leave without giving credit to those upon whom the burdens of his commands fell. "There are no words to a sailorman more expressive of the highest commendation than the Navy's 'Well Done.' With great pride, gratitude, and thankfulness, I give to each and every one of you my sincere and heartfelt 'Well Done.'" He assured his men that, "To you belongs the credit and I shall do all within my limited powers to see you receive it."[1]

It was no surprise that Halsey directed so much of his victory speech to the young men, some yet in their teenage years, who comprised his crews. As one top-ranking officer concluded, while some commanders are known as an admiral's admiral, throughout the Navy, Halsey carried a reputation as being a sailor's admiral.

That mutual fondness, however, reveals only a part of Halsey's essence. For four long years of war Halsey was also the citizens' admiral, a leader whose aggressiveness sated a nationwide vengeance sparked by the enemy's startling December 7, 1941, assault on Pearl Harbor. In towns large and small, from his New Jersey birthplace to the West Coast, people related to the man's stirring words and swift actions. Young and old, men and women, adopted Halsey as theirs, for at a time when the nation most needed a battler on the front lines, Halsey stood tall.

A 1944 note from a man called Owen Cedarburg of Bonne Terre, Missouri—one of the thousands of letters from citizens that inundated Halsey's flag bridge during the war—reflected the fondness with which the nation embraced Halsey. Rejuvenated by Halsey's valiant actions in the Pacific, Cedarburg wrote, "Ever since I heard of your exploits I have liked you. I like your seagoing looks and the manner in which you fight and just about everything else." He added that, "when you went in the Japs went out."[2]

CHAPTER 1

"I HAD NO OTHER THOUGHT EXCEPT GOING INTO THE NAVY"

William F. Halsey came by his combativeness honestly, for belligerence had nourished a family tree spotted with sea dogs and sinners. Though he counted spirits tame and bold among his forbearers—"On one side I had a lot of Puritans and on the other a hard drinking, hard living set from around New York"—the latter clearly caught his fancy. Halsey loved to relate anecdotes of those ancestors he described as "seafarers and adventurers, big, violent men, impatient of the law, and prone to strong drink and strong language."[1]

Halsey could have been talking of himself, for he exhibited those same traits throughout his life. He loved action the way previous generations of Halseys did. He resorted to profanity and drink, and when he thought of the sea, he thought of his ancestors' manner of seamanship—sailors chanting sea ditties as they labored while sails snapped in the wind, and audacious captains staring adventure and danger in the face. Men were men, which to Halsey meant going where the fight and the grog flowed freely.

He felt a special kinship with individuals of strong, almost reckless, will combined with a penchant for the bottle. Captain John Halsey of Massachusetts especially intrigued the future admiral. After attacking

French shipping for the British as a privateer during Queen Anne's War (1702–1713), Captain Halsey continued his raiding in peacetime as an independent buccaneer. William Halsey later wrote, "I enjoy reading how his little brigantine once took on four ships together and captured two of them, with $250,000 in booty."[2]

Halsey could even point with pride to the page mentioning his ancestor in a 1926 book on brigands, *The History of the Lives and Bloody Exploits of the Most Noted Pirates.* According to the volume, when John Halsey died of a fever in Madagascar in 1716, fellow sailors revered him so highly that they placed his sword and pistol in the coffin with the body and mounted a 46-gun-salute to honor the 46-year-old veteran of the seas. The book concluded that Captain Halsey "was brave in his person, courteous to all his prisoners, lived beloved, and died regretted by his own people."[3]

A century later, Captain Eliphalet Halsey added to family sea lore when in 1815 he became the first to sail a Long Island whaler around South America's Cape Horn into the Pacific. The Halseys had thus made a name on the Seven Seas in both the eighteenth and nineteenth centuries. The current Halsey hoped that he, too, could record similar deeds in the twentieth century.

Halsey's paternal grandfather, Charles Henry Halsey, was both a lawyer and an Episcopal minister. He married the daughter of the president of Columbia College, Eliza Gracie King, and they had either six or seven children depending upon which person or record you believe. The youngest, William Frederick Halsey, became the admiral's father. While still in his early teens, William mentioned his desire to enter the Naval Academy. With the assistance of a family friend, he received an appointment to Annapolis and graduated in 1873.

In 1880 William Halsey married his childhood friend Anne Brewster, a direct descendant of William Brewster, the famed spiritual leader of Plymouth Colony. On October 30, 1882, the couple welcomed their firstborn child—William Frederick Halsey Jr., who was born in Elizabeth, New Jersey.

While he inherited a love of the sea from his father, Halsey's mother proved to be the dominant influence in his life. The Navy might dispatch her husband to foreign ports—Halsey lived in six cities before he reached his teenage years—but she held the family together, dispensing advice to young William and his sister, Deborah, and making ends meet on the miserly income provided officers in the 1880s and 1890s. "She always had very sterling qualities of right and wrong," he noted in his memoirs, "and God only knows how she raised two children on $200 a month which we lived on for much of my childhood."[4]

After residing for two years in Elizabeth, New Jersey, while working at a hydrographic office, Lieutenant Halsey was assigned to duty aboard a survey vessel based in California. Anne Halsey remained behind to pack the family belongings, then accompanied the children for the grueling trip to California. The trio first boarded a transport that took them down the U.S. East Coast, then switched to a train to endure a sweltering crossing of the Isthmus of Panama, a dreaded stretch during which Anne constantly worried that her son and daughter would contract the deadly yellow fever. Once the family reached the west side of Panama, they boarded a second transport for the sea voyage north to California.

Despite the rigors of this journey, the younger Halsey, not yet of school age, loved the excitement offered by life at sea. His inquisitiveness prodded him into impromptu scouting expeditions, excursions that not only broke the monotony that came with lengthy voyages but also permitted him to inspect what lurked in the ship's hold. On one of his outings he suddenly disappeared, causing a frantic Anne to worry that he had fallen overboard, but a thorough search by the ship's crew unearthed the youth below, watching the ship's butcher kill livestock for the day's meal. "It is reported that they found me with my shoes and stockings off wading in blood,"[5] remembered Halsey of his youthful adventure.

The family eventually settled in Coronado, California, a short distance from the Mexican border. There, Halsey entered kindergarten, where his boisterous nature often clashed with the classroom's strictures and his fellow students' taunts. His body seemed tailor made for heckling: a powerful upper torso featuring a barrel chest, muscled arms, and oversized head balanced precariously on short, stocky legs. Classmates delighted in calling him "Billy Big Head" in attempts to provoke a reaction. Being more Bowery Boy than altar boy, Halsey willingly obliged.

The sunny sojourn in California ended in 1891 when the Navy transferred Lieutenant Halsey to Annapolis, Maryland, to teach physics and chemistry. The young Halsey wasted little time finding trouble on the quaint city streets. He joined a neighborhood football team that called themselves "Little Potatoes" because "we considered ourselves hard to peel,"[6] and he received a spanking from his father after breaking a string of street lights with his slingshot.

Halsey loved Annapolis. Ships cluttered the waters, sailors prowled the city streets, and in the midst, sparkling and shiny on its waterfront perch, stood the Academy. The more he absorbed the salty atmosphere, the more determined Halsey became to follow his father into the Naval Academy.

He selected a challenging path, for rarely in his school career did he let academics interrupt his fun. If classmates needed help in math or history, they looked elsewhere, but if they wanted someone to fire up the football team or to guarantee an amusing afternoon or evening, Halsey was their person.

"MADAM, YOUR PRAYERS HAVE BEEN ANSWERED"

As he approached his fifteenth birthday, the earliest a young man could then enter the Naval Academy, Halsey's interest in attending Annapolis intensified. "I had no other thought except going into the Navy," he recalled. "I always intended going in the Navy ever since I can remember."[7] The youth faced a monumental problem, however—since his father's frequent relocations had constantly uprooted the family, he lacked the necessary political connections to gain a Congressional nomination. Undeterred, the young hopeful wrote every politician he could think of—including the president of the United States, William McKinley.

The fourteen-year-old Halsey pleaded his case in a January 26, 1897, letter to the president. "I want to ask you, if you have not already promised all your appointments to the Naval Academy that you will give me one." He explained that the appointment from his district had already been filled, that his father currently served as a naval officer, and added, "I know people do not like to give important positions such as this is away without knowing the person they are giving them to. But then you know that a naval officer would not keep his position long if he were not the right kind of man." Hoping to impress the president, Halsey mentioned a family connection with the current secretary of the Navy, then turned to sentiment. "I have been with my father on shore and on ship board a great deal, and have always wanted to enter the Navy." Pulling out all stops, Halsey ended the letter with a hearty helping of flattery. "It is almost needless to congratulate you on your grand victory [the presidential election of 1896] which every good American sees is for the best. It has been told you so many times by men it is hardly worth while for us boys to say it."[8]

The letter, remarkable for someone just entering high school, nevertheless failed to provoke a response from the president. Disheartened but not defeated, Halsey penned more letters to officials. When in the following summer his father returned from four years of duty in the Far East with the Asiatic Fleet, he added his entreaties, but lacking the appropriate connections, all failed. Lieutenant Halsey even enrolled his son in one of the numerous preparatory schools that existed solely to ready boys to take the harsh Academy entrance examinations, but that tactic also fell short of drawing an appointment. Near desperation, the family sent their son to medical school, hoping the step might permit easier entrance into the Navy as a medical officer. So in the fall of 1899, Halsey entered the medical school at the University of Virginia. But try as he might—and he never tried all that hard—Halsey could not put the classroom above his favorite pastimes. As he did throughout his military career, he applied himself to what he thought was important and avoided what he considered frivolous. Histology class lacked appeal, especially when fun and football lurked. The real Halsey appeared on the football field, a legal arena for the roughhousing and aggression he so loved. Though Halsey lacked the size and talent of a first-stringer, the coaches loved his spirit and recklessness. He charged through practices and games as if each play determined victory or defeat.

Halsey received a break in 1900 when Congress passed a bill permitting the president to name five additional appointees to the Academy. Anne Halsey sought the aid of family friend Edgar Grigg, then New Jersey's attorney general. Grigg escorted Anne to the White House where, according to her son, she "camped out in President McKinley's office until she secured a promise of an appointment for me." The president agreed to meet with Mrs. Halsey, who told McKinley of her desire to see her son follow his father into the Navy and that, "I have been praying. I have been praying very sincerely." McKinley replied, "Madam, your prayers have been answered."[9]

With only the entrance exams standing between him and Annapolis, Halsey immersed himself in textbooks for one of the few times in his student life. "I had to cram like the devil to pass the entrance examinations, but I managed to and was sworn in on July 7, 1900."[10]

THE SPECTACULAR SHOWING by the U.S. Navy during the Spanish-American War of 1898, in which its exploits handed the nation a ready-made Pacific empire, created both a feeling of pride in the Navy and a desire among politicians and the people to expand American interests around the globe. The elevation in 1901 of Theodore Roosevelt to the presidency handed the Navy a worthy ally. The young executive had avidly read Captain Alfred Thayer Mahan's seminal *The Influence of Sea Power upon History, 1600–1783,* and at age twenty-four he had written a highly regarded book about the Navy during the War of 1812. Roosevelt quickly turned his persuasive powers to convincing Congress to approve funds for one battleship a year and for expansion at the Naval Academy.

It was during this time of transition and expansion that Halsey entered the Academy. His was the last class to contain fewer than one hundred members, and after his group, the students would be called midshipmen, the term employed by Great Britain's Royal Navy, rather than naval cadets.

Starkness and rigidity defined the Academy. Founded in 1845, the institution rests on the shores of the Chesapeake Bay, which provides a perfect location for training seamen. Cadets lived in spartan rooms that contained wooden table desks, unpainted chairs, a wash basin, and iron beds. A book titled *Regulations of the United States Naval Academy* listed hundreds of infractions in twenty-two pages of small print.

Halsey quickly made a mark at the Academy—as always, outside the classroom rather than inside. Fellow cadets continued the process begun by Halsey's elementary school tormentors by teasing him about his immense head, but updated the criticism by stating that he "looks like a figurehead of Neptune."[11] A photograph of the time shows that a heavy jaw dominated the lower half of his face, while thick eyebrows camouflaged deep-set, piercing blue eyes. Neatly combed hair swept to the right across his forehead, underneath which beamed a face exuding confidence.

Halsey, now grown to six feet, encountered few difficulties adapting to the rigid atmosphere. Whenever a social event occurred, the fun-loving Halsey could be found directly in the middle, laughing and slapping classmates on the back. He considered demerits for infractions a necessary evil to be tolerated, not a deterrent to fear. In his second year alone he amassed an alarming number of demerits, usually for offenses such as smoking, being late for formations, or talking in the ranks. Not surprisingly, at a time when 4.0 was perfect and 2.5 was considered barely passing, Halsey floundered in the lower half of his class, often perilously approaching failing grades.

Halsey could not comfortably operate in a rigid curriculum that stifled individual initiative and creativity, qualities he had in abundance. Since instructors lacked experience in classroom skills, having typically been career naval officers rather than educators, they usually taught in the same fashion as their predecessors, with a heavy emphasis on memorization. For a free spirit such as Halsey, who would have better thrived in an environment that challenged pre-existing ideas and formulated fresh ways to examine problems, the Academy's dry tedium was oppressive.

The only time Halsey's ears perked up was when classroom discussion focused on one topic. With U.S. possessions scanning the Pacific from Hawaii to the Philippines, instructors often debated strategy with their next likely enemy—Japan. They also pointed to British Admiral Horatio Nelson as the model officer to emulate. Nelson, said Halsey's teachers, best combined the attributes of triumphant leaders—the willingness to fight, an absolute trust in the officers under him, and a concern for the welfare of his men.

A controversy that rocked the Navy in the early years of the century would later benefit Halsey. Following the spectacular naval defeat over Spain in 1898 two American commanders—Commodore Winfield Scott Schley and Acting Rear Admiral William T. Sampson—distastefully vied for the honors that ensued. Their vehement arguments, in which each man contended that he had been in charge for the crucial victory in Santiago, Cuba, split the Navy into two camps, provoked an official court of inquiry, and turned the Navy into a laughingstock in the nation's newspapers. Only President Theodore Roosevelt's edict to end the quarreling prevented the feud from becoming worse.

Though Halsey took little apparent notice of the Sampson-Schley controversy, another midshipman at the Academy did. One year behind Halsey, future Fleet Admiral Chester W. Nimitz hated watching his beloved Navy torn apart. He vowed that if he ever became a commander, he would never allow a similar controversy to demoralize the Navy as this one had done. In 1944, Nimitz would face such a predicament involving Halsey.

Football led the list of his extracurricular activities. The coaches admired his grit, which even monstrous athletes could not break, but a lack of talent and size confined Halsey to the bench until an injury to the starting fullback handed him the opportunity to play. Halsey held the spot for the next two years.

One activity that held Halsey's attention was the annual summer cruise. Rather than some obscure piece of information to be memorized for a classroom examination, summer cruises offered Halsey a practical application of knowledge, something tangible that could be used by a seaman. Let others scrutinize past campaigns and memorize elaborate equations—he would take the open seas and action any day.

He called the cruises "a delight" and claimed they turned cadets from "landlubbers to real sailormen."[12] Veteran officers and sailors passed along the intricacies of life at sea to Halsey and his classmates, from the engines in the ship's bowels that powered the craft to the signal flags high above. The ships were floating classrooms, but Halsey relished the experience, for here he was doing what he had come to the Academy to learn. He rapidly excelled in navigation, surpassing the performances of fellow cadets who routinely posted better grades in the classroom.

Like every other cadet, Halsey spent half his time on a steamship, normally the battleship USS *Indiana* or USS *Massachusetts,* and the other on a sailing ship, usually the USS *Chesapeake.* The leadership talents that had lain dormant in an academic setting burst into life on the water, and Halsey steadily received more responsibilities with each cruise. By the time of his third and last cruise, Halsey had been placed in charge of the main top, the second highest job that could be given a cadet in his final year. Classroom instructors may not have noticed anything spectacular about Halsey, but superiors at sea spotted inherent leadership talent. Halsey appeared to have a natural gift for command.

During one of the cruises, filled with a sense of importance over finally being at sea, Halsey and a group of friends decided to get tattoos. They headed to the ship's unofficial tattoo artist, a sailor then in the brig for drunkenness, who agreed to etch an anchor onto their shoulders. The anchor's chain formed an "04," Halsey's graduation class, with a red "USNA" perched on the crown. "It was hard to tell which was filthier," Halsey wrote of the sailor who drew his tattoo, "he or his instruments, and Lord knows why we all didn't die of blood poisoning."[13]

"I WISH YOU ALL THE LUCK IN THE WORLD"

Halsey's 1904 yearbook, *Lucky Bag,* described him the way his fellow students viewed the budding officer—full of life and ready for action. The yearbook mentioned that Halsey, nicknamed Willie or Pudge, was involved in as many activities as anyone in the class and held offices in numerous clubs. For his efforts, Halsey received the Thompson Trophy Cup, awarded each year to the first-classman who most promoted athletics. "A real old salt,"[14] the *Lucky Bag* called him.

In order to hasten new officers into Roosevelt's refurbished Navy, Halsey's class graduated on February 2, 1904, rather than in June. His ranking of forty-third out of the sixty-two who graduated to become passed midshipmen was far from illustrious. Other than his successes in the summer cruises, he had achieved little to mark him as a man to watch. At the graduation ceremony the Chief Master at Arms at the Academy, a gruff ex-Marine sergeant whose ferocious demeanor kept every cadet at arm's length, shook Halsey's hand and said, "Mr. Halsey, I wish you all the luck in the world, but you can never be as good a naval officer as you[r] dad."[15]

Halsey had a chance to disprove the chief's opinion with his first post—duty aboard the battleship USS *Missouri* (BB–11), one of the most coveted spots in the Navy. Since the ship was due to leave for Cuba for winter training only five days after graduation, Halsey had to forego the normal one-month leave granted graduates and race to join the ship. Fittingly, forty-one years later Halsey would end his seagoing career aboard another vessel bearing the same name.

Halsey's first night at sea, where he served the mid-watch on the bridge during a stormy night, severely tested the young officer. He battled nerves, the uncertainty of a new duty, and the elements. "I didn't like anything about the Navy after those first four hours up there in the cold, the rain, and the blizzard and my trying to do something and not knowing what to do or what I was supposed to do."[16]

From Cuba, the battleship steamed to Pensacola, Florida, for target practice, where an incident occurred that affected Halsey for the rest of his life. On Friday, April 13, 1904, while he served as junior officer of the deck, a deadly explosion in the 12-inch gun turret during target practice killed thirty-six men. Upon hearing the eruption, Halsey glanced behind to see a sheet of fire shoot several hundred feet into the sky from the top hatch. Flames engulfed one enlisted man standing on the turret, who either jumped or was thrown overboard by the explosion. Halsey watched helplessly as the man, shrouded in flames, disappeared beneath the waves.

A second blast, stronger than the first, rattled the ship when burning powder plunged down the turret well into the handling room and ignited four 90-pound powder bags. The fierce explosions blackened the handling room and roasted to death the men working there. Sailors rushed in with fire equipment, but the damage had already been done.

Superiors ordered Halsey to investigate the scene as soon as the fires had been extinguished. The task, which required him to wade in the hip-deep water littered with charred bodies and debris, sickened him. "I went down to the handling room and it was rather a God-awful sight. The water by that time was somewheres [sic] between the waist and knees. There were bodies floating around in this water."[17]

The aftermath was just as traumatic for Halsey. Crew members carried the wounded, many horridly burned, to sick bay, and gently rested the dead on the superstructure deck. The ship immediately turned back to Pensacola, where every available civilian physician and a large volunteer citizen group rushed over to assist. Assigned to supervise the undertakers that came aboard that night to prepare the bodies for burial, Halsey faced another unsettling duty that was compounded the next day when, still gaining his sea bearings as a neophyte officer fresh out of the Academy, he stood with the surviving crew as the ship conducted a mass funeral for the thirty-six men who had perished.

Halsey never shook the effects of that tragic day. He wrote forty-three years later that the incident "still looms monstrous in my memory. Indeed, it has cast a shadow over the rest of my life. I dread the thirteenth of every month, and if it falls on Friday, my apprehension almost paralyzes me."[18]

THE NEXT TWO autumns Halsey returned to safer and more comfortable ground when he was detached for temporary duty at the Academy as assistant backfield coach for the football team. Shortly after the 1905 pigskin season ended, Halsey received orders for duty aboard the *Don Juan de Austria,* a gunboat salvaged from Manila Bay after the United States defeated Spain in 1898. The vessel had orders to hasten to the Caribbean as a deterrent to European nations who were considering dispatching military forces to the Dominican Republic to collect money owed to them by the bankrupt nation.

President Roosevelt intended to prevent other nations from encroaching upon a section of the world that he considered an American sphere. Roosevelt cautioned the European countries that only the United States would intervene in the Dominican Republic, but he promised that the money owed would be repaid. He sent military forces to the nation to take over the customs collecting and set aside more than half of the receipts to pay off the debts. For six months, Halsey and the *Don Juan de Austria* steamed Samana Bay in the Dominican Republic, doing nothing but collecting customs and showing the flag, a duty Halsey called "stupefying in its monotony."[19]

One proud interlude occurred when the passed midshipman became an ensign on February 2, 1906. The promotion gave him added benefits in case of injury, a raise in pay, and enabled him to wear a gold stripe on his cuff. Halsey walked the decks, proud of the stripe that now adorned his uniform.

Later that year the *Don Juan de Austria* returned to the Norfolk Navy Yard in Virginia for repairs. One afternoon, as Halsey barked out orders while drilling his squad on the ship's deck, a female visitor, standing next to the wife of the ship's executive officer, noticed him.

"Who is that young officer over there who takes himself so importantly?"[20] she asked her friend. When told, the girl tossed her muff at Halsey to gain his attention, sending his cap flying. With his squad stifling laughter, Halsey retrieved the muff and turned to its owner but refused to hand back the item until she told him her name. Frances Cooke Grandy of Norfolk promptly identified herself.

The two started a courtship. Halsey was at first drawn to her beauty—others considered her one of the most attractive of available females—but he also loved her lively spirit and her tendency to speak what was on her mind. Even though her family, still proud of its Confederate heritage, raised objections about the young officer from the North, Halsey soon overcame their doubts, and the two became engaged.

"A FEAST, A FROLIC, OR A FIGHT"

As often happens to military officers, world events influenced the path of Halsey's career. Though just a young upstart fresh from the Academy, Halsey hopped directly into a Navy buoyed with renewed enthusiasm and vigor. The victorious war against Spain in 1898, which saw the Navy register resounding victories at Santiago, Cuba, and at Manila in the Philippines, brought a string of Pacific possessions under U.S. control and increased popularity to the military arm that had registered the most gallant deeds. Congress approved funding for eight sparkling new battleships, the linchpins of an enlarged Navy, and President Theodore Roosevelt employed every opportunity to emphasize that his aggressive foreign policy depended on the existence of an intimidating Navy. The early 1900s offered excitement and action to a young officer. Fortune, it seemed, smiled on Halsey.

In March 1907 Halsey reported to the new battleship USS *Kansas* a sparkling behemoth sporting four 12-inch guns, eight 8-inch guns, and twelve 7-inch guns. The Navy rushed to finish the ship so that it could become a centerpiece in the planned world cruise of the U.S. fleet ordered by President Roosevelt. Roosevelt, who announced that the lengthy circumnavigation was nothing more than an extensive training mission for his new vessels, actually held loftier goals. He intended to flex the nation's newfound naval strength to rivals in Europe, especially Germany and Great Britain, and in the Pacific, where the Japanese government threatened to disrupt Western dominance in the Far East.

Advocates for manifest destiny who supported spreading American might about the globe feared that a Japanese military buttressed by its victory over the Russians in the Russo-Japanese War of 1904–1905 might turn its gaze toward Hawaii and other American possessions in the Pacific. Some national newspapers even hinted at the possibility of war with Japan.

On December 16, 1907, sixteen battleships and five destroyers formed two columns at Hampton Roads under the command of Rear Admiral Robley D. Evans, the Commander in Chief Atlantic Fleet. At 8:00 A.M. all sixteen battleships boomed a simultaneous 21-gun salute to President Roosevelt, who watched the impressive spectacle aboard the presidential yacht, *Mayflower.* Aboard his flagship, Admiral Evans announced to reporters that his men were ready for "a feast, a frolic, or a fight."[21] That spirit infused the entire fleet, including a young Ensign Halsey.

BOLD ACTION, QUICKLY EXECUTED

As the juggernaut churned through the Atlantic toward its first destination, Halsey settled into his routine. During the lengthy stretches at sea, which frequently lasted from ten to fourteen days between ports of call, he supervised drills and participated in maneuvers orchestrated by Evans's staff. Though the constant exercises were arduous, Halsey noticed that they improved the fleet's efficiency, for its response and execution improved steadily. Halsey, who liked to joke that the time at sea provided a welcome relief from the monotonous string of balls and parties the men had to attend at each stop, tucked that information away for the time when he would command his own ships.

After spending Christmas in Trinidad, the fleet continued on to Rio de Janeiro, through the Straits of Magellan to Valparaiso, Chile, on the

Pacific side of South America, and north to cities on the U.S. West Coast, including San Diego, San Francisco, and Seattle. Enthusiastic crowds greeted the ships at each stop—one million residents welcomed the sailors in San Francisco alone—and the trip gained so much attention that Roosevelt's fleet garnered publicity in national and world newspapers.

While the cruise may have been a public debut for Roosevelt's navy, the voyage served as a preparatory school for Halsey, helping to fashion the traits marking the young officer and to establish a reputation he would maintain throughout his entire career. After witnessing the benefits of Evans's intensive training, Halsey gained more experience in formidable Punta Renas, Chile, a raucous town originally designed as a penal colony for Chilean criminals, where he commanded his first shore patrol.

"You are forced to learn much about handling men," he later claimed of his time ashore at Punta Renas. One night he led a patrol to one of the town's most forbidding sectors, ripe with houses of prostitution that lured sailors and visitors alike. Recent disturbances caused Halsey to be especially vigilant, and when a group of American sailors, feeling their oats after a night of drinking and visiting brothels, dared the young officer to arrest them for public drinking, Halsey took swift action. Instead of trying to detain the entire group, which would have incited a free-for-all, Halsey arrested the man he judged to be the ringleader, the toughest and most vociferous man there. When he had the sailor forcibly returned to the docks and ordered that the fees for a carriage required to take the offender back to his ship be deducted from the man's pay, the rest of the group backed down. With minimal disruption and no bodily harm, Halsey had defused the situation. "This soon ended the troubles in the district,"[22] he later boasted.

"If handled promptly, and with decision, a man will rarely ever get out of hand," Halsey wrote. During one liberty in New Zealand during the same cruise Halsey confined in a shed any sailor who caused disturbances until a boat arrived to transfer the group back to their ships. As he and his men guarded the structure, a large commotion from inside caused Halsey to rush in and investigate. A frightening hulk of a sailor, brandishing a two-by-four chunk of wood, dared anyone to approach him. Halsey stepped a few paces toward the man and ordered him to drop the club. "No son-of-a-bitch can make me," he snarled at Halsey.

Halsey refused to back down, despite ceding a weight and height advantage to the sailor. He drew to within an arm's length, all the time glaring straight into the offender's eyes. "Those next two or three steps were the longest miles I ever walked in my life," Halsey wrote in his memoirs. The intrepid tactic worked however, and the man backed down. "As I expected, when I reached him, he dropped the weapon and he was immediately put in charge of a strong guard and returned to his ship."[23] Bold action, quickly executed, became the centerpiece of Halsey's command style.

Halsey relished everything about being an officer, from the mundane tasks aboard ship to donning his uniform and strutting about the various towns. On a parade through the streets of San Diego with other naval officers, however, he learned, though, that not everyone shared the lofty impression. "I was a proud and stout Ensign in command of a company," he wrote, "and thought not too badly of myself. Out of the corner of my eye I suddenly spied two little urchins sitting on the curb stone and heard one say to the other, 'Pipe the guy with a face like a bull dog.' I did not hear the last of that from my friends for many a day."[24]

"THE GRANDEST NAVAL PAGEANT"

After stopping in Hawaii in 1907, the fleet veered southwest into waters that would become all too familiar to Halsey during World War II. Ports of call in Australia, the Philippines, and Japan—all crucial to the outcome of the future conflict—proved welcome interludes to the long sea voyage.

As the fleet neared the Japanese Home Islands, though, tension mounted aboard each ship. Every officer, including Halsey, had studied Japan's history. They knew of the Japanese penchant for surprise attacks, as shown in 1894 against the Chinese and again in 1904 against the Russians. When the fleet entered Tokyo Bay on October 18, 1908, some wondered if they were headed straight into a trap.

When their arrival unfolded without mishap, Halsey and his fellow officers embarked upon the customary rounds of banquets that marked every stop along the cruise. During one party aboard the Japanese battleship *Mikassar*, after diplomats and naval officers exchanged toasts, Japanese officers grabbed their American counterparts, tossed them into the air, and caught them as they came down. Halsey and a handful of others hoisted Admiral Heihachiro Togo, who had defeated the Russian fleet in the 1905 Battle of Tsushima Strait, and returned the favor. "We picked him up and instead of lifting him gently into the air, we threw him to an appreciable altitude, giving a lusty *Banzai* with each heave. If we had known what the future held," Halsey concluded later, "we wouldn't have caught him after the third one."[25]

A brief stop on the Riviera preceded a gathering at Gibraltar, which served as their final staging area before entering the Atlantic Ocean and the path home. Festivities marked the return when Halsey and the fleet appeared at Hampton Roads on Monday, February 22, 1909—Washington's birthday. Hundreds of small craft gathered to welcome the ships in what the *New York World* called "The Grandest Naval Pageant in American History."[26] At a signal from the flagship, 26 warships boomed a simultaneous 21-gun salute to the president, then again passed in review while Roosevelt watched the seven-mile-long column from the *Mayflower.* Ashore, a band played "There's No Place Like Home."

"Not until some American fleet returns victorious from a great sea battle will there be another such homecoming," proclaimed Roosevelt. He added that the cruise had "immeasurably raised the prestige not only of our fleet but of the nation."[27]

Benefits accrued from the exercise. The Navy bolstered its self-esteem by setting numerous world records: the fleet was the largest conglomeration to circumnavigate the globe; it had traveled farther—46,000 miles—than any other fleet; it had experienced no major breakdown; it had been away from home waters for 436 days; it had crossed the equator five times and visited twenty-six nations.[28]

The American public, which had closely followed the lengthy voyage in newspapers and magazines, saw the value of a strong Navy. The trip sparked pride in the service, increased interest in international events, and notified other nations that the United States could no longer be ignored on the world scene, especially in the Pacific. Officers, including Halsey, gained valuable experience handling the Navy's newest ships and training the crews. Frequent drilling and gunnery practice turned the fleet into an efficient, tightly-run operation. The lesson was not lost on the young officer—Roosevelt had taken firm action to send the Japanese a message, one that caused them to bide their time in the Pacific.

Upon completion of the voyage, Halsey traveled to the Philadelphia Navy Yard, where he sat for the arduous week-long examinations for promotion to lieutenant (jg) and full lieutenant. Seven officers sat for the examination, and four—including Halsey—passed. Though he normally would have worn the uniform of a lieutenant (jg), the Navy faced a shortage of full lieutenants and swore Halsey in at that rank with the effective date of February 2, 1909. He was about to enter his first command as a naval officer.

"I AM LOOKING AROUND FOR A JOB"

If Halsey had any illusions about his place in the Navy's hierarchy, the scrawny torpedo boat USS *Du Pont* clarified matters. When Halsey arrived at the Charleston Navy Yard, the twenty-six-year-old officer stared at what he described as "one of a motley assemblage of old buckets that had been laid up for years." Nevertheless, the rusty *Du Pont* was his, and the man who would go on to supervise history's mightiest fleet later stated that "no subsequent command is ever as important or as thrilling as your first, and I was a proud man when we hoisted the colors and the commissioning pennant on the *Du Pont*."[29]

As far as Halsey was concerned, the crew, consisting of Passed Midshipman A. R. M. Allen and twenty-three men, matched the magnificence of hundreds serving aboard battleships or cruisers. Except for a brief stint as executive officer of the battleship USS *Wyoming* and his time on shore duty, Halsey would have a twenty-three-year-long love affair with torpedo boats and destroyers that began with the *Du Pont*.

From the first day, Halsey implemented a clear, firm system with his crew. He believed that the men would perform more efficiently if they knew their commander could show leniency toward minor infractions while dealing firmly and swiftly with major offenses. He thus usually chatted with offenders of lesser violations, offering them second chances if they vowed not to repeat their missteps, but he showed little mercy on serious issues. Halsey drummed one sailor out of service for repeated drunkenness and replaced him with a mess attendant.

Halsey had more on his mind than the torpedo boat, however. With the pay raise that came from his promotion to lieutenant, Halsey felt financially able to ask Francis, or Fan, as he called her, to marry him. In the fall he left the *Du Pont* for one month to make arrangements for the December 1, 1909, wedding in Christ Church in Norfolk, Virginia. Following the Episcopal ceremony, the couple honeymooned in New York City.

Two years of mundane service ended in August 1912 when Halsey was named the commander of the destroyer USS *Flusser.* There was a certain romance attached to the sleek destroyers, compact corsairs that turned on a dime and sliced through the waves. The diminutive, aggressive ships perfectly matched the demeanor of the pugnacious young officer. Brimming with a mixture of pride, elation, and excitement, Halsey stepped aboard his first destroyer.

During his time with the *Flusser,* the novice skipper enjoyed the first of his sporadic encounters with a man who would later wield much power over his career. An early assignment took Halsey and his destroyer to Campobello Island, Canada, an island off the Maine coast, where he reported to then Assistant Secretary of the Navy Franklin D. Roosevelt, a rising political star in the Democratic Party and an avid sailor.

As Halsey ferried Roosevelt through the strait that separated Campobello Island from the mainland, Roosevelt asked if he could take the helm. Halsey hated to reject the assistant secretary's plea, but being responsible for the safety of his ship and crew as it maneuvered through the tricky waters, he was hesitant. Though he wondered if Roosevelt, who had experience in smaller craft, could handle a larger vessel, he reluctantly granted the request but kept a close watch as Roosevelt took over. His fears soon dissipated, however. "As soon as I saw that he checked his course and turned by observing the stern," wrote Halsey, "I was assured that he was capable of handling the ship."[30]

Halsey took command of his next vessel, the destroyer USS *Jarvis,* in August 1913. The ship steamed to Guantanamo, Cuba, for winter maneuvers, where Halsey served under the influential Captain William S. Sims. A rising star in the Navy, Sims was known for advocating various reforms in gunnery, naval administration, and ship design, but it was Sims's manner of command that most impressed Halsey. Sims insisted on constant, rigorous training of the men and ships under his command, and he detested long-winded, wordy orders, instead issuing his dictates in crisp, brief sentences.

In the spring of 1914, while the crew enjoyed shore liberty in Pensacola following winter maneuvers, a ship's clarion summoned everyone to their posts. Deteriorating conditions in Mexico, where a group of U.S. sailors had been detained in Tampico, caused President Woodrow Wilson to demand that Mexican president General Victoriano Huerta resign. When Huerta refused, Wilson ordered warships and ground forces to the scene. Halsey had two responsibilities—to support the forces going ashore and to evacuate American citizens from Tampico.

Halsey supervised the evacuation with his usual efficiency. After gathering American citizens from their residences, he placed them aboard a destroyer tender, a ship that normally provided maintenance support for destroyers, which whisked them back to the United States. With the civilians out of danger, Halsey concentrated on his other task and remained off the Mexican coast, ready to bring supporting fire should violence flare ashore. Though the episode ended without hostilities, Halsey gained valuable experience in commanding men in a crisis situation.

For instance, as commander off Mexico, Halsey encountered what he described as "the hardest man I ever had to handle." A fireman from his crew known for his fondness for alcohol, twice jumped ship and returned drunk. Exasperated that his warning to the man after the first episode had made no impression, Halsey told the sailor, "If you want to be treated as a man, act like a man. If you want to be treated like a dog, act like a dog and I'll chain you up like a mad dog."[31] The man promised to improve but soon relapsed, forcing Halsey to have him court-martialed.

The start of hostilities in Europe in the summer of 1914 brought the prospects for war front and center. The United States remained neutral in what was basically a European problem, but the excitement of nations at war and the possibility of combat tantalized Halsey. In the meantime, he bided his time patrolling New York Harbor with the *Jarvis* to prevent belligerents, especially from Great Britain and Germany, from purchasing and removing any of the speedy privately owned yachts that rested in the harbor's waters.

A shore command momentarily derailed Halsey's hopes for an active sea post in 1915 when he returned to the Naval Academy, where as part of the discipline department, he enforced the many regulations that governed the midshipmen's lives. Halsey figured that, since he had once attended the Academy, he knew all the tricks and could stay a step ahead of his charges.

Robert B. Carney, who later served as Halsey's chief of staff in World War II, recalled the fairness with which Halsey enforced his discipline. During his inspection rounds Halsey purposely allowed his sword to clank and make noise so that the midshipmen would have enough time to straighten their quarters and remove objectionable items. Carney stated that Halsey's tactics achieved what Halsey wanted—clean quarters—without the threat of punishment.

Events on the Halsey home front ameliorated his frustrations at being removed from sea duty. On September 8, 1915, his son, William Frederick Halsey III was born, joining daughter Margaret Bradford, who had arrived on October 10, 1910. Fan had her hands busy with the two youngsters, especially as her husband was often away at sea or on Navy business, but Lieutenant Halsey could not have been happier.

In 1916 Congress passed a bill enlarging the Navy, making Halsey eligible for promotion. When he handily passed the oral exam for lieutenant commander, he faced a bright future, especially with much of Europe at war.

"SOME HAD TEARS IN THEIR EYES"

Halsey yearned to be a part of the fighting. He knew the nation was far from ready to engage in hostilities in 1914, both militarily and politically, but as war fever mounted, mainly because of German submarines that flouted United States neutrality, his hopes correspondingly rose. By April 1917, with the United States only weeks from entering the war, Halsey remained anchored at the Naval Academy. "Time was passing and there was still no seeming hope of getting to sea."[32] The April declaration of war opened the floodgates for hundreds of officers to cross the ocean to the combat zone, yet Halsey remained on the sidelines.

Halsey waited impatiently for a change of orders that never arrived. Finally, near desperation, in November he took matters into his own hands. After learning that the commander of U.S. naval forces in Europe, Admiral William S. Sims, had placed Halsey's name on a list of desired officers, Halsey convinced the Academy's superintendent to let him go. On December 26, 1917, he was detached from Annapolis with orders to proceed to Ireland and duty aboard destroyers.

On January 7, 1918, Halsey boarded the liner *New York* for the trip to Liverpool, England. As the senior naval officer aboard the liner, Halsey was responsible for matters pertaining to the Navy, but an uneventful trip unfolded. When the ship arrived in Europe later that month, Halsey reported to Captain Joel R. P. Pringle, the senior American naval officer; he assigned Halsey to the destroyer USS *Duncan* under the supervision of Commander Roger Williams. Halsey hoped to soon be in the midst of the fighting, and he even started a diary on January 18 in anticipation of recording momentous events, but to his dismay the *Duncan* did little more than escort ships coming into or departing from European waters, conduct rescue missions, and unsuccessfully search for German submarines.

On February 1 Halsey was promoted to the temporary rank of commander, and twelve days later he proudly assumed command of his first wartime ship, the destroyer USS *Benham*. His pride all but disappeared when he first inspected the vessel, which he judged to be shockingly subpar. He recorded in his diary on February 25 that he gathered his officers and "read the riot account" to them because of the ship's poor condition. "They are a good crowd of youngsters," he confided about the officers under his charge, "but have been badly lead [sic]. The ship is filthy dirty, including wardroom and the people on watch do not keep in uniform. No one turned out in morning."[33] Halsey took immediate steps to remedy the situation. He ordered the crew to appear on deck by 8:00 A.M., ready to scour the vessel from bow to stern, and he warned that he expected the ship to be in tip-top shape within six weeks.

The chastened men responded so favorably that by March 17 Halsey wrote that he was pleased with the vast improvement, in both the crew's punctuality and the ship's cleanliness. "She is beginning to look like a real destroyer,"[34] he proudly added. Within a few additional weeks he claimed that the *Benham* no longer resembled the shoddy warship he had boarded in February.

All was not work, however. Halsey capably blended in fun to relieve the tedium and drudgery of life at sea. On February 24, for instance, he enlivened target practice by painting the German flag and the words "Kill the Kaiser" on the target raft.

Brief moments of excitement—none involving the enemy—substituted inadequately for combat. Anticipation rose on March 15 when lookouts reported a large wake crossing the starboard bow. Halsey studied the spectacle from the bridge, and in the heat of the moment thought he had finally locked horns with his first submarine. Just as he was prepared to drop depth charges he noticed that the wake, rather than remaining in a tight pattern as would a torpedo, suddenly jumped around and spread out. Instead of the enemy, a school of fish was headed toward his craft. Halsey had mistaken the aquatic migration for a submerged submarine or the wake of a torpedo.

Halsey finally had his chance three weeks later when, on April 9, he dropped his first depth charge after a supposed sighting. No member of the crew actually spotted a ship, but since he stood in wartime waters the impatient Halsey attacked "on general principles. First egg I have laid."[35]

Halsey's stint with the *Benham* ended in the middle of May 1918, when he received orders to take command of the destroyer USS *Shaw*. He assembled the *Benham*'s crew to speak to them for the last time, a moment that touched him.

"I remember when he was detached from the destroyer," recalled the executive officer, Lieutenant Julian Wheeler, "he'd only been in command a few months, why, every man on the ship manned the rails and some of them had tears in their eyes when he left."[36]

"IGNOMINIOUSLY TOWED BY A TUG"

With a fresh ship under his charge, Halsey made a five-pound wager with Commander Alan S. Farquhar of the USS *Sterett* that he would be the first to destroy a German submarine. Much to Halsey's dismay, the competition fizzled. On June 1, which Halsey called "one of the most distressing days I have ever had," the *Shaw* raced to aid the *Sterett* when the latter vessel reportedly spotted a submarine. Instead of a sea chase, Halsey turned away from what might have been his first action and limped back to port when a tube split and ruined the ship's condenser. "Was certainly a most disappointing day, particularly as it was the first chance to ever get near a sub that I had had. Came in ignominiously towed by a tug."[37]

Matters only deteriorated. Halsey dropped a depth charge when the *Shaw* struck a submerged object on July 8, and reacted elatedly when oil bubbled to the surface, indicating that a ship had been ruptured. Halsey radioed for assistance, but when he dropped two more depth charges, a keg bearing the markings USS *Reserve,* a ship out of Aberdeen, popped into view. Halsey had apparently come across the site of an earlier sinking rather than an enemy submarine. He returned to port on July 10 to find that news of his "attack" had preceded him. Fellow officers called him the Duke of Aberdeen, and wrote a ditty containing the lyrics, "The finest sight I have ever seen was Bill Halsey's submarine from Aberdeen."[38] Halsey accepted the taunting as an occupational hazard, but the ribbing had to gall him.

The enemy might have been eluding him, but Halsey used the time to sharpen his leadership skills. When he was given temporary command of three other ships in June, Halsey, who labeled himself "king of the Irish sea [sic]," relished the chance to coordinate ship movements among four combatants. "Had the time of my life bossing them around," he wrote in his diary. "I was as proud as a dog with two tails."[39] His "armada" engaged in no hostilities, but no one could deny that Halsey had a natural penchant for command. A war correspondent from the *Saturday Evening Post,* Peter Macfarlane, closely observed Halsey on several of his patrols and liked what he saw in the young officer. Macfarlane later told his son that the two figures to look out for in the future were Franklin Roosevelt and William Halsey.

Halsey learned much during his wartime service under Admiral Sir Louis Bayley, a British officer who allowed his subordinate commanders freedom to determine their paths of action. Bayley believed that because his commanders were at sea, rather than back at headquarters where he was, they possessed a clearer image of the action and could thus better formulate a response. Bayley trusted his men to use their initiative and do what had to be done.

Halsey liked this approach. Never a textbook type of commander, Halsey relied more on instinct than on proper naval doctrine. Halsey believed in a simple policy—assess the situation, inform your superiors of what you intend to do, then act. Bayley's example provided a beacon for Halsey as he made his way up the command ladder.

"He always pointed out that the man on the spot has so much better information than the man at headquarters," Halsey wrote of Admiral Bayley, "and it was impossible for the man at headquarters to give adequate and proper instructions. This is a lesson that has stood by me all through my naval career."[40]

To Halsey's chagrin, the fighting in Europe ended without his engaging in combat. He received the Navy Cross for his guidance of destroyer crews and for his escort of Allied shipping, but he discounted the honor. Unlike in World War II, when the Navy Cross meant something, during World War I the medals were handed out to almost every destroyer commander. As he traveled home across the Atlantic, Halsey wondered if he would ever participate in a surface engagement with an enemy force.

AFTER A BRIEF sojourn with Fan and their two children in Washington, D.C., and Atlantic City, Halsey headed to Philadelphia to receive command of a new destroyer, USS *Yarnall.* Instead of remaining in home waters, Halsey requested escort duty as part of the force accompanying President Woodrow Wilson to Europe for the peace conference. On December 4, 1918, the collection of ships, including Halsey's *Yarnall,* left the United States to great fanfare.

Halsey spent six months in Europe delivering messages between England and the mainland. He visited Paris and the sites of recent monumental battles in his free time, and he renewed his acquaintance with Franklin Roosevelt when he transported him to a mainland meeting.

Halsey did not hesitate to take a firm tack when the occasion warranted it. When he learned that most of the crew had raided a captured German ammunition dump and brought back to the ship a supply of ammunition as souvenirs—enough to blow the ship clean out of the water, according to his informant—Halsey ordered an inspection of the ship, seized the explosives, and had them tossed overboard.

In January 1919, Halsey received orders to exit the port of Lisbon, Portugal. He debated the wisdom of the order, as heavy storms shrouded the area, but he reluctantly followed his superiors' orders. Shortly after the ship departed, heavy waves swept three men overboard.

Halsey was certain that, had he been able to keep the *Yarnall* in port, as he had thought best, he would not have lost those men. He became more convinced than ever that, as Bayley contended, whenever possible the man on the spot should make the crucial decisions.

NAVAL AVIATION entered Halsey's life while the *Yarnall* steamed off Spain in 1919. Three flying boats piloted by a trio of Halsey's friends—Commander John H. Towers, Lieutenant Commander Patrick N. L. Bellinger, and Lieutenant Commander Albert C. Read—left Newfoundland in May, determined to complete the first transatlantic crossing by air. As part of the mission, a line of sixty American ships took station at various spots along the route in case one of the aircraft splashed down.

Halsey took position north of Spain, where he eagerly watched the NC–4 flying boat piloted by Read when it flew overhead. Towers and Bellinger had been forced to make emergency landings and did not complete the crossing, but Halsey's admiration for aviators and for the risks they willingly took grew as the years passed.

With the conclusion of the peace conference the next month, Halsey's *Yarnall* escorted President Woodrow Wilson on his return voyage. After a few days' leave with his family, Halsey took the destroyer to Hampton Roads to join the new Pacific Fleet then being assembled under Admiral Hugh Rodman as a countermeasure to growing Japanese power. Shortly before the fleet departed, Halsey took the next step upward in the naval hierarchy when he was named a division commander and placed in charge of six destroyers.

Commander Halsey was about to make a name for himself.

CHAPTER 2

"SHOOT FIRST AND WE'LL ARGUE AFTERWARDS"

Although the 1920s handed Halsey experience in commanding destroyers and involved him more fully in aviation, the decade opened with little promise. Like every other career military man in the United States, Halsey stared at diminishing prospects in a postwar world eager to return to normalcy. The government slashed military budgets and pared its military to the minimum. The Navy placed scores of ships in reserve, and others operated with reduced crews.

At the same time, this tightening drew Halsey and his fellow officers closer together. In the face of the budgetary strictures, they circled the wagons and reminded themselves that they were all that stood between their nation and their country's foes. The Japanese embarked on suspicious moves in the Pacific, and a growing number of officers contended that the harsh terms of the Versailles Treaty imposed on Germany at the end of the last war would inevitably lead to another conflict. Meager appropriations could not last forever. Halsey would bide his time, learn, and be prepared when opportunity arose.

"A DARING AND SKILLFUL DESTROYER MAN"

Halsey was fortunate to serve under a dynamic leader. Rear Admiral Henry A. Wiley, the commander of destroyers in the Pacific, insisted on strict discipline from every destroyer commander and on proper execution of maneuvers. He refused to allow his men to use tight budgets as an excuse for not being professional. As a result, his high-spirited squadrons were among the best-trained units in the Navy.

Halsey quickly fell under Wiley's spell. He wrote in his autobiography that Wiley's "leadership, his discipline, and his insistence on smartness made them [his destroyers] the proudest ships in the fleet." He added in his memoirs that, "The destroyers had great pride not only in their ships but that by their appearance could be distinguished from any other group in the Navy."[1] Halsey and his fellow destroyer commanders forged a close association. They comported themselves in an almost "us versus them" demeanor, one anchored in the boast that few in the Navy could match them.

Halsey's team at this time, which included a young Commander Raymond Spruance, exhibited a freestyle, dynamic approach that was the envy of other officers. Halsey's destroyers barreled at flank speed in navigating tricky maneuvers, veering as one at the sign of a signal flag, ignoring heavy seas and howling winds to achieve their objective. According to Spruance's biographer, Thomas Buell, if a darling of the fleet existed, it operated under Halsey's orders.

Robert Carney, later to be Halsey's chief of staff, said Halsey's work in destroyers gained notice with the naval hierarchy. "In destroyers he found an outlet for his command talent, his inherent boldness, and his gift for dealing with people," recalled Carney after the war. "Before long, he enjoyed a reputation as a daring and skillful destroyer man." Carney added that Halsey's ability to connect with the men under his command "was felt and understood down to the lowest rank and rating. They sensed his sympathetic understanding of people, and they responded to his demand for bold and aggressive action."[2]

In his own division, one of three six-destroyer divisions in the squadron, Halsey drilled his men day and night and conducted torpedo practices, the main offensive weapon carried by destroyers. Since most of his ship captains remained with Halsey for long stretches, they were able to learn each other's tendencies and capabilities and forged a tight team. Throughout the week they worked together and on weekends with their wives, they played together, mainly in boisterous alcohol-fueled parties filled with light-hearted banter, songs, and laughter.

Despite being almost his complete opposite, Halsey felt particularly close to Spruance. Halsey loved the soft-spoken commander's professionalism and vast knowledge of naval tactics, while Spruance admired Halsey's seamanship and his fighting spirit. Halsey, who had a reputation for brutal honesty in writing fitness reports on the officers in his command, penned glowing remarks about his subordinate, calling him an able, bright officer who was "one of the best all around officers I have ever served with. He is quiet, efficient, always on the job, and with a clear thinking brain always working. His judgment is excellent, and I invariably seek his opinion on knotty problems."[3]

Halsey's aggressive method of command did not always pay off. In the spring of 1921, as commander of Destroyer Division Fifteen, Halsey stepped in for the ill destroyer squadron commander for a mock attack between Halsey's nineteen destroyers and a group of four battleships. Halsey took his flotilla out 30,000 yards from the battleships, now shrouded in smoke, and ordered an attack. He had asked a senior officer beforehand if any rules restricted his movements against the larger ships and was elated when told that none stood in his way.

Halsey built speed to 25 knots and attacked in two columns, intending to flank the battleships between his columns and place them under fire from both sides. To avoid damaging the battleships, the torpedoes featured soft metal nose heads that crumbled when hitting their targets, but Halsey maneuvered his destroyers too close before launching. One torpedo struck the USS *Texas* in the compartment below her steering engine room and, instead of crumbling, impaired the ship's electrical gear. Two other torpedoes damaged the USS *Mississippi*'s propellers, and another smacked into the USS *New Mexico* and caused minor flooding.

Halsey later wrote, with devilish satisfaction, that when the battleships emerged from the smoke, they "were not in the pretty formation they were in when they entered the smoke." Superiors, on the other hand, were less impressed with the attack, which caused $1.5 million worth of damage in under two minutes. Halsey had to appear before a board of inquiry, but he declined an offer for a lawyer by stating that his defense was simple—"I was ordered to attack. I attacked."[4] A brief investigation found no reason to enter any incriminating remarks in his record, but the board coldly advised him to avoid another such incident.

On this occasion and others, detractors pointed to another of Halsey's shortcomings—a loathing for paperwork. He avoided it whenever possible, preferring instead brief meetings where, face-to-face, he could make his feelings known to his officers and open discussions produced solutions. He believed paperwork prevented him from carrying out his main responsibilities—running a tight, clean ship and, in wartime, chasing the enemy. As a result, whenever Halsey left one of his ships for a subsequent post, his relief found the files all but empty of correspondence.

"I WAS EATING, DRINKING, AND BREATHING AVIATION"

Halsey spent the next three years on shore assignment. After a year laboring in the Office of Naval Intelligence, the only time in his career that he saw duty in the nation's capital, in October 1922 Halsey received orders posting him to Europe as naval attaché. For two years, from posts in Germany, Norway, Denmark, and Sweden, he studied Europe's fleets and new naval developments so he could better advise American officials. Fan and the two children, now twelve and seven, accompanied Halsey to Germany, which was still so ravaged by the devastation of the previous war that the family had difficulty purchasing bread, milk, and butter.

Halsey's years with Naval Intelligence ended in 1924 with his commands of the destroyers USS *Dale* and the USS *Osborne*, then stationed in Europe to show the flag around the Mediterranean. For the next sixteen months Halsey traveled to ports along the Atlantic and Mediterranean coasts, parading an American presence to a politically fluid continent.

While willing to rebuke officers and men when required, Halsey tried to run a happy ship. Laughter, friendly chatter, and profane jokes filled Halsey's wardroom, and Halsey addressed everyone by their first names, unlike other officers in the Navy who relied on formality and rigidity. When Ray Spruance was set to relieve Halsey as commander of the *Osborne* in 1926, Halsey cautioned his men against judging his taciturn friend too hastily. He told them that although Spruance would conduct a quieter ship and address the men by their last names, they would quickly gain admiration for his efficient, professional manner.

After a year as executive officer aboard the battleship USS *Wyoming,* in 1927 Halsey returned to the Naval Academy as commander of the *Reina Mercedes,* a ship captured during the Spanish-American War that was used to house Academy discipline problems. Halsey, who had had intimate knowledge of the Academy's code of behavior as a student, now faced the task of enforcing it with midshipmen who bore a strong resemblance to his younger self.

"It was one of the most pleasant tours of duty in my entire naval career,"[5] he later wrote of his three and one-half years at Annapolis. A cook and steward attended to his family's needs, and as few midshipmen committed serious enough offenses to be long incarcerated aboard the vessel, Halsey could freely pursue his interests. He and Fan loved being in the midst of the Academy's social gatherings and dances, and with Washington, D.C., and Baltimore close by, he could easily travel to those places for entertainment and friendly calls on naval associates.

"My whole naval career changed right there," Halsey stated in February 1927, when the Academy's first permanent aviation detail was placed under his command aboard the *Reina Mercedes.* Until then he had been an impartial witness to aviation events, but now his role took on a more active stance. He pestered the unit's officers, Lieutenant Dewitt C. Ramsey and his executive officer, Lieutenant C. A. F. "Ziggy" Sprague, to take him flying at every opportunity and fired a stream of questions their way. A thrilling new world opened to him. "I flew as often as Duke or 'Ziggy' Sprague would give me a ride," he wrote. "It wasn't long before they were letting me handle the controls, and it wasn't much longer before I thought I was an ace. . . . Soon I was eating, drinking, and breathing aviation, and I continued to do so during the remainder of my duty on the *Reina.*"[6]

Ramsey and Sprague needed all the help they could find to combat deep-seated opposition inside the Navy. Older admirals adamantly believed that battleships formed the Navy's backbone, and they resented the intrusion of the infant aviation branch. Naval aviators, who daily faced the hazards inherent in the early days of flying, responded to the derision by banding together in a tight-knit group. Aviators like Sprague and Ramsey did all they could to promote aviation, and commanding the detail at Annapolis gave them an opportunity to bring aviation's benefits to the men who would become the Navy's next generation of leaders.

They had a long way to go, however. Convincing raw recruits out of the Academy was one thing, but winning over upper echelon commanders was another. Thus Ramsey, Sprague, and other fliers considered Halsey a key recruit. In the spring of 1930, when Rear Admiral James O. Richardson, the chief of the Bureau of Navigation, offered Halsey the opportunity to take the aviation course at Pensacola, he jumped at the chance. Unfortunately, Halsey failed the eye exam and was not admitted to the course.

AN AMAZING THESIS

In June 1930 Halsey was detached from his duties at the Academy and given command of Destroyer Squadron 14, a collection of nineteen destroyers stationed in the Atlantic. Halsey loved returning to sea, but because of his time with Sprague and Ramsey, he was now more attuned to developments with the air arm. During torpedo practices, for instance, when aircraft spotted for his destroyers, instead of remaining on his flagship's bridge, he spent half the time observing from the bridge and half the exercise watching from the air.

Back with his beloved destroyers, Halsey added to his Navy-wide reputation for risk taking. While other commanders concentrated on the escort duties of a destroyer, Halsey emphasized the ship's offensive capabilities. His intense training focused on night exercises, where he operated at high speeds and relied on whistles to relay course changes. Officers and crew who had not been accustomed to such energized maneuvers saw new potential in the speedy vessels.

He displayed the same forceful demeanor in war games. During Fleet Problem XIII, an exercise designed to test naval theory and strategy, in March 1932, Halsey's destroyers escorted two aircraft carriers whose task was to repel an assault on the West Coast by two other carriers. Rather than accept a merely passive role in protecting his force's carriers, Halsey executed a perfect dummy torpedo attack on the USS *Saratoga.*

Halsey's long tenure with destroyers—he had by this time spent more time at sea aboard destroyers than had any other officer in the Navy—ended in June 1932 when the Navy sent him to study at the Naval War College in Newport, Rhode Island. The move indicated that the Navy considered Halsey a prospect for higher command and wanted him to study naval tactics and strategy with other bright young officers.

Halsey enjoyed his year at the War College, which is perched on a luxuriant shoreline crag on Rhode Island's southern coast. The twelve months gave him time to debate naval tactics with classmates and, as he put it, to "test any wild theories you have on the game board."[7] For the first time, Halsey read professional journals and reflected on great naval leaders of the past, on their campaigns, and on their tactics. He studied the Orange Plan, the naval strategy in the Pacific to counter Japanese strikes against American possessions, particularly in the Philippines, and he became more knowledgeable about events in a portion of the globe that might be a future battleground.

The pivotal year in Newport provided Halsey with the opportunity to think about his future and to formulate a set of command principles. Elaborated in a May 16, 1933 essay titled "The Relationship in War of Naval Strategy, Tactics, and Command," the remarkable eleven-page document, which has been overlooked by most historians and biographers, foreshadows Halsey's evolution as a commander in the Pacific War and, in a general manner, predicts his controversial moves off San Bernardino Strait in October 1944. Amateurishly written and containing the normal padding tactics so beloved by college essay writers through the years (he begins with a quote lasting almost two pages), the latter half of the document is remarkably prescient, almost as if the young Halsey hinted at what the older Halsey was going to do. Had other officers, particularly Chester Nimitz, been aware of this essay, the events of October 1944 might have turned out differently.

In this paper, the student Halsey claimed that while three principles—strategy, tactics, and command—guide military leaders during wartime, "the greatest of these is command." Sound plans provided the foundation, but a battle's course rested upon the shoulders of the officer who stood on the bridge while the shells exploded rather than the staff planner hundreds of miles away in headquarters.

A prime way for a commander to prepare for action, according to Halsey, was to conduct frequent conferences with his subordinates rather than issuing a stream of written orders, for "Ideas can never be so clearly conveyed in writing, as they can by personal and intimate discussion." Halsey contended that frank discussions among the senior officer and subordinates crystallized the objectives of an engagement and the desires of the commander. In that manner, wrote Halsey, the commander gains the opportunity to "impress his personality upon his subordinates."[8]

He argued that "a good plan, not understood, is worse than useless," and contended that plans "may be written, verbal, *or of common understanding* [italics the author's]."[9] That last phrase emphasized Halsey's belief that an officer should enjoy wide latitude to interpret plans in his own manner, a practice he would clearly rely on during the war.

Halsey added that a commander had to forge a tight team with his subordinates so that every officer knew his role and how it affected those about him. "No matter how many stars are gathered together, if the team is being continually shifted, it will be an easy victim for a mediocre opponent. It is of paramount importance that unit groups be not broken up, except by urgent necessity. We have all seen this violated many times and always to the detriment of the team."[10] The events surrounding the Battle of Leyte Gulf eleven years in the future lent credence to these words.

Halsey then stated that besides proper organization a commander had to insist upon frequent training for, all other factors being equal, "the battle will go to the more ably commanded and better trained fleet." Once ready, the commander should be prepared to move quickly, a fact Halsey supported by resorting to the words of Civil War cavalry General Nathan Bedford Forrest, "Get there furstest with the mostest men."[11] He favored aggression over hesitation, action over inaction—precisely the traits that most distinguished Halsey in the Pacific during the first two years of that conflict.

Halsey next addressed the issue of who should make decisions once a battle begins. He contended that after clearly conveying his plan to subordinates and assigning each man his duties, a commander must grant discretion to those subordinates to execute the plan.

"In this day of easy and fast communications, the temptation of a commander to interfere with a subordinate acting independently, is very great. From the information available, it is very easy to size up the situation in a distant theatre. It is also easy to size up this situation entirely wrong. The man on the spot may have information not available to the commander that gives an entirely different picture. The subordinate must be trusted, or if not trusted removed." Halsey also issued a caveat to the subordinates. "By the same token, the man on the spot must act and act now, and never commit the unpardonable offense of asking instructions. He has all the available information, and knows or should know the commanders [sic] intentions." Halsey added that the Navy should adopt the slogan, "Tell him what to do, but not how to do it."[12]

This paragraph could have been written by Halsey in the aftermath of Leyte Gulf to justify his actions. Halsey longed for the days when captains freely sailed the seas and attacked targets of their own choosing, but in light of modern technological advances, his superiors held Halsey at the end of a communications leash.

Halsey also listed seven traits that a successful commander needed. He added that a commander should be someone his men would willingly follow into battle, and that he "must have a pleasing personality, rigid uprightness of character, a niceness of personal appearance, and be a strict disciplinarian, tempering justice with mercy." Halsey's final two traits stipulated that a commander should be the officer and gentleman expected by the Naval Academy, and that "His courage both moral and physical must be unquestioned."[13]

This thesis predicted not only Halsey's aggressive spirit that so aided the American cause in the war's first two years and turned him into a national hero, but also his penchant for dashing off on his own that marked the latter phase of the war. In 1933, Halsey clearly outlined how he would react in the future if presented with a certain set of circumstances.

Following his productive year at the Naval War College, Halsey headed to the Army War College in Washington, D.C., for more study.

Halsey worked with bright Army prospects, including Omar Bradley and Jonathan Wainwright, studying military campaigns from the viewpoint of the men who guided the forces.

Halsey was now ready, through years of sea duty and almost two years of intensive study, to command one of the Navy's newest and most promising weapons—the aircraft carrier.

"THE STUFF THAT LOYALTY IS BUILT ON"

Near the end of 1933, Halsey was offered command of the aircraft carrier USS *Saratoga,* but to be eligible, he first had to complete an aviation observer course in Pensacola. The Navy required that any man receiving command of a carrier or a naval air station had to be an aviator, but in 1933 most of the experienced fliers in the Navy were too junior in rank to assume such important posts. The Navy established the aviation observer course as a solution. Halsey or other senior officers would take the course, which offered the same training aviators experienced without the need to solo, and thereby meet the Navy's requirements.

"The world of aviation suddenly reopened to me," enthused Halsey. "I was so excited that I regarded the privilege of commanding the *Sara* [sic] merely as a pleasant bonus."[14]

The fifty-one-year-old Halsey, by now a grandfather, was determined to perform well at Pensacola. He knew that he would be attending classes and competing with young naval officers in the prime of health, and that everyone would be watching to see how the "old man" performed. The last day of June 1934, one day before starting classes in Pensacola, Halsey swallowed a glass of Scotch then swore off alcohol until he had successfully completed his course.

Close to seventy men joined Halsey when the class gathered on July 1. The group spent half the time on the ground and half in the air, learning navigation, radio, gunnery, mechanics, and other skills. After a few days, Halsey changed his status from student observer to student pilot, a more rigorous course that required the student to solo. He thought that if he was going to command aviators and send them into battle, he should at least know firsthand what it was like to fly a plane and to experience the dangers they faced.

Fan exploded upon learning that her husband intended to fly aircraft. "What do you think the old fool is doing now?" she shouted to a family member after reading Halsey's letter containing the information. "He's learning to fly! It must be that flying is the only thing left that will make him feel young again. He can't turn somersaults on the ground any more, so he's going to turn them up in the air."[15]

Halsey successfully completed the instruction and became the final man in the class to solo. Pensacola tradition called for the group to toss the tailender, clothes and all, into the harbor, but Halsey's classmates hesitated to dunk a captain twice their age and possessing enough power to impede their careers. Halsey solved their dilemma by ordering them to follow tradition, at which the young aviators hoisted Halsey and, amidst enthusiastic cheering and laughter, chucked him into the water.

After soloing, Halsey learned how to handle biplanes, patrol craft, and fighters. During one landing Halsey hit a soft spot on the runway and flipped the aircraft onto its back. A crash truck and ambulance rushed to the scene but Halsey, angry with himself and unleashing a torrent of cuss words, stepped out without a scratch. He was more concerned that the event might dampen his eagerness to climb back into a plane, so rather than return to his quarters and rest, as everyone urged, he hopped into another plane to test his nerve.

Halsey's irregular flying, partly the result of an abhorrence for wearing his eyeglasses, gained him an "award" that he used as both a motivation and a reminder. The Royal Order of the Flying Jackass, an aluminum plate featuring a winged donkey standing on a boundary marker, was handed to any pilot who taxied into a boundary light. The pilot had to wear the emblem until another aviator committed the same offense. It was not long before Halsey demolished a marker and had to don the emblem. When Pensacola's commanding officer, Captain Rufus F. Zogbaum, asked Halsey to accompany him during an inspection, Halsey put on his uniform and the accompanying medals, an impressive array from three decades of service. As he paced through the assembled pilots, none could avoid laughing as, proudly draped around his neck, overshadowing his other honors, rested the Flying Jackass. Francis D. Foley, who later rose to the rank of rear admiral, explained that Halsey "endeared himself to everyone by being one of the boys."[16]

A few weeks later Halsey refused to yield the motif when a fellow pilot taxied into another light. "I won't wear it around here any more," he told his instructor, "but when I take command of the *Sara* [sic], I'm going to put it on the bulkhead of my cabin. If anybody aboard does anything stupid, I'll take a look at the Jackass before I bawl him out and I'll say, 'Wait a minute, Bill Halsey! You're not so damn good yourself!'"[17]

On May 15, 1935, at the completion of the course Captain Zogbaum pinned the coveted wings onto Halsey's uniform. Now a naval aviator and feeling more qualified to command an aircraft carrier, Halsey traveled to Long Beach, California, and reported to his next post, the USS *Saratoga,* in July 1935. The *Saratoga,* along with her sister ship, USS *Lexington,* held title to the largest warship in the world. The mammoth vessel displaced 33,000 tons and carried a crew of 3,373 men.

Halsey pondered how he, a man more accustomed to commanding between 250 and 300 men, would manage a ship holding ten times that number. Rather than create a new set of rules, he concluded that a carrier was nothing more than a destroyer on a grander scale, and he decided that he would follow the same command techniques that gained success on destroyers—fairness in discipline, insistence on a sparkling ship and on training, and making the men feel important.

In June 1937 Halsey received orders to return to Pensacola as the base commander. During his time in Florida Halsey was selected as rear admiral, a promotion that brought with it a loftier post. In May 1938, Halsey was named commander of Carrier Division 2, a unit consisting of the new twin carriers, USS *Yorktown* and USS *Enterprise,* in Norfolk, Virginia. A lengthy love affair thus started between Halsey and the *Enterprise,* the ship on which he first gained fame.

Halsey attracted attention in January 1939 with his actions during Fleet Problem XX, conducted in the Caribbean. Sent by his superior to locate an enemy cruiser force, Halsey did one better by launching a strike against the foe that judges ruled would have sunk the cruisers. Afterwards, President Franklin D. Roosevelt, who witnessed some of the maneuvers, hosted twenty flag officers aboard his ship. When Halsey spoke to his longtime associate, Roosevelt congratulated him on the fine showing and warned him to be alert to the activities of Germany and Japan.

Halsey's answer was to intensify the training his forces received. He utilized time in port assembling the carrier pilots in a large circle for informal discussions about world events, naval tactics, and other items. The pilots, most of whom were two decades younger than Halsey, felt during these chats that they were engaging in a bull session with their buddies. "Everybody was crazy about Admiral Halsey, I think, because he could kind of get with it, let us say," explained then Lieutenant Thomas M. Moorer, who later rose to the rank of admiral. "So there wasn't such a separation between the junior officers and the admiral. He had a knack of involving everybody in the discussion."[18]

In May 1939 Halsey switched from Carrier Division 2 to Carrier Division 1, where he rejoined the *Saratoga* in time for joint maneuvers with the Army. Rather than merely escorting troops to California beaches, as his orders stipulated, Halsey staged a surprise pre-dawn carrier air attack on an Army base at Reno, Nevada, 200 miles from the scene of the maneuvers. Halsey's aviators easily swept in to complete their mock destruction of the base, which took the Army commander by surprise. The pilots rubbed salt in the Army officer's wounds by dropping alarm clocks attached to parachutes with notes teasing him about being asleep. Halsey praised his young fliers while Army generals and battleship admirals fumed at the audacity of the unplanned attack. With his ingenious raid, Halsey foreshadowed another pre-dawn aerial assault that would drag the United States into war two years later.

In April 1940 the Battle Fleet, including Halsey's ships, steamed to Hawaii. Two months later he was promoted to the temporary rank of vice admiral and appointed Commander Carrier Division 2 (ComCarDiv 2) as well as Commander Aircraft Battle Force (ComAirBatFor). Halsey was now responsible for all the Pacific aircraft carriers and their air groups, heady duties in light of the developments bubbling in the Pacific. He attacked his new duties with typical enthusiasm, ordering his officers to reconsider tactics and notions that might no longer apply in light of recent world developments. "We improvised our formations, our tactics, our instructions," said Lieutenant William Ashford, "and changed them to meet particular conditions and certain operating problems."[19] Ashford recalled that most of the old tactical manuals disappeared from the shelves as Halsey coaxed his units to examine problems in new ways.

Halsey shrank from no decision, no matter whose feelings might be ruffled. One of his young squadron commanders, John S. Thach, was due to lead his squadron to the *Enterprise* shortly before a fleet problem, but Thach badly needed additional training for his inexperienced pilots, who had not even had the chance to fire their guns. Thach attempted to explain the problem to Lieutenant Commander Miles Browning, then Halsey's operations and war plans officer, but Browning ignored Thach's request. In a move that enraged Browning, Thach took the issue directly to Halsey. When he told Halsey that his men needed more time in the air, Halsey asked whether that afternoon would do. He was willing to grant additional training to Thach, even though in doing so Halsey could no longer employ Thach's squadron in the fleet problem. His men, not the exercise, mattered more to Halsey.

In his new post Halsey granted great leeway to his carrier commanders, but he expected them to use their initiative. Captain Ernest D. McWhorter, skipper of the *Yorktown,* failed to meet Halsey's standards. McWhorter, a newcomer to aviation, appeared hesitant on the bridge, which was the mark of death as far as Halsey was concerned. One day as his aircraft circled the carrier, McWhorter worried that an approaching rainstorm might toss the landings into disarray, even though his staff believed the planes could easily set down. Rather than make the decision on his own, McWhorter walked to the flag bridge to consult Halsey. According to Gerald F. Bogan, the *Yorktown*'s navigation officer, McWhorter's staff held its breath in anticipation of Halsey's eruption at being bothered by something so inconsequential, but Halsey calmly said, "Well, Mac, I don't care. If you're not in a hurry, why don't you go around [the storm]. It'll only take a few minutes." McWhorter prepared to leave, then turned back to Halsey and asked, "Admiral, shall I use right or left rudder?"[20]

That final query doomed McWhorter. Halsey vowed to block any promotion that came McWhorter's way, a promise he later abandoned, but the incident showed that Halsey expected commanders on the spot to make their own decisions.

At the same time, Halsey displayed a willingness to shoulder blame, even if he was not directly involved. During the ensuing maneuvers, a staff officer committed a navigational error that slowed the launching of aircraft from the *Yorktown.* Halsey received a message from his superior,

Admiral Ernest J. King, requesting the name of the officer responsible for the delay, but Halsey took full responsibility. That a senior commander would so readily place the blame on his own shoulders rather than single out a young officer impressed one onlooker. "He takes it without passing it on," said the man. "For my money, that's the mark of greatness in a naval officer. It's also the stuff that loyalty is built on."[21]

On the eve of war, Halsey the commander was taking shape. The traits he had developed through the years would be especially vital as 1941 dawned, since across the ocean another nation was flexing its military muscles.

"WAR WAS INEVITABLE"

Japan's role in the Pacific and the Far East was more complex than that of the United States, which enjoyed spacious land into which her population could spread. If Japan were to grow, the island nation required land beyond her borders. When expansionists studied the nearby areas, most eyes turned west toward the Asian mainland and China.

From early 1936 on, militarists had gained such influence in the government that an alarmed American ambassador to Japan, Joseph Grew, sent warnings to Washington. He cautioned his superiors that militarists intended to expand to China and other areas and that the course of events in the Pacific appeared ominous.

Halsey agreed with Grew. "I probably had felt for a great many years that war with Japan was inevitable," he wrote in his memoirs. "There were too many points of conflict, both economic and ratial [sic]."[22]

German dictator Adolf Hitler had already plunged Europe into a war that threatened to embroil the United States. When the German army swiftly defeated the French in June 1940, Congress appropriated $4 billion to build a two-ocean navy, one stationed in the Atlantic and the other in the Pacific.

In February 1941, Admiral Husband E. Kimmel took command of the Pacific Fleet, based out of Pearl Harbor, Hawaii, as a deterrent to Japanese aggression, while Halsey continued to direct operations for the Pacific's carriers and their air arms. Halsey chastised the isolationist trends so dominant in the United States in the 1930s for leading to stringent budgets that now, with Germany and Japan rattling their swords, placed the military in dire straits. Halsey admitted that had it not been for Franklin Roosevelt's perceptive views on foreign policy and his determined efforts to enlarge the military, the United States would be in even worse shape in the Pacific.

Admiral Kimmel reorganized the Pacific Fleet into three task forces. Halsey commanded Task Force 2, with Vice Admiral William S. Pye and Vice Admiral Wilson Brown directing Task Force 1 and Task Force 3 respectively. Kimmel kept at least two of the three task forces at sea at all times to avoid losing his entire carrier force to a single attack, although he relaxed his restrictions on weekends, when most ships crowded into Pearl Harbor for liberty.

Additional signs pointed to war. On April 4, 1941, Halsey received a dispatch from headquarters ordering the removal from all ships of any flammable materials such as canvas awnings and linoleum, as well as items that might splinter in the event of an explosion. Crews scraped regular paint from interior bulkheads and applied fireproof paint, mounted protective shields around guns, and installed submarine-detection equipment. Sailors painted ships a dull dark gray to better blend in with the sea and avoid recognition from enemy aircraft. "I believe by this time everyone in the fleet was conscious that war was inevitable, the only question was where and when it would strike,"[23] Halsey wrote in his memoirs.

When Japanese troops moved into Indochina in July 1941, President Roosevelt cut off all trade with Japan, including the flow of oil. He promised to maintain the embargo until Japan withdrew from both China and Indochina and renounced the Tripartite Pact. Japanese Prime Minister Hideki Tojo replied that the nation had more than 100,000 dead and wounded and that they could not now repudiate such sacrifices.

Japanese leaders faced two alternatives. They could settle with the United States and reopen the supply line from that nation, or they could continue to expand and risk war. With only an eighteen- to thirty-six-month supply of necessities, the leaders had to carefully weigh the route they would take.

Japanese Admiral Isoroku Yamamoto offered a solution. As the fastest-rising star in the Japanese Navy, Yamamoto had long understood that air power had replaced the battleship as the Navy's principle offensive arm. Because of his advocacy of additional naval air power, by the latter half of 1941 the Navy possessed six large aircraft carriers.

Yamamoto studied Japanese war plans and concluded that it was useless to attempt to lure the U.S. Navy into a decisive battle, which he believed handed the initiative to the United States and failed to properly employ Japan's new aircraft carriers. In its place he proposed a bold plan that would have delighted Halsey for its audacity—an attack against the American Navy at its base in Pearl Harbor. Yamamoto argued that only by delivering a strong opening blow could the Japanese hope to succeed in forcing the United States to the bargaining table. He cautioned that if the outcome were not decided in the first days, all could be lost.

Yamamoto's critics wondered how such a huge array of ships could sneak across the Pacific and unleash a surprise attack on a foe that was certain to be on the alert. Yamamoto, though, had scrutinized reports from agents operating in Hawaii and noticed that the American fleet, like clockwork, steamed into port every weekend for liberty. This, he believed, handed the Japanese an opportunity to strike when the United States least expected it. When the highly respected Yamamoto threatened to resign if his plan was not adopted, the general staff of the Japanese Navy assented in November 1941.

Yamamoto was all too aware of the risks, and he hoped to avoid war with a giant. As the United States possessed ten times the capacity to manufacture war matériel that Japan did, they would undoubtedly win any drawn-out struggle. Japan would have to deliver a knockout blow in the early stages or face defeat. As Yamamoto told the Japanese prime minister, "I can guarantee to put up a tough fight for the first six months, but I have absolutely no confidence as to what would happen if it went on for two or three years."[24]

"STEADY NERVES AND STOUT HEARTS ARE NEEDED NOW"

Military leaders in Japan agreed that if diplomats could not convince President Roosevelt to lift the embargo on oil and other products by the first week in November, they would start their operations against the

United States and the European powers. They only possessed enough oil reserves to last one year, and poorer weather after December would impede proposed landings on the Malay Peninsula and in the Philippines. While negotiations continued, the military prepared for war.

Japanese diplomats informed their American counterparts that if Roosevelt resumed oil shipments to Japan, Japan would halt her military action in Indochina. Alerted by intercepts of coded messages that Japanese troops were already embarking on transports for shipment to the Dutch East Indies and Southeast Asia, the American government spurned the proposal. In late November, Secretary of State Cordell Hull briefed Roosevelt and his cabinet to prepare for the likelihood that military action would be required.

On November 27 Kimmel received a dispatch from the Navy Department alerting him to the imminent threat of war. The message referred to Southeast Asia, the Philippines, or Borneo as the likely avenues of advance.

Kimmel took fast action. That same day he ordered Halsey to ferry twelve Marine fighters, under the command of Major Paul A. Putnam, to Wake Island in an attempt to bolster that outpost's defenses. "We fully expected that the trip with these Marines was leading us into the lion's mouth and that an overt act might occur and war be precipitated at any moment," Halsey stated in his memoirs. When he asked Kimmel what action he could take should he encounter any Japanese on the way to Wake, Kimmel gave him a free hand. "Goddam [sic] it, use your common sense," he replied.

Halsey needed little prodding. His Academy classmate had just given him orders that were tantamount to telling him to start the war should the opportunity arise. He appreciated Kimmel's faith in him, as Halsey would be the man on the spot and could better determine the proper reaction in a crisis. "I think that was as fine an order as a subordinate ever received and there was no attempt to pass the buck,"[25] explained Halsey.

Halsey guided Task Force 2 out of Pearl Harbor on November 28, taking every precaution to make it appear as if he were leaving on another training exercise. Once he reached the open sea, Halsey split his force into two parts. He would rush ahead with the faster vessels of Task

Force 8, consisting of the *Enterprise*, three heavy cruisers, and nine destroyers, while Rear Admiral Milo F. Draemel remained behind in command of the slower ships of Task Force 2.

Once out of range of Draemel's ships, Halsey issued Battle Order No. 1, a brief, bombastic message. Straight out of Halsey's playbook, it stated that "The *Enterprise* is now operating under war conditions" and that the crews should be prepared for action at any time, day or night. The order mentioned the possibility of encountering Japanese submarines and ended with the admonition, "Steady nerves and stout hearts are needed now."[26]

Halsey approved the arming of torpedoes, ordered aircraft to carry a full allotment of bombs and ammunition, and granted his pilots permission to shoot at any ship or aircraft they encountered. Lieutenant Clarence E. Dickinson, a member of the carrier's Scouting Squadron 6, listened with pride as his commander relayed Halsey's orders to the aviators. "Anything we saw in the sky was to be shot down, anything on the sea was to be bombed," Dickinson recalled of Halsey's orders. Halsey let them know that if they fired the opening shots of the war, they did so with his complete blessing and were not to worry about any reaction in Pearl Harbor. "Admiral Halsey had made it clear to us repeatedly that under any circumstances he stands behind us. Right or wrong, if we act he takes the responsibility."[27]

When Halsey's operations officer, Commander William H. Buracker, read the order, he asked Halsey if he had authorized the directive. Halsey replied that he had, at which Buracker asked, "Do you realize that this means war?" Halsey indicated that he did. Stunned, Buracker added, "Goddammit [sic], Admiral, you can't start a private war of your own! Who's going to take the responsibility?"

"I'll take it," growled Halsey. "Shoot first and we'll argue afterwards. I am going to if anything gets in my way."[28]

Halsey intended to prevent any Japanese ship or scout aircraft from radioing a report of their location. He also conjectured that, in light of the recent war warnings, all other ships in the area were hostile. "I believed that war was a matter of days, possibly hours, and that if we had to fight, our only chance of survival—and even of getting off an alert to the Commander in Chief before our ships were annihilated—was to strike the first blow. I felt that I would be completely justified in striking it."[29]

At 7:00 A.M. on December 4, with his force 200 miles from Wake Island, Halsey launched the twelve Marine fighters, then turned his ships toward Pearl Harbor. If all went well, he would enter the channel at 7:30 A.M. on Sunday, December 7.

Halsey could do little about the weather, however. When heavy seas and brisk winds delayed the refueling of his destroyers and retarded the force's progress, he alerted Pearl Harbor that he would not arrive until the night of December 7.

By dawn on December 7, Halsey stood 200 miles from Hawaii. He watched the launching of eighteen aircraft that would land at Ford's Island in Pearl Harbor, then stepped below to shower, change his uniform, and enjoy breakfast. He looked forward to reaching port, where a drink and a good dinner with friends would offer a respite from the tension.

Inclement weather proved an affable ally for Halsey, as it prevented him from being berthed inside Pearl Harbor when the Japanese attack started. Halsey's ships steamed safely at sea while Japanese aircraft dropped their bombs on slumbering ships.

With negotiations failing, the Japanese turned to their military as the only way to avoid being economically strangled. Though Roosevelt made one final attempt to keep talks going by sending a personal note to Japanese Emperor Hirohito on December 6, no response followed. When American codebreakers intercepted a Japanese message to diplomats in Washington ordering them to destroy sensitive documents and to present a note to the United States at 1:00 P.M. on December 7, Roosevelt knew war was imminent.

In the United States, reporters and editors applied the final touches to the last peacetime issue of *Time* magazine. Not surprisingly, thoughts of war dominated the pages. "Everything was ready," stated the publication. "From Rangoon to Honolulu, every man was at battle stations. . . . A vast array of armies, of navies, of air fleets were stretched now in the position of track runners, in the tension of the moment before the starter's gun." The magazine somberly concluded, "A bare chance of peace remained—of a kind of peace very close to war but not quite war."[30]

CHAPTER 3

"ADMIRAL HALSEY'S SEAGOING COMMANDOS"

"THIS IS NO DRILL"

The serenity with which December 7, 1941, dawned created a surreal mood for what was about to unfold. At 7:58 A.M., as Halsey ate breakfast with his flag secretary, Lieutenant H. Douglas Moulton, the telephone rang. Moulton answered, then as the blood drained from his face, turned to Halsey.

"Admiral, the staff duty officer says he has a message that there's an air raid on Pearl!"

Halsey jumped to his feet and, thinking that Pearl Harbor's guns had mistakenly identified the eighteen *Enterprise* aircraft, exclaimed, "My God, they're shooting at our own planes. Get the word to Kimmel."[1]

Before Moulton could comply with Halsey's instruction, at 8:12 Halsey's communications officer, Lieutenant Commander Leonard J. Dow, rushed in with a dispatch from Kimmel. "Air raid on Pearl Harbor. This is no drill."[2]

Halsey immediately called for general quarters and ordered that the carrier's battle flag be hoisted. The United States—and Admiral Halsey—were at war.

WITHIN THE HOUR, Admiral Kimmel named Halsey, then 150 miles west of Pearl Harbor, the commander of all the ships at sea. Until the situation calmed and further decisions could be made, besides his own Task Force 8 Halsey was to take charge of Task Force 3, consisting of the heavy cruiser USS *Indianapolis* and escorting destroyers then off Johnston Island 700 miles southwest of Hawaii; and of Task Force 12, comprising the carrier USS *Lexington,* three cruisers, and escorting destroyers then steaming northwest of Hawaii to deliver aircraft to Midway Island. In addition, all ships inside Pearl Harbor that could reach the open sea were to sortie as Task Force 2 under Rear Admiral Milo Draemel, still in command of the battleships and destroyers that Halsey had detached before heading toward Wake. The orders handed Halsey every offensive weapon then at sea. In the Pacific War's opening hours, Halsey comprised the sole barrier between the Japanese and the West Coast.

At 9:15 A.M. the first wartime combat air patrol of the Pacific, consisting of four F4F fighters, lifted off the *Enterprise.* Six minutes later Halsey ordered Task Forces 3 and 12 to rendezvous with him near Niihau Island to Hawaii's west. Halsey had no idea how the enemy had drawn so close to the Hawaii bastion or how much damage the Japanese had inflicted inside the anchorage, but he intended to meet the enemy and make them pay a price for their brazen attack.

A maddening day ensued as Halsey chased imaginary foes based upon erroneous reports. At first the enemy was seen southwest of Hawaii, then to the south, and finally to the northwest. Halsey sent ships or aircraft in pursuit after each sighting, but found only empty ocean. He received so many diverse reports that he wondered if enemy spies operating in Hawaii had sent them.

"The confusing and conflicting reports that had poured in on us all day had succeeded only in enraging me," Halsey wrote in his autobiography. "It is bad enough to be blindfolded, but it is worse to be led around the compass."[3]

Worse still to be chasing one's own forces. Confused *Enterprise* aviators in scout planes, unnerved by the war's first day, spotted Rear Admiral Draemel's ships, which they speedily misidentified as Japanese. Halsey's staff relayed this information to Draemel, along with orders to locate and attack the Japanese. For a part of the afternoon, in a caper the Keystone Kops would have relished, Draemel unwittingly chased himself.

Around 1:30 P.M. Halsey learned that Japan had declared war on the United States. "The dirty little bastards!" bellowed Halsey, irate that Japan's opening attack had preceded her announcement. "Japan attacks, kills our citizens, shoots down our planes, sinks our ships; then bows and tells us, 'Excuse, please, but have decided to declare war!'"[4]

Halsey's anger became a driving force in the war that elevated him to national attention. Already known for aggressiveness within naval circles, Halsey would be adopted by a nation seeking a response to December 7. The factory worker, mailman, or housewife back home, as well as the Navy in the Pacific, could not yet strike back at the Japanese, but in the interim they had Halsey. He became their reply, the tip of their sword pointed at Tokyo, until the country's military machine roared to life. If the United States could not answer with bullets and bombs, at least Halsey would respond with words.

The day's frustrations infuriated Halsey. Friends and Academy classmates fought and died at Pearl Harbor at the hands of an enemy who, by his reckoning, had to be somewhere close by. He wanted revenge, but on December 7 Halsey never located the enemy.

"If I had had more information as to the whereabouts of the enemy fleet, I could have and would have intercepted them and attacked," Halsey wrote in his memoirs. He admitted that he could have done little harm with the forces he commanded—a carrier, a handful of cruisers, and some destroyers—and that he was low on fuel, but he believed "my few remaining planes might have accomplished some damage." He added that while he never fired a shot on December 7, "I have the consolation of knowing that, on the opening day of the war, I did everything in my power to find a fight."[5]

Halsey's angst was the U.S. Navy's and the nation's good fortune. Had Halsey met the enemy on December 7, a catastrophe would have resulted. The six Japanese carriers and their iron blanket of escorts would have handily sent Halsey and his smaller collection of warships to the ocean's bottom. Had that calamity occurred, the thin naval line between Yamamoto and the West Coast would have been eliminated. Sometimes avoiding an encounter can be as crucial as engaging in one.

"YOU'RE ALL WE'VE GOT LEFT"

As dusk neared, Halsey split a group of aircraft that had been sent to attack a Japanese force reported south of his position. The planes failed to locate anything, but in their lengthy search consumed most of their fuel. Halsey ordered six fighters to continue on to Pearl Harbor rather than attempt a difficult night landing on a carrier, then positioned the *Enterprise* to take on the dive-bombers and torpedo planes that lacked enough fuel to reach Pearl Harbor. The pilots would have to set down on a rolling carrier at night while still carrying their torpedoes.

As Halsey watched from the bridge, a Devastator torpedo plane landed hard and sent a torpedo skipping dangerously along the flight deck. The missile barely missed the island on its path toward the bow, where it came to a sudden stop. Crew rushed out and disarmed the torpedo before it could explode.

The six fighter pilots faced a rougher ordeal. Even though the *Enterprise* had notified Pearl Harbor about the planes, jittery antiaircraft gunners inside the harbor did not take any chances. As the fighters flew above Battleship Row, gun crews filled the nighttime sky with tracers while soldiers lined the shore to fire vintage World War I–era Springfield rifles. In the confusion, three of Halsey's pilots died, including Ensign Herbert H. Menges, the first naval fighter pilot to perish in the war.

These first casualties of the war under his command were bitter pills for Halsey, especially as they came from friendly fire instead of at the hands of the enemy. He understood that frightened young gunners had spent a difficult day battling the Japanese, and "When you have actually seen your ships treacherously attacked and injured and your comrades killed, no planes look friendly to you and you shoot first and ask questions afterwards."[6] Still, the losses hit him hard. Throughout the war the deaths of young sailors and men under his command kept Halsey awake at night.

At dusk on December 8, as his ships inched into Pearl Harbor, Halsey braced for what he knew would be a shattering spectacle.

Flames consumed ships and buildings while billowing black smoke formed a somber canopy shrouding the mangled base. The hulls of Halsey's ships brushed aside debris in the narrow channel as they moved toward berths cradling charred vessels. The odor of burning oil and seared bodies sickened some of the crew that stood along the edge of the flight deck, while the sights, sounds, and smells moved many to tears. The battleship USS *Nevada* lay grounded by the stern, and water swept across the decks of its fellow battlewagon, the USS *California,* which had settled to the bottom. In the spot where the *Enterprise* would have berthed had she arrived as originally scheduled, the battleship USS *Utah,* rent to a twisted heap by Japanese torpedoes, lay belly-up in the water. Halsey quietly surveyed the carnage, absorbing the incredible destruction, then blurted through clenched teeth, "Before we're through with 'em, the Japanese language will be spoken only in hell!"[7]

Hundreds of soldiers manning their posts at Hickam Field watched the *Enterprise* and her escorts return. Some, still numb from the Sunday fighting, stared without muttering a sound. Others vented their rage. "Where in hell were you?" shouted a soldier in the carrier's direction, while another yelled, "You'd better get the hell out of here or the Japs will nail you too."[8]

Robert J. Casey, a newspaper reporter observing the events, concluded that the Japanese could not have wasted many shots in light of all the destruction he witnessed, which he called "startling, stupendous, and disgraceful." The images created the nightmare scenario of an enemy free to roam the Pacific while the United States stood helplessly by. "You got the impression that whatever the inventory of damage, the United States wasn't going to hit back because the United States couldn't hit back." He added, "We began to wonder, as many a person was wondering in Honolulu right at that time, if we weren't totting up the score for a war that had ended before it began."[9]

Halsey commandeered a boat and hurried to Kimmel's headquarters. The emotion and trauma of the wrenching forty-eight hours showed in the exhausted, unshaven faces and grimy uniforms of Kimmel and his staff. Halsey thought that while Kimmel looked haggard, he kept his chin up and maintained his composure as he directed subordinates.

Kimmel briefed Halsey on the latest developments, then reiterated that, to avoid being caught in a follow-up attack, Halsey could not risk his carrier by remaining in the harbor. He had to refuel and re-provision as quickly as possible and head back to the open seas.

A trickle of good news brightened the gloom. Though the Japanese had inflicted serious damage to the fleet, they had also left valuable targets untouched. They had missed the carriers, which had been at sea instead of in the harbor. Many of the sunken ships, including the battleships, could be salvaged for later use. Most important, the Japanese had not targeted three crucial assets—Pearl Harbor's repair shops, the submarine base, and 4.5 million barrels of fuel oil. Had the Japanese destroyed these resources, the United States would have been forced to withdraw its remnants to the West Coast, a step that would have delayed the war's end by months, if not years. As it was, the Navy reeled under the losses, but at least it had carriers, submarines, and fuel. Until the time came when American factories produced the needed weapons to take the fight to the enemy, the carriers and submarines would have to bear the load.

Halsey returned to the *Enterprise* to oversee the repair work. By working nonstop, the crew completed the refueling and re-provisioning in eight instead of the normal twelve hours. Just after 5:00 A.M. on December 9, the task force departed.

Before they left, a soldier on shore remarked to a member of the crew, "It's up to you carrier boys now. Pearl Harbor must be held, and you're all we've got left in the Pacific!"[10]

WHILE HALSEY STRUGGLED with the scenes of destruction at Pearl Harbor, a combination of anger, fear, and determination gripped the country. *Time* magazine labeled the attack "premeditated murder masked by a toothy smile" and stated that though Japan had brought instant unity to the nation, trying moments lay ahead. The Navy "was caught with its pants down"[11] at Pearl Harbor, absorbing greater naval losses in one morning than it had in all of World War I.

The magazine noted, however, that the country would have to wait for a meaningful response from a hamstrung military. "Like a boxer who is slammed before he can get off his stool, the Pacific Fleet had first to get itself up. From that time until the day when it can report its first victories over the Japanese, its role is primarily defensive." The magazine concluded that in light of the drastic circumstances, "a revolutionary strategy" was required of the military. "When Japanese bombers whipped over the frowning fastness of Diamond Head last Sunday morning the book of traditional U.S. naval strategy in the Pacific was torn to shreds."[12]

In calling for an innovative strategy, the magazine described a situation that was made for Halsey. If any officer could smash the traditional restrictions and head into uncharted territory, something not seen on the war boards of the Naval War College, it was Halsey. Free to improvise, Halsey became a master irritant to the Japanese, an unquenchable fly buzzing about the perimeters of the Japanese advance. In the process, Halsey rose to national fame, established a reputation as a ferocious battler, and unconsciously fashioned an image that would, in one October morning off the Philippines, haunt him.

For the next week Halsey and the *Enterprise* task force steamed off Hawaii, checking on reported sightings and guarding the avenue to the islands. The constant activity placed a heavy burden on his aviators, who had to endure long hours in the skies. Some had flown through thick antiaircraft fire and enemy bullets to land at Pearl Harbor on December 7. Others had watched aircraft burst into flames and seen friends die.

Halsey sensed the toll. On December 10 he made a surprise appearance in the aviators' wardroom to lift their spirits. He delivered a stirring talk in which he expressed his confidence in the men and in ultimate victory. "True, the Japs got lucky at Pearl, gentlemen" said Halsey, "but it will be and is their downfall. We are going to fight vigorously and viciously until we've drilled them into the God damn ground!"

Halsey's optimism impressed the young aviators, causing one to exclaim, "Those Japs had better look out for that man." Lieutenant Richard Best listened with growing confidence as "the old man" delivered his pep talk. "Halsey won respect not with his good looks—he truly looked like a bulldog—but with his attitude," recalled Best. "He clearly carried the emotions of everyone with this speech." Best then summed what may have been Halsey's most significant contribution to them at that moment and to the home front later—boosting their morale with positive assertions. "That mirrored Halsey in everything he did, in every operation he led. Right from the start of the war, he grew a 'Get them' attitude in the *Enterprise* crew from the lowest black gang kid to the Captain."[13]

Halsey registered a minor victory. On December 10 seven Japanese submarines maneuvered into position to intercept Halsey as his force steamed north of Oahu, but a dawn search from the *Enterprise* detected the invaders. Aircraft bombs forced to the surface the submarine *I–70,* which sank later in the day. The other six Japanese boats launched torpedoes, but they churned harmlessly by the *Enterprise.*

When Halsey returned to Pearl Harbor on December 16, he learned that his longtime friend and classmate, Admiral Kimmel, had been relieved and replaced by Admiral Chester W. Nimitz. Until Nimitz could report for duty, Admiral William S. Pye took over in temporary command.

"WHERE, OH WHERE, IS THE UNITED STATES NAVY?"

At least one light pierced the gloom. In the bleak days following Pearl Harbor the Marine defenders on Wake Island repulsed a December 11 landing attempt and held on to the tiny atoll against near-daily bombing attacks. In the process, the Wake Islanders lifted home-front morale and injected confidence into their fellow military.

Before being relieved, Admiral Kimmel formed Task Force 14 to rush additional supplies and men to the besieged defenders. Consisting of the *Saratoga* and fourteen escorting vessels commanded by Rear Admiral Frank Jack Fletcher, Kimmel risked losing his valuable ships should a stronger enemy naval force appear, but he felt the impact on morale for both the military and the public back home outweighed the negatives. The Wake Island Marines needed help.

Kimmel's temporary successor, Admiral William S. Pye, more reluctant than his predecessor to risk such a large portion of the Navy's remaining resources, at first hesitantly went along with the scheme when he replaced Kimmel. On December 18 he ordered Halsey to stand near Midway so that he could protect the right flank of the ships racing to Wake. At that location he would be able to rush southwest to Wake Island or southeast to Hawaii in case either required assistance.

Great expectations quickly crumbled. As the relief force steamed across the Pacific, a cautious Pye kept a wary eye out for the Japanese Navy, especially their aircraft carriers, and was ready to recall the unit should any significant opposition appear. His apprehension increased when Admiral Harold R. Stark, the Chief of Naval Operations, informed Pye that the Navy Department considered Wake a liability and that the decision to relieve the garrison rested solely in his hands. Pye correctly read between the lines. He could continue the operation to save the atoll's defenders, but his superiors would hold him accountable should the Pacific Fleet, already badly harmed, suffer significant losses. Admiral Pye weighed his options and ordered the relief expedition back to Pearl Harbor.

The recall produced angry outbursts among Marine and Navy personnel aboard the ships at sea, who urged superiors to ignore the order and steam to the rescue of the brave Marines. On the bridge of the *Saratoga* Rear Admiral Aubrey Fitch retreated to his quarters so he would not hear possibly mutinous talk and be forced to take action. One Navy officer aboard the *Enterprise* dejectedly wrote, "It's the war between two yellow races." Even in Japan, propagandist Tokyo Rose ridiculed the Navy by sarcastically asking in a broadcast, "Where, oh where, is the United States Navy?"[14]

Halsey supposedly swore for half an hour when informed of the decision, which he viewed as a betrayal of gallant men. He considered disregarding Pye, but cooler heads among his staff dissuaded him. "Why we were diverted I still don't know," he wrote after the war. "All we knew was that the war was only fifteen days old, and we had already lost Wake and Guam."[15] Halsey, irritated at missing the enemy on December 7, believed Pye's timidity blinded him to an opportunity to damage the enemy. Halsey re-entered Pearl Harbor on the last day of 1941, eight days after Wake's fall, still lacking an encounter with the enemy.

In his unpublished memoirs, Halsey divided his wartime career into three distinct phases. The first—lasting from the attack at Pearl Harbor until his hospitalization in June 1942—covered his time as commander of a task force at sea. The second phase—his stint as an area commander in the South Pacific—started in October 1942 and lasted until June 1944, at which time he assumed command of the Third Fleet, an immense conglomeration of men, ships, and aircraft.

A more accurate assessment of Halsey as a wartime commander would split his service in half, each producing vastly different results—the no-holds-barred commander who, in the bleak days of 1942 and into 1943, rallied his fellow Americans at home and in the service at a time when national morale and hope were at their lowest, and the Third Fleet commander who, in 1944–1945, helmed the mightiest naval assemblage in warfare at a time when the conflict's outcome, unlike 1942–1943, was rarely in doubt. Although Halsey created controversy and criticism in the latter years, his words and deeds in the war's first two years guarantee his place with John Paul Jones and the other great naval commanders in United States history.

To comprehend the significance of Halsey's contributions to victory in 1942 and 1943, one must understand the country's mood in the weeks after Pearl Harbor. Not only was much of the nation's military capability lying in the mud at Pearl Harbor, but citizens struggled to digest what had occurred, how it could have happened—and wondered when the military would respond. A pessimism bordering on defeatism gripped many. Americans, who took pride in the knowledge that the nation had never suffered a defeat, now stared at images of mangled ships littering a smoking Pacific harbor.

Correspondent John Lardner described a country that scrambled for answers, a nation of immense buoyancy that had suddenly had the rug pulled from underneath its feet. He wrote of "the picture of a country and an army and a navy at war but innocent of knowledge of war, full of fight but uncertain how to flex a fist, earnest, awkward, stumbling, getting up and falling down again, learning from day to day and learning always the hard way—aware of potential might and resources to come, but aware too of the crying needs and desperate lacks of the moment."[16]

In early January 1942, a *Time* magazine article titled "Where Is the Fleet?" quoted citizens who worried about the nation's capacity to respond. In the article, noted military correspondent Hanson Baldwin warned that, "The Pacific Fleet is not capable of conducting a major foray today against Japan." John Lardner agreed with the assessment, stating that, "We did what we could with the tools at hand, in the early weeks of defensive war."[17]

Military commanders in the Pacific faced the quandary of how to respond with the meager resources then available. Admiral Kimmel shepherded his carriers east of the 180° meridian to patrol the crucial triangle between Wake Island, Midway, and Hawaii. His successor, Admiral Pye, hoped to stage minor raids to keep the Japanese on the defensive, but as another admiral stated, "We were to fight a holding war—but there was little to do the holding with."[18]

While testifying before the Roberts Commission, established to investigate the debacle at Pearl Harbor, Halsey provided a hint of the tactics they could expect of the man. "I think General Forrest's [Civil War General Nathan Bedford Forrest] description is the best thing I know, to get to the other fellow with everything you have and as fast as you can and to dump it on him. You have to scout out and find it, and as soon as you find it, send everything you can at him and hit him with it."[19]

Within a few months American households would cheer Halsey's name for precisely those tactics.

"WILD BILL WILL TRY ANYTHING ONCE"

In elevating Chester W. Nimitz as fulltime replacement for Kimmel as Commander in Chief Pacific Fleet, Admiral Ernest J. King, the newly appointed Commander in Chief United States Fleet, issued clear instructions. He drew a heavy line on a map that the Japanese could not be allowed to cross—the demarcation ran from Midway Island straight down to Samoa, southwest to Fiji, and on to Australia. Nimitz had to protect the crucial Midway-Johnston Island-Hawaii triangle from further attack, and more important, guard the vital lines of communication connecting the United States mainland with Australia and New Zealand. Should those lines be severed and Australia fall to the Japanese, Allied ability to mount an offensive against Japan might suffer a fatal blow.

King, sensing the American public's hunger for good news and knowing that the Navy must strike back to show the country that someone stood guard in the Pacific, added, "Undertake some aggressive action for effect on general morale."[20] He left the details to Nimitz's discretion, but emphasized that the nation needed to read about American, not Japanese, daring.

Nimitz possessed few resources with which to implement an attack. It would be foolish to jeopardize his carriers. At this stage of the war, the fighter aircraft aboard the carriers were slower and less maneuverable than the Japanese Zero, while the stodgy, slow torpedo planes made tempting targets. Despite the shortcomings, Nimitz had to team his carriers with the right leader and hand him a mission that made sense.

Halsey cemented his relationship with Nimitz during a January 8 meeting at headquarters. Halsey and his cruiser commander, Rear Admiral Raymond A. Spruance, attended the discussion, during which Nimitz and his staff debated what steps to take next. Intelligence indicated that the Japanese intended to send aircraft from new bases in the Gilbert Islands to strike the lines of communication to Australia.

To counter this, Nimitz proposed that carriers rush reinforcements to Samoa, then veer north to strike at the Gilberts and the Marshalls. Some of Nimitz's staff objected to the move, asserting that the Navy could ill afford to lose any of its valuable carriers. The officers, leftovers from Kimmel's staff, argued that if Nimitz lost the carriers, the West Coast of the United States would be vulnerable to attack.

Nimitz could simply order any mission he desired, but he preferred to avoid that step. He had only been in Pearl Harbor a few days, while the staff had devoted months to Pacific strategy. Besides, as he was not an aviator and had never commanded an aircraft carrier, Nimitz felt he could not yet press his arguments too strenuously to men who possessed aviation experience.

Halsey, the aviator and carrier commander, stifled the defeatist atmosphere with a few sentences. He stated that in the current condition, with the nation reeling from news of Japanese victories, to do nothing was not only worse than risking the carriers, but was alarmingly defeatist. Every operation entailed risk, he added, and he exhorted the men to consider Nimitz's plan to attack the Gilberts. Halsey's eloquence suppressed further objections from his fellow aviators and convinced the staff that action was preferable to inaction.

Nimitz never forgot Halsey's firm stand in his behalf. On January 9 he ordered Halsey to attack the Gilberts and Marshalls. After escorting reinforcements to American Samoa, Halsey and Task Force 8 centering around the *Enterprise*, joined by Rear Admiral Frank Jack Fletcher's Task Force 17, anchored by the *Yorktown*, would turn north to strike the Japanese island bases.

Nimitz's astute move provided the perfect answer for King's dictate to conduct a bold offensive action. As Robert E. Lee had Stonewall Jackson in the Civil War, and as Dwight Eisenhower would later have George Patton, Nimitz now teamed with Halsey to take the fight to the enemy. Halsey would be his offensive arm in the war's early months. In elevating Halsey to direct America's initial response, Nimitz all but guaranteed that Halsey would become the war's first hero.

Halsey led his force out of Pearl Harbor on January 11. Escorted by three heavy cruisers—*Chester, Northampton,* and *Salt Lake City*—seven destroyers, and one oiler, the *Enterprise* steamed from Hawaii and veered south to rendezvous with Admiral Fletcher north of American Samoa.

On January 24 the task force, with Fletcher and Task Force 17 steaming 150 miles astern of Halsey's Task Force 8, altered direction and headed northwest for the approach to the Gilberts and the Marshalls 1,600 miles distant. Robert Casey observed on the *Salt Lake City* that the officers grew more nervous as each mile brought the men closer to their first taste of combat. "After all it's unexpected to find an abiding calm among the officers of this crate. Not one of them has ever heard a shot fired for business purposes."[21]

The original plan called for Fletcher to strike Makin Atoll in the Gilberts and Jaluit and Mili in the southern Marshalls, while Halsey attacked Wotje and Maloelap in the northern Marshalls. However, when a submarine reported on January 27 that the Marshall Island chain was lightly defended, Halsey, following the advice of his chief of staff, Miles Browning, added another target. Even though the change would require Halsey to navigate directly into the midst of the Marshalls and bring his force within striking range of Japanese land-based aircraft, Halsey directed an attack against Kwajalein itself. On February 1 his aviators would hit airfields on Kwajalein, Maloelap, and Wotje, while his cruisers bombarded Wotje and Maloelap. As long as he could attain surprise, Halsey concluded that the benefits justified the risks. "It was one of those plans which are called 'brilliant' if they succeed and 'foolhardy' if they fail,"[22] wrote Halsey.

The men readily embraced the changes and their attendant perils. "As far as steaming close to danger goes, that didn't mean anything to Admiral Halsey," stated one man. Others boasted that, "Wild Bill will try anything once."[23]

Halsey divided Task Force 8 into three groups. Rear Admiral Spruance's Task Group 8.1, consisting of the cruisers *Northampton* and *Salt Lake City* escorted by the destroyer *Dunlap,* would strike Wotje, while Captain Thomas M. Shock's Task Group 8.3, with the destroyers *Balch* and *Maury* escorting the heavy cruiser *Chester,* hit Maloelap. Halsey would take Task Group 8.5, consisting of the *Enterprise* and three escorting destroyers directly into the Marshalls for the main assault against Kwajalein and for secondary attacks against Wotje and Maloelap.

Few civilians knew the name Halsey, nor did they expect to wake up to headlines that heralded a triumph rather than another defeat. In a few days, however, the nation would have its victory and its first wartime hero.

As Commander T. P. Jeter, the executive officer of the *Enterprise,* wrote on January 31:

"An eye for an eye,
A tooth for a tooth,
This Sunday it's our turn to shoot."[24]

"HAUL ASS WITH HALSEY"

Halsey's concerns rose as his ships neared their targets. In adding Kwajalein to the list of objectives, Halsey had to bring the *Enterprise* dangerously close to Japanese-held islands, at times even steaming between atolls containing enemy aircraft.

On January 31, 1942, the eve of launching, a Japanese scout aircraft flew within thirty-four miles of the task force, but haze fortunately prevented the pilot from sighting the ships. Halsey, delighted that he had escaped detection, asked his staff to pen a message for his opponent, translate it into Japanese, and have it dropped during the bombing raids. "From the American Admiral in charge of the striking force, to the

Japanese Admiral on the Marshall Islands," the note began. "It is a pleasure to thank you for having your patrol plane not sight my force."[25]

At 6:30 P.M. on January 31, Halsey embarked on the final approach to what would be his first experience in combat. "The night was clear and calm, and I was the exact opposite. As a commanding officer on the eve of his first action, I felt that I should set an example of composure, but I was so nervous that I took myself to my emergency cabin, out of sight. I couldn't sleep. I tossed and twisted, drank coffee, read mystery stories, and smoked cigarettes. Finally I gave up and went back to flag plot."[26]

At 3:00 A.M. *Enterprise* aviators awoke and ate breakfast. Forty-five minutes later flight quarters sounded, and within the hour each pilot was ready to launch. After a frustrating two months in which the Navy had attempted to recover from the shock of December 7, Halsey was providing the answer to the home front's question about where the Navy had gone.

At 4:43 A.M. only thirty-six miles off Wotje, Commander Howard L. Young led nine *Enterprise* torpedo bombers, carrying 500-pound bombs for their targets at Kwajalein, and thirty-seven dive bombers, armed with 500- and 100-pound bombs for Roi. While his aviators attacked Roi and Kwajalein and his cruisers under Admiral Spruance blasted Wotje and Maloelap, Admiral Fletcher attacked Jaluit, Makin, and Mili.

Halsey, wearing a leather windbreaker and a white sun helmet as he waited for the results, listened through earphones as his fliers shouted encouragement and warnings to each other and celebrated as their bombs tore into ships and buildings. At one point the *Enterprise* steamed so close to Wotje that Halsey easily observed antiaircraft fire rising from the island and the columns of black smoke billowing from targets.

Halsey mounted twenty-one strikes while maneuvering the carrier inside a tight rectangle five miles by twenty-five miles. He knew the risks of an enemy air attack rose the longer he lingered, but he kept his ships inside the rectangle for nine hours to give his aviators as much time as possible over the objectives.

Halsey's pilots inflicted light damage on the Japanese, dispatching one transport and two smaller vessels while damaging eight others.

Though the raids were unspectacular, especially when compared to future operations, Japanese pride suffered a blow. Rear Admiral Matome Ugaki, Yamamoto's principal adviser, wrote in his diary on February 1, "They have come after all; they are some guys!" He added that the Americans had chosen wisely as the Japanese had focused on the Southwest Pacific and "the defensive strength in the Marshalls was thin."[27]

Halsey had all but dared the Japanese to come out with his bold decision to remain in hostile waters for nine hours. Around 1:00 P.M. Lieutenant Commander William R. Hollingsworth, the commander of Bombing 6, arrived at the bridge to make his report. After completing his assessment of the results, Hollingsworth added, "Admiral, don't you think it's about time we get the hell out of here?"

"Boy," replied Halsey, "I think you got something. Let's go."[28] Halsey issued orders for the force to turn back to Pearl Harbor.

Captain G. D. Murray described in his Action Report that the *Enterprise* "took up a retiring course at high speed." Robert Casey wrote in his diary, "This is the fastest I've ever traveled except in a speedboat somewhere on a calm lake. We are sticking our nose into it and flinging spray over the bridge."[29] Sailors coined a new phrase by boasting of membership in the "Haul Ass with Halsey" club. The first brush strokes painting the image of Halsey as a legend had been applied.

At 1:38 P.M. five Japanese twin-engined bombers, led by Lieutenant Kazuo Nakai, attacked. On the open bridge, Halsey followed the bombs' paths until Browning shouted the order for everyone to drop down. "I gladly obeyed," wrote Halsey, who later stated he felt a mixture of fear and anger—"I admit I was . . . madder than hell"—as the enemy missiles drew closer. "I was the fustest and the fastest on the deck and when I finally arose I had most of the footprints of the other people who were on the flag bridge, on my back."[30]

Captain Murray swerved the carrier out of the way to avoid direct hits. Explosions from near misses produced 200-foot geysers that shook the *Enterprise,* and shrapnel ignited the fuel and killed Boatswain's Mate 2nd Class George H. Smith.

The five pilots turned away after dropping their bombs, but Nakai, apparently with a damaged aircraft, veered back in a suicidal attempt to crash into the *Enterprise.* The Japanese pilot avoided the curtain of antiaircraft fire and smashed into the deck, scraping the port edge of the flight deck opposite Halsey with the plane's wingtip and ripping off the tail of a Dauntless. With Halsey watching the scene directly below, the right wing split from Nakai's plane and skidded into the port catwalk. The rest of the bomber sprayed fuel everywhere as it spun madly across the deck before disappearing over the side.

Halsey joked about his fear during this first action, but his staff claimed that once the shooting began, Halsey kept his composure. Browning even once cautioned Halsey about the white sun helmet he wore, explaining that the unusual headgear might draw the attention of the Japanese gunners, but Halsey growled, "Gives 'em something better to shoot at!"[31]

The most direct route to Pearl Harbor was to head northeast, a path that enemy submarines or scout planes were certain to comb, but Halsey's flag lieutenant, Lieutenant William H. Ashford, offered a tempting alternative. One hundred miles from the Marshalls, the officer spotted a squall to the northwest and suggested Halsey hide among its mist to evade the Japanese. Halsey agreed and ordered a course change toward the covering.

For the next few days the task force traveled with the squall, which benevolently masked them from searching Japanese eyes. A few times radar tracked Japanese planes—Yamamoto had sent three carriers from Truk to chase Halsey—as they searched nearby, but not once did they find Halsey.

As the task force neared Hawaii and with the country's first offensive strike in his pocket, Halsey sent a message to all hands. "Well done! You have made history in the Marshalls. I am proud to have the honor to command you. God bless you!"[32]

"ALL HANDS, WELL DONE"

For the first time in the war, a victorious American task force returned to the warm reception of a grateful nation. On February 5, when the ships steamed into Pearl Harbor, sailors of the task force again saw men of the naval base aligned along the shores, but this time cheering their exploits rather than shouting derogatory remarks as they had in the immediate aftermath of December 7. At Hospital Point, nurses and doctors rushed outside and waved to the returning victors. Ships anchored in Pearl Harbor blew their whistles and sirens while crews manned the railings to catch a glimpse of the warriors. The frustrations of December 7 dissipated in the wake of America's initial victory. Halsey's operation brought hope to military and civilian alike and replaced defeatism.

"We had been whipped in the attack that opened the war and had been on the defensive ever since," Halsey wrote. "Now the offensive spirit was reestablished; officers and men were bushy-tailed again. So, presently, was the American public. At last we had been able to answer their roweling question, 'Where is the Navy?'"[33]

Halsey tried unsuccessfully to check his emotions as he witnessed the powerful scene. "Naturally this filled us all with pride of accomplishment," he wrote. "The men in the task force tried to cheer back but choked up. I myself cried and was not ashamed of it." Admiral Nimitz hastened to the *Enterprise* to congratulate Halsey, and Rear Admiral Robert A. Theobald, commander of the Pacific destroyers, waved a finger in Halsey's face and exclaimed, "Damn you, Bill, you've got no business getting home from that one! No business at all!"[34]

This raid handed the press what they had been seeking. The nation needed a hero, and in Halsey the newspapers and magazines found one, a protagonist who charged into battle, hurling shells and quotable phrases in equal measure. Halsey was the smiling, swearing antagonist to Yamamoto who symbolized action over timidity and optimism over defeatism.

In a ceremony aboard the *Enterprise,* Nimitz pinned the Distinguished Service Medal on Halsey for his execution of the raid, an award he deflected to his staff and men. Halsey told his staff they were as much responsible for the award as he was, and that evening he joined the carrier's crew on deck to watch a movie. Before the film, the crew asked Halsey to say a few words. Halsey proudly held up his medal and told the young Americans that he was honored to wear it on their behalf. He paused as emotions swelled to the surface, then added, "I just want to say that I have never been so damned proud of anyone as you."[35] The ship's crew erupted in such raucous applause and cheering that one officer stated that it was the most moving demonstration of fondness from crew to leader that he had ever witnessed.

People in the United States rejoiced that their military had finally struck back. A relatively unknown admiral had handed them something to cheer, and overnight, the nation had its hero—a role Halsey was more than happy to fill. Until February, doubt and fear had dominated hopes, but Halsey had replaced that with the belief that the Japanese could be vanquished.

"U.S. Pacific Fleet Batters Japanese Bases in Marshall and Gilbert Isles" ran the *New York Times* headline for a story filed February 2. The paper stated that the news, "received in official Washington with great satisfaction, was regarded in many quarters as an answer—and probably only a preliminary and token answer—to the question long raised and repeated frequently by critics: 'Where is our Navy?'"[36]

As commander of the assault force that delivered America's first attack of the war, Admiral Halsey received the lion's share of praise. Reporters labeled him "Bull" Halsey, the man who like a bull charged fearlessly into the enemy's den and safely extricated his ships after inflicting an embarrassing blow. The *New York Times* heralded Halsey "for planning and conducting these brilliant and audacious attacks on Japanese strongholds and for driving them home with great skill and determination."[37] One reporter labeled the intrepid leader and his force "sea-guerrillas." Halsey was the home front's darling.

HALSEY WAS SOON out on another island raid. When the Australian government reported that the Japanese might try to seize Nouméa, 600 miles off Australia's eastern coast, Admiral King ordered a task force to the area and sent Halsey to hit Wake Island in a diversionary attack.

Two cruisers, seven destroyers, and an oiler accompanied the *Enterprise* as the carrier left Pearl Harbor on February 14. On February 24 they struck a blow for the abandoned Marine defenders when Spruance's cruisers blasted Wake's installations from 16,000 yards while aircraft from the *Enterprise* damaged a few installations during erratic bombing.

As Halsey retired from the Wake operation, headquarters radioed him the option to add Marcus Island as a target. A raid against Marcus, fewer than 1,000 miles from Tokyo, would place his force within striking range of Japanese aircraft based at Iwo Jima, but the audacity of a raid so close to the enemy's home islands appealed to Halsey. He approved the new mission, stating later that "we figured that by raiding a spot that close to the main islands of the Empire, we might upset them a bit. It bore resemblance to a thumbing the nose gesture and was very important for the morale of our people."[38]

The aviators who would have to strike so deeply into Japanese territory trusted Halsey's instincts. One man aboard the *Enterprise* wrote that "every one in the task force believed we were going into the lion's den with no assurance we were going to be taken care of as well as Daniel. But we did have great trust in Admiral Halsey." The aviator added, "The admiral is a daring man but he uses his head. We knew he was proud of us and we knew he would never send us to a place from which we were not coming back unless it was absolutely necessary . . ."[39]

From 125 miles northeast of Marcus, on March 4 Halsey launched thirty-two bombers and six fighters that destroyed a radio station and damaged a handful of buildings. The meager results failed to dampen Halsey's enthusiasm, however; he was elated to learn that his raid had caused an air alert in Tokyo.

Six days later Halsey re-entered Pearl Harbor. Robert Casey, who labeled the task force "Admiral Halsey's Seagoing Commandos," had no doubt where the praise should rest—with the crusty, chain-smoking officer. "The Navy was definitely on its way to a new, interesting and profitable phase of accomplishment. Its past didn't seem to count any more. And maybe, you think looking back on it, the Commander was right—'Forget Pearl Harbor.'" Casey suggested that in the future, should any politician want a strike, they will look to one man only. "Halsey! That's it, Admiral Halsey!"[40]

Other reporters joined Casey in proclaiming Halsey the country's best weapon. The press called him "Knock-'em Down Halsey," and Clark Lee stated that Halsey "was all the United States Navy needed. The Navy had always had the guns and the gunners and the guts, it had the ships and it could shoot. It needed the confidence that comes with knowledge that you are attacking and not retreating; fighting aggressively instead of defensively."[41]

The nation, so long mired in miserable news and embarrassed by their military's stodgy reaction, now had two reasons to cheer because of Halsey. *Time* magazine concluded that "U.S. citizens waited hopefully for the next time Bill Halsey's task force turned up at its home port,"[42] bringing news of yet another successful sortie. In Japan, where Halsey's raids had raised the specter of attacks against the Home Islands, doubts festered. Yamamoto started to outline an advance toward Midway Island, both to secure Japan proper and in hopes of luring American carriers into a decisive sea clash. Admiral Ugaki predicted that the United States would follow with additional raids, "for it is the easiest for them and the most effective." He concluded that, "It was fortunate for us that the enemy only scratched us on this occasion and gave us a good lesson instead of directly attacking Tokyo." He then added, with what would prove to be amazing prescience, "And the most probable move they would make would be an air raid on our capital."[43]

CHAPTER 4

"THIS FORCE IS BOUND FOR TOKYO"

"AMERICA HAD NEVER SEEN DARKER DAYS"

On December 7 of the previous year, President Franklin D. Roosevelt sat in his White House study, an aging leader suddenly appearing older and wearier. Only moments before, the secretary of the Navy, Frank Knox, had informed him that much of the Pacific Fleet stationed in Hawaii now rested on Pearl Harbor's bottom. The secretary of labor, Frances Perkins, could see the anger and dismay. "It was obvious to me that Roosevelt was having a dreadful time just accepting the idea that the Navy could be caught unawares,"[1] she recalled.

The leader who had lifted the nation's morale in the bleakest days of the Great Depression quickly rallied. Top on his list was a strike on the Japanese homeland, an answer in kind for the destruction wrought upon U.S. territory in December 1941. Roosevelt prodded his military leaders daily to find a way to bring the war directly to Japanese shores.

Little came to mind. The United States possessed no airfields that were close enough to Japan for American bombers to take off, and the other option—a raid by carrier-borne fighters—appeared suicidal as it required ships to steam within 300 miles of the Home Islands and their Japanese land-based aircraft. Nimitz could not risk losing one or two carriers to execute a single bombing raid over Japan.

Roosevelt and Nimitz had their answer by January 10. Captain Francis S. Low, a member of the staff of Admiral Ernest J. King, the Commander in Chief of the U.S. Fleet, mentioned to King the revolutionary idea of launching bombers from aircraft carriers. By late January a tentative plan had been drawn up, and the head of the Army Air Corps, General Henry H. "Hap" Arnold, called to his office the man he had selected to organize the operation.

Lieutenant Colonel James Doolittle's place in aviation had already been assured by the time World War II broke out. A veteran test pilot, Doolittle established numerous records in the 1920s, including a pioneering flight across North America in less than twenty-four hours. Arnold often sought his counsel in aviation matters, and he now divulged the details of the mission he wanted to carry out. After lifting off from carriers and striking Japan, Army bombers would fly on to airfields held by friendly Chinese forces under the command of General Chiang Kai-shek.

If successfully executed, the raid carried benefits that far outweighed the drawbacks. A bombing raid over Japan would demolish the myth of invincibility that cloaked the Japanese military. No foreign invader had ever assaulted Japan, and Tokyo had assured its citizens they need not fret about an attack on the homeland.

All that was needed was to find was an admiral crazy enough to take those bombers to Japan's shores.

AT NIMITZ'S CINCPAC (Commander in Chief, Pacific Fleet) headquarters on March 19, Commander Donald B. "Wu" Duncan, an air operations officer on Admiral King's staff, briefed Nimitz, Halsey, and Halsey's chief of staff, Captain Miles Browning, on the coming mission. After listening to the details, Nimitz asked Halsey if he thought it could succeed.

"They'll need a lot of luck," replied Halsey.

"Are you willing to take them out there?" Nimitz asked, already knowing the answer.

"Yes, I am," Halsey quickly replied.

"Good! It's all yours!"[2]

Duncan sent a dispatch to his superior, General "Hap" Arnold, informing him that the operation was set. "Tell Jimmy to get on his horse,"[3] the note read.

By accepting an assignment that would bring the war to Hirohito's doorstep, Halsey would be taking half of Nimitz's carrier strength perilously close to Japan. Should ill fortune befall the force, Nimitz would be hamstrung by the loss of Halsey and another future star, Rear Admiral Raymond A. Spruance, the able commander of Halsey's cruiser screen.

Before heading into such a risky enterprise, Halsey wanted to size up the man who commanded the bombers. Nimitz sent Halsey and Browning to San Francisco, where on March 31 they met Doolittle in the Fairmont Hotel. The two officers immediately warmed to each other, bound by a shared love of the daring. They debated how closely they should take the carriers into Japanese waters before launching. Doolittle, who wanted to shorten as much as possible the distance his bombers had to fly, proposed that Halsey ferry him to within 400 miles of the coast while Halsey, sensitive to the threat posed to his carriers by enemy picket boats, countered that the carriers should not draw closer than 800 miles. Much like labor negotiators at the table, the two compromised on 500 miles, with the stipulation that should the Japanese detect their presence before reaching the launch point, they would follow one of two courses. They would launch an attack if they were still within striking distance of Tokyo, but if outside that range, the bombers would either be flown to Midway or Hawaii if close enough or be shoved overboard so the *Hornet*'s flight deck could be used by its complement of fighters.

Halsey heartily endorsed the target selections. In five separate sections, Doolittle's bombers would strike military facilities and factories in northern and southern Tokyo, installations in the Tokyo Bay region, relevant facilities in five other cities, and the navy yard at Yokosuka near Tokyo.

On April 1, one day after Halsey and Doolittle met, massive hoists in San Francisco lifted the B–25 bombers onto the *Hornet*'s flight deck for the trip across the Pacific. The *Hornet* departed from Alameda Air Station near San Francisco on April 2, accompanied by two cruisers, four destroyers, and one oiler. Gleaming on her decks, in plain view of civilian spectators along the shoreline as she passed under the Golden Gate Bridge, stood the sixteen B–25 bombers, being ferried, explained military authorities to the press, to Hawaii. The aircraft occupied so much of the carrier's deck that the tail of the last bomber protruded over the ship's stern.

Once the task force was out of sight of the mainland, Captain Marc A. Mitscher announced to his naval personnel aboard the *Hornet* and to the other ships via semaphore that "this force is bound for Tokyo." Doolittle recalled that at the stunning declaration, "Cheers could be heard all over the ship"[4] as Navy seamen and officers realized they were finally getting a crack at the enemy's homeland.

"ALL THE ELEMENTS OF MYSTERY"

On April 8 Halsey steamed out of Pearl Harbor with Task Force 16. Two heavy cruisers, four destroyers, and one oiler flanked the *Enterprise* as the flotilla headed westward toward Japan. The unit would rendezvous with *Hornet* and Task Force 18, then escort the ships to the launching point. America's most crucial weapons were now in Halsey's hands.

Unlike Mitscher's crews, no one in Halsey's task force yet knew their destination. Scuttlebutt favored another of Halsey's by-now famous island raids, and everyone admitted that with Halsey in charge, action of some sort was guaranteed.

Their query was answered dramatically at 6:00 A.M. on April 13 when an *Enterprise* lookout spotted the *Hornet* and her accompanying ships approaching from starboard, 800 miles northwest of Midway Island and 2,600 miles east of Tokyo. Men crowded the rails to catch a glimpse of the ships and paused when they saw Army B–25 Mitchell medium bombers cramming the *Hornet*'s deck. What purpose could bombers, which had never before lifted off carriers, possibly serve with the task force?

"We could not believe what we were seeing as the *Hornet* slipped into close range," stated *Enterprise* sailor AOM1 James C. Barnhill. "She was carrying sixteen North American B–25s. We knew those planes would have problems in taking off from the *Hornet,* and we knew for certain if they got off the deck, they would never be able to return."[5]

With the *Hornet*'s arrival came a renewed plea from Doolittle to ferry the force closer to Japan. Halsey discussed the issue with his staff and, though reluctant, advanced the launch point to within 400 miles. He cautioned the aviator, however, that he would order an immediate launching of the bombers if the task force was sighted, no matter how many miles separated them from their Japanese targets.

Halsey now felt comfortable in announcing the mission's purpose to the *Enterprise* group. Using semaphore to notify other ships while the news blared from the carrier's public address system, Halsey electrified crew members by saying, "'This force is bound for Tokyo.' In all my experience in the Navy I have never heard such a resounding cheer as came up from the ship's company."[6]

Sailors, excited at being the first modern force to attack the Japanese Home Islands, hopped to their tasks with renewed vigor. "Trust Wild Bill to take us to Tokyo!" they proclaimed. "And, by God, Bill Halsey will see us out again."[7] The news had added significance as it arrived only four days after American forces surrendered at Bataan in the Philippine Islands.

With the safety of his men and the mission's success on his mind, Halsey's main concern was to avoid detection, at least until after Doolittle's men had left his carrier. Rough seas buffeted the ships for three days, benevolently shielding the vessels while foreshadowing a harsh launching, but Halsey's unease grew on April 16 when Radio Tokyo scoffed at British news reports that three American bombers had dropped bombs on Tokyo. Though the Japanese dismissed the news, Halsey worried that the affair might prod the Japanese Navy into taking extra precautions in defending its Home Islands. Might he encounter a more vigilant picket line as the ships closed in on Japan?

The day before launching Halsey handed Doolittle a collection of medals he hoped the aviator would deliver. Halsey and other officers involved with the Great White Fleet had received them when they visited Japan, and though Halsey had subsequently lost his own, his Navy buddies hoped to return the items to their previous owners. Sailors attached the medals to bombs and chalked messages for their enemy. "I don't want to set the world on fire, just Tokyo," and "You'll get a BANG out of this!"[8] exhibited the glee with which the men viewed America's first offensive strike of the war against Japan proper.

AT 7:15 ON April 18, the pilot of a patrol plane returned and dropped a message that he had sighted a Japanese patrol vessel forty-two miles ahead. More alarmingly, the pilot added that he believed the vessel had spotted him. Halsey, still hoping to reduce the distance for Doolittle's group, ordered a course change and continued toward Japan. Uncertainty about being seen by the enemy dissipated at 7:44 when lookouts on the *Hornet* observed a patrol craft only 10,000 yards ahead.

Halsey had drawn close to the *Nitto Maru,* one of Yamamoto's picket ships that prowled the seas 600–700 miles out from Japan to provide an early warning system. Aboard the diminutive vessel Seaman 2nd Class Nakamura Suekichi awakened the captain, Gisaku Maeda, to report "Sir, there are two of our beautiful carriers now dead ahead."

Maeda rushed from his quarters and gazed at the spectacle through his binoculars. "Yes, Suekichi, they are beautiful but they are not ours."[9] Maeda sent a message alerting Tokyo to the presence of American carriers.

When the *Hornet* intercepted the Japanese message, Halsey ordered the cruiser *Nashville* to sink the enemy craft while his carriers turned into the wind to prepare for a launch. "Shells are tossed like machine gun bullets," reporter Robert Casey scribbled in his diary of the *Nashville*'s lumbering 15-inch guns taking aim at the tiny vessel, "eight salvos in the air at once."[10]

His presence now known, Halsey had to launch Doolittle immediately and reverse course for Hawaii if he were to evade the inevitable search ships and aircraft sent out to locate and destroy his carriers. He also figured that the Japanese, assuming that the American carriers had to draw within fighter range of the Home Islands, did not expect an attack until the next day. An early launching might hand Doolittle the chance to slip in and complete his mission against an unsuspecting enemy.

Halsey issued the launch order at 8:00 while Doolittle was still 650 miles from Japan. "To Colonel Doolittle and his gallant command:

Good luck and God bless you,"[11] Halsey signaled from the *Enterprise* to the *Hornet.*

Doolittle raced to the *Hornet*'s bridge for a few last-minute words with Captain Mitscher, then dashed to his cabin shouting, "Okay, fellas, this is it! Let's go!"[12] Doolittle's eighty men grabbed their gear and hurried toward their bombers.

Sixteen bombers awaited them on the flight deck. The first, Doolittle's aircraft, rested within 500 feet of the forward end of the deck, while the tail end of the final bomber extended beyond the stern. Two white painted lines, one for the left wheel and the other for the nose wheel, guided the bombers along a flight deck designed for much smaller aircraft. By correctly following the lines, each pilot would miss the carrier island to his right by a scant six feet, a difficult task in normal conditions but one made more perilous by the 26-knot winds and swirling seas.

Doolittle climbed into his bomber. A stiff wind buffeted his plane, and the sea intermittently stormed over the carrier's ramps while Doolittle stared at the brief distance separating him from the ship's edge. At 8:20 Doolittle flashed the thumbs-up signal to the deck launching officer to indicate that he was ready. As the bomber lurched forward, Doolittle steered the aircraft along the white line that had been painted along the carrier deck, jerked the bomber straight up so severely that the plane almost stalled, and lifted into the sky with room to spare. Doolittle veered to the right, circled low over the carrier while the crew waved and cheered, then turned toward Tokyo.

With winds gusting to 40 knots and heavy swells pounding the *Enterprise,* Halsey observed a liftoff he later described as "most spectacular." He added that, "The wind and the sea were so strong that morning that green water was breaking over the carriers' ramps. Jimmy led his squadron off. When his plane buzzed down the *Hornet*'s deck at 0825, there wasn't a man topside in the task force who didn't help sweat him into the air. One pilot hung on the brink of a stall until we nearly catalogued his effects,"[13] but all sixteen bombers departed safely and were soon on their way to Tokyo.

Halsey wasted no time before turning back to Pearl Harbor to extricate his two carriers from danger. Less than five minutes after Doolittle's final bomber took off, he changed course for Hawaii at 25 knots.

"TERROR HAD ARRIVED IN TOKIO"

Halsey had successfully shepherded the force toward Tokyo, a tricky feat in itself, but now, with Japan soon to be seeking vengeance for the startling raid on their capital, Halsey faced stiffer odds. He had to once more evade detection from the Japanese picket line, then elude any force that might pursue him along the path to Hawaii.

The Japanese spotted him by early afternoon, when two Japanese picket ships appeared in the distance. *Enterprise* aircraft sank one of the vessels, but when the second remained afloat, Halsey ordered the *Nashville* to turn its large guns on the lone target.

While Halsey steamed east with all due speed, radio rooms closely monitored Tokyo broadcasts to gauge the enemy's reaction. At first all seemed normal in Tokyo, as Japanese radio stations at 12:55 P.M. aired the usual musical programs. An announcer bragged that of all the nations currently at war, only Japan had been free from enemy attack. Japan, he boasted, would never be attacked. The announcer added, "And in our invincible security, we ask ourselves, 'What has become of the advertised American air power? What has become of the British and American fleets, if any?'"[14]

The announcer would soon eat his words. By 2:00 P.M. the programming suddenly halted as the sound of air raid sirens filled the airwaves. At 2:30 a Japanese commentator broadcast the news that enemy bombers had hit and destroyed schools and hospitals. Men aboard the *Enterprise* cheered, not because schools and hospitals were hit, for they knew Doolittle's targets were industrial, but because the bombers had obviously made it to Tokyo.

The radio broadcasters' tones spoke volumes. Rather than talking in a calm manner, terror marked their voices. One Japanese commentator speculated that the United States possessed a super carrier with a flight deck a quarter mile long that could launch big bombers. Others pointed to airfields in the Philippines or China as the likely point of origin, and one even suggested that the Americans had taken off from a secret airfield inside Japan itself.

Casey explained that no one knew how much actual damage Doolittle's bombers had inflicted, "But had we based our estimates on what we heard that night as relays of hysterical announcers pushed a somewhat unintelligible commentary in English over the beam to America, we should have thought the whole of Japan in ashes." Casey added that "you'd have known that the terror had arrived in Tokio." Though they knew few details of the raid, Casey stated that the event was what everyone back home "had been waiting for since the morning of December 7."[15]

The Japanese failed to locate Halsey's task force, though certainly not for a lack of trying. Yamamoto diverted a submarine squadron from the Bonin Islands to the south, dispatched a cruiser force from the main fleet base at Yokosuka, and sent two armed merchant cruisers off Honshu in pursuit. Even the *Kido Butai* and its mighty carrier force then returning from successful operations in the Indian Ocean received a summons to race back to the Pacific, but Halsey enjoyed too great a lead to be caught.

Darkness on April 18 could not arrive soon enough for Halsey. Had the Japanese found him in daylight, Halsey would have had to rely on his fighter groups and antiaircraft batteries to shield the *Enterprise* and the *Hornet*. Night, however, with its refuge into which he could disappear, was his ally, for the enemy could then conduct no air search until daybreak, ten hours distant. By that time Halsey would have added another 200 miles to the distance between him and his pursuers.

Aboard the *Hornet* Chaplain Edward B. Harp published a special edition of the ship's daily news bulletin. Beneath a large headline proclaiming, "REMEMBER PEARL HARBOR" rested a cartoon showing Uncle Sam spitting a mouthful of bombs across the Pacific Ocean onto an island. Neatly printed below the island were the words, "Japan, or what's left of it."[16] The raid came nowhere near inflicting the damage depicted by the cartoon, but it was at least another daring move designed to knock the Japanese off balance.

In contrast to the welcomes on Halsey's returns from his earlier island carriers raids, no soldiers or sailors lined the docks and no military bands awaited when he returned to Pearl Harbor on April 25. Officials later informed the American public of Doolittle's involvement, but they kept the role of Halsey's carriers out of the press for another year. Having no idea that the Japanese had already extracted the information from captive pilots who bailed out of downed aircraft, they wanted to keep Tokyo guessing as to where the bombers had originated and hoped that Japan might conclude that the United States possessed a fleet of super bombers capable of flying long distances.

"THE HARD-BOILED FIGHTER FROM NEW JERSEY"

News of the bombings caused celebration in the United States. "DOOLITTLE DO'OD IT" dominated the front page of the *Los Angeles Times.* "It was electrifying," wrote reporter Clark Lee at the time, "almost too good to be true after we had been waiting so many long, bitter weeks for the United States to get started."[17] Hollywood soon started production on a film, *Thirty Seconds over Tokyo* starring Spencer Tracy, that extolled the raid's accomplishments.

In addition to boosting American morale, the raid shattered Japan's sense of invincibility—the Japanese homeland had been assaulted in an act once considered unthinkable. Admiral Ugaki wrote in his diary on April 18 that, "the enemy force seemingly withdrew to the east after launching the planes. We have missed him again and again. This is more than regrettable, because this shattered my firm determination never to let the enemy attack Tokyo or the mainland."[18]

Halsey correctly extolled Doolittle, terming the flight one of the most courageous deeds in history, but Halsey was the one who had imbued the task force with the belligerence required for such a risky endeavor, providing evidence to the nation and to Japan that the United States had risen from Pearl Harbor to continue the fight. Halsey lifted the nation and its military, first with his island raids and then with this April mission. The debacles at Pearl Harbor, Wake Island, and Bataan had not been forgotten, but their punches carried less sting.

When reporters asked Roosevelt the location of the airfield from which the bombers had taken off, the president replied with a mischievous grin that they had come from Shangri-La, the mythical setting for James Hilton's novel *Lost Horizon.* The War Department released additional information one year later, when secrecy was no longer an issue, identifying the *Hornet* as the carrier from which the planes launched, and stating that the commander of the task force "was Admiral William F. Halsey, Jr., who had already achieved fame as a skillful and bold leader of naval raids upon Japanese bases in the Pacific."[19]

In reporting the information, the *New York Times* concluded that, "It was an audacious raid, and one that took the Japanese by surprise. At that stage of the war no one had dreamed—or at least had not executed the dream—of sending big land bombers careening off naval carriers, built to accommodate smaller aircraft." The article added that the raid proved "to the Japanese that their isle was not impregnable, . . ." and that it was commanded by Halsey, "the hard-boiled fighter from Elizabeth, N. J. . ."[20]

When the hard-boiled fighter learned that the Japanese had executed three of Doolittle's pilots, Halsey promised vengeance for the atrocities. "He stuck out that ram-bow jaw and he ground his teeth," said Lieutenant Ashford, Halsey's flag lieutenant. "Those eyebrows of his began to flail up and down. I wouldn't swear that St. Elmo's fire didn't play about his ears. All he could choke out was, 'We'll make the bastards pay! We'll make 'em pay!'"[21]

Payback had already begun. Feeling guilt and shame over a raid they told their nation could never happen, Japanese military leaders took steps to ensure it would not be repeated. To make the enemy appear more heinous they spread rumors that the bombers had targeted schools and gunned down innocent civilians. They reassigned four fighter groups from island bases to the Home Islands and diverted thousands of troops from military operations to search for Doolittle.

Halsey's actions, both during the island raids and here, produced benefits far beyond what the United States expected, emphasizing the value of boldness at a time that seemed to call mostly for defense. More audacity would soon be needed. As Halsey hurried back to Pearl Harbor from the raid, events in the South and the Central Pacific conjoined to form a perfect storm.

"SHORT BY ONE DAY"

Back at Pearl Harbor, in April 1942, Admiral Nimitz had come to a startling conclusion. Based on information culled from eavesdropping on

Japanese radio traffic, his top two analysts, Joseph J. Rochefort and Edwin T. Layton, had determined that the Japanese would soon launch an operation into the Coral Sea, northeast of Australia, to seize the important port facilities at Port Moresby on New Guinea's southeast coast. The two predicted that three carriers would escort Japanese transports headed for Port Moresby. Rochefort suggested that the Japanese would then launch an even more substantial operation in the mid-Pacific.

Nimitz faced a quandary. Just when he most needed the combative Halsey and his carriers, Halsey, who had been sent out on the Tokyo bombing mission, was unavailable. The only tools on hand rested on the decks of Task Force 17's two aircraft carriers. The major responsibility for halting the Japanese in the Coral Sea fell by default to its commander, Admiral Frank Jack Fletcher.

Nimitz flew to San Francisco on April 24 to meet with Admiral King. Both considered Fletcher an overcautious man, but they doubted that Halsey could return to Pearl Harbor from his current operation, replenish, and rush out to the South Pacific in time to contribute. They ordered Fletcher to be prepared for action in the Coral Sea by late April and, on the slim hope that the Japanese might fall behind schedule, they also instructed Halsey that after he arrived at Pearl Harbor, he was to hurriedly re-provision his ships and leave for the South Pacific.

Halsey entered Pearl Harbor on April 25, prepared to turn about in five days and race toward the Coral Sea some 4,000 miles away. If he joined Fletcher before the Japanese arrived, Halsey was to assume command, in which case he would have under his control all four remaining aircraft carriers in the Pacific—his own *Enterprise* and *Hornet* as well as the *Lexington* and *Yorktown* from Fletcher.

A crucial sea battle loomed, but the prospects meant nothing if Halsey could not arrive in time. Anticipation over participating in the war's largest carrier battle mixed with frustration. Might the Doolittle raid deny him the opportunity to engage enemy carriers?

His impatience aggravated a skin rash that spread over much of his body, denying Halsey sleep at night and causing discomfort by day. Eating little as a result of the pain that came with each movement, the admiral lost twenty pounds in less than two months. "This is a most annoying disease," Halsey concluded of the dermatitis in his memoirs, one that "became progressively worse." He described the ailment as "a general eruption of the skin and a tremendous itching. It took more will power than I had to prevent an occasional scratch, although I knew it was the worst possible thing to do."[22] To counter the effects, inflamed by the tension and pressure under which he operated as a battle commander, he had begun taking baths in oatmeal mixed with water, but they brought little relief.

On April 30 Halsey took Task Force 16, comprised of two carriers, five heavy cruisers, eight destroyers, and two oilers, to sea. He chafed at his inability to control events as his ships churned southwestward through the Pacific. He could do nothing for the next few days but wait while he closed the gap between his force and the Coral Sea at 20 knots per hour.

Halsey, perturbed with the frustrating race to reach the Coral Sea, ordered additional drills so his crews would be at peak capacity. If his luck held out only a few more days, he just might be waiting when the Japanese carriers appeared over the horizon.

WITH TASK FORCE 16 steaming south of the Phoenix Islands, on May 6 Halsey learned that Fletcher's *Lexington* and *Yorktown* had already begun to engage the enemy. The news dashed any chance for his participation, as he could not possibly close the distance between him and Fletcher. "Our race to reach the Coral Sea and join up with Fletcher's force fell short by one day,"[23] Lieutenant Ashford later wrote of the disappointing time. For the man who most wanted to find a fight, the near miss in the Coral Sea was maddening.

In two days of action Fletcher succeeded in checking the Japanese advance toward Port Moresby, a crucial outcome for the embryonic Allied war effort then assembling in Australia, but in the process lost both carriers. Rather than operating together in the same screen, protected by an enhanced ring of destroyers and more concentrated antiaircraft fire, Fletcher allowed the two to maneuver independently. The *Yorktown* had to return to Pearl Harbor for repairs, while the *Lexington* sustained such heavy damage that American destroyers sank her after the battle.

Though Halsey missed the critical clash, he nonetheless gained additional acclaim back home. In its May 18, 1942, issue *Time* magazine asserted that since for security purposes the Navy could not recognize the commander on the scene in the Coral Sea, the magazine guessed it most likely included the man who first brought cheer to the home front, and that Nimitz "could thank his task-force commanders, sea dogs like bushy-browed Vice Admiral William Frederick Halsey, Jr., a naval aviator who knows the potency of the swift attack, sighted and powered from the air; . . ."[24]

Even in absentia Halsey, the home front hero, benefited. He alone—not Nimitz, Fletcher, Spruance, or any other lesser-known naval officer—symbolized America's fighting spirit. In the war's first six months the nation looked to Halsey as its warrior on the front line.

FOR THE NEXT five days Halsey prowled the South Pacific attempting to locate an enemy task force supposedly heading southeastward toward Ocean and Nauru Islands near the Gilberts or through the Solomon Islands for an assault on Samoa or the Fijis. Halsey had 1,400 miles of the Pacific to comb, but if the Japanese were out there, he intended to find them.

Task Force 16 once again sailed toward unknown perils. According to Lieutenant Clarence E. Dickinson on the *Enterprise,* "there were shipboard rumors that Admiral Halsey was going in to attack three or four different Japanese bases and wind up in Rabaoul [sic]." He added that everyone aboard felt that, "here we go, to the lion's den once more," but that there was only "one Daniel and lots of lions."[25]

Halsey missed a possible engagement with the enemy when the Japanese invasion force turned back after an American submarine sank the flagship. However, more important developments were brewing. On May 14 Nimitz sent Halsey another message ordering him to steam close enough to the Gilbert Islands that he could be certain that Japanese patrol planes had located him, then to immediately withdraw and set a course for Pearl Harbor. Nimitz's intelligence team concluded that the Japanese intended to strike Midway with a force that included most of her aircraft carriers. Nimitz hoped that if the Japanese saw Halsey in the South Pacific, they would assume he could not possibly participate in the Midway operation.

"RAY SPRUANCE WITHOUT HESITATION"

In the coming operation Yamamoto planned to lure American aircraft carriers toward Midway, where his battleships, cruisers, and carriers would ambush the unsuspecting American forces. Once he had destroyed the U.S. Navy and seized Midway, Hawaii would be his for the taking, and the West Coast would be vulnerable, two specters that Yamamoto hoped would nudge Roosevelt to seek peace.

As Task Force 16 barreled its way at top speed toward Hawaii, officers and sailors vainly tried to decipher the strange occurrences. Nimitz's dictate on May 16 to expedite Halsey's return reinforced Halsey's notion "that trouble was brewing in another area." Crews aboard both carriers figured that only a major threat would cause Halsey to consume precious fuel by maintaining top speed for the eleven-day voyage, and aboard the *Enterprise* Lieutenant Clarence E. Dickinson deduced that the sudden change in orders meant that action could not be far away. "What was in the wind?" he wondered. "Something exciting, surely."[26]

Halsey, weakened by a lack of sleep and exhausted from being at sea almost constantly since the war's start six months earlier, arrived in Pearl Harbor on May 26. The rash so assailed the admiral's entire body that Lieutenant Ashford tried to conjure ways to alleviate the exasperating itching. A gaunt Halsey claimed the itching "was becoming increasingly violent and I was getting little or no sleep."[27] Halsey objected when his medical officer remarked that he would have to immediately enter the hospital at Hawaii, but the physician rebuffed all arguments. When it came to the admiral's health, he told Halsey, he would decide what was best.

The crew of the *Enterprise* witnessed a disturbing sight when the carrier berthed in Pearl Harbor. Halsey, the commander who had been with them for every engagement since December 7, the man who had flouted the Japanese by navigating his carriers right under their noses, now lay frail on a stretcher as a group of sailors helped him off the ship. Some men whispered that the admiral would never leave the *Enterprise* unless he was dead or the ship was sinking, but here he was, too feeble to walk off on his own.

When Halsey shuffled into Nimitz's office, the commander took one look at the drained warrior and ordered him to the hospital. The pair first discussed who should replace him for the crucial battle about to unfold. Without hesitating, Halsey suggested Ray Spruance, his cruiser commander. The selection momentarily surprised Nimitz as Spruance, a non-aviator who had never helmed an aircraft carrier, would be handed the controls for the war's most important carrier action. Nimitz could have insisted that Halsey choose one of the more senior aviator officers from Task Force 16, but instead he followed Halsey's instincts. Halsey had worked with Spruance during their destroyer days as well as in the heat of combat, and he knew that the man's calm ability to command would compensate for any deficiencies in his knowledge of aviation.

Knowing how controversial his choice would be, especially to the air admirals, Halsey carefully orchestrated the selection of Spruance. Fearing he might be relieved once he reached Pearl Harbor, Halsey had begun to prepare his staff for the switch on the way back from the South Pacific. Members of the crew noticed the frequency with which he praised Spruance, and in a May 25 letter to Admiral Fletcher, Halsey commented that Spruance "has consistently displayed outstanding ability combined with excellent judgment and quiet courage. I have found his counsel and advice invaluable. From my direct close observation I have learned to place complete confidence in him in operations in war time."

Expecting that his choice would especially anger those with more seniority than Spruance, Halsey extolled his subordinate's qualities, hoping that his words might counter any fears that existed over Spruance's lack of aviation experience. "I consider him fully and superbly qualified to take command of a force comprising mixed types and to conduct protracted independent operations in the combat theater in war time,"[28] he added to Fletcher.

With this endorsement, coming from the war's first naval hero, Halsey in effect admonished other aviator officers to lay off Spruance. He could have selected someone with more carrier knowledge, but Halsey believed that Spruance's command abilities, which included an amazingly analytical mind that operated well under pressure, was more important than experience operating a carrier. Knowing he had made the right decision did not lessen Halsey's pain. On the eve of the largest naval clash against Japan, he had to step to the side and watch as his underling, a non-aviator, took his carriers into battle. In doing so, though, Halsey ensured that, in spite of his forced absence, he would contribute significantly to the outcome of the Pacific War's most crucial naval battle. At that moment, Halsey grasped the big picture. Victory, not who achieved it, was all that mattered. Ignoring in-service politics, Halsey selected the man best able to execute the task—Raymond Spruance. The warrior's hand might not be orchestrating the actions during the June battle, but his fingerprints were all over the design.

Upon emerging from his meeting with Nimitz, Halsey ordered Lieutenant Ashford to "Go back to *Enterprise* and tell Ray Spruance he is to take the task force out tomorrow, using my staff. Tell him to shift his flag to the *Enterprise*."[29] With that final piece of business concluded, Halsey gingerly stepped into a waiting car for the ride to the hospital.

The news that Spruance had replaced Halsey sent shock waves through the task force. Halsey, who had confidently guided them in a series of bold raids since the war's opening salvos, would be absent for what lay ahead. His replacement, Spruance, had built a reputation commanding destroyers and cruisers, not carriers. Officers and men throughout Task Force 16 wondered how he would hold up under the enormous strain.

Both Halsey and Spruance understood the enormity of the coming battle. The Pacific War boiled down to a handful of June days, a time when the Navy had to register a victory. Nimitz's Command Summary, the so-called Greybook that was CinCPac's official daily synopsis of events occurring throughout the Pacific, recognized this when it stated on June 3, "The whole course of the war in the Pacific may hinge on the developments of the next two or three days,"[30] agonizing hours that Halsey would have to spend in bed while others engaged the enemy and executed the fighting he had so badly sought.

From his hospital bed on May 28 Halsey watched as Task Force 16, with Raymond Spruance in charge of the two carriers Halsey had led in the war's first major offensive strikes—*Hornet* and his beloved *Enterprise*—exited Pearl Harbor and veered toward its destination point near Midway. Like a concerned father, Halsey could only observe from a distance as his charges navigated outside his grasp. "And from the Naval hospital at Pearl," Halsey wrote in his autobiography, "'itching'—as Chester put it—'to get into the fight,' I watched them sortie on May 28 to win the crucial carrier duel of the war."[31]

Halsey remained in the hospital until June 5, when he and Lieutenant Ashford boarded the light cruiser USS *Detroit* for the trip to San Francisco and treatment by Stateside experts. While Halsey's cruiser receded over the eastern horizon, 1,000 miles to the northwest Spruance turned to the formidable task of halting the Japanese.

"YOU'RE FAMOUS!"

The climactic Battle of Midway reversed the fortunes of war for both the United States and Japan when Halsey's Task Force 16 sank four enemy carriers and turned back Yamamoto's invasion fleet. The American press and public heralded Midway's results. Robert Casey, the correspondent who had expressed a nation's doubts about its Navy, marked the battle as a turning point. "Let us not toy with the fact that the most outstanding surprise of this war to quite a lot of us has been the discovery that the Navy is really as good as we used to think it was on, say, December 6." The reporter continued that, "In other words, we who a couple of months ago were shuddering at the sight of Pearl Harbor, have taken control of the Pacific."[32]

Halsey's joy that his navy had mauled the Japanese at Midway was tinged with melancholy. "This was a sad occasion for me," he wrote in his memoirs, "as it prevented my taking part in the Battle of Midway where I would have been the senior officer present." Then, with an emotion that can still be felt years later, he added, "This was my greatest regret in the whole war."[33]

HALSEY WAS HAPPY to leave Pearl Harbor. The cramped captain's quarters aboard the *Detroit* offered a pleasant alternative compared to his hospital room, where fine coral dust wafting in from a nearby construction site aggravated his discomfort. Covered in grease to combat the itching, Halsey remained in bed the entire voyage. Lieutenant Ashford noted that the severe rash so exasperated Halsey that he could not even don the most comfortable of pajamas.

When the ship arrived at the Alameda Naval Air Station near San Francisco, the senior medical officer on the staff of the commandant of the 12th Naval District in San Francisco informed Halsey that he had already arranged treatment from the country's leading allergist, Dr. Warren W. Vaughan of Richmond, Virginia. Doctor Vaughan's effective treatment permitted Halsey to leave the hospital within one week. The physician warned Halsey, though, that he remained under his care for the next six weeks and that during that span the admiral must relax, an unwelcome rest that annoyed Halsey almost as much as the skin inflammation. "Under a new treatment my dermatitis abated, but whereas it had made me writhe I continued to writhe at my enforced inactivity."[34]

Though the Navy hoped to keep Halsey's presence secret, the numerous visitors who poured into his hospital room made that impossible. He treated the sojourn as a vacation, visiting family in Delaware and enjoying his grandchildren. One Sunday his grandson, Halsey Spruance, rushed in to his celebrated grandfather as he sat with a cocktail and shouted, "You're famous! Here you are in the funny papers!"[35] In his hand the grandson held the day's comic section, containing a strip about the admiral's exploits.

Halsey had fully recovered by August 5. The Navy, taking no chances with their most renowned admiral, ordered him to enjoy the remainder of the month before reporting for duty. The period gave him time to gauge the mood of the nation; despite his actions in the island raids and the victory at Midway, the country faced hard obstacles on the road to defeating Germany and Japan.

In a June 8, 1942, article titled "The First Six Months," *Time* magazine analyzed the war's initial half year. Alongside a photograph of Halsey, the article listed the few bright spots, including "the brilliant raids led by Vice Admiral Halsey on the Marshall and Gilbert Islands, on Wake and Marcus" and "Jimmy Doolittle's raid on Tokyo, an action of limited military importance but a brilliant tactical success."

The article stated that while there was a lull during which both the United States and Japan rebuilt for the next phase of operations, the country could take hope in the performance of its vast industrial base, which "was now performing prodigies. The spring of 1942 may some day be looked back on as the real turning point of the war. That was when the U.S. first began to demonstrate that it could really make munitions."[36]

Those signs of hope, though, brought disappointment for Halsey. A warrior like him, accustomed to action over organization, would become less relevant. The same arsenal of democracy that gushed a torrent of ships, planes, and other weapons to the Pacific would require oversight by admirals more suited to entrepreneurship than to bold charges. As Halsey recuperated from his dermatitis, the war was passing him by.

With his skin condition considerably improved, Halsey sent clear signals to his superiors. On August 31, before a captive audience of midshipmen at the Naval Academy, Halsey admitted that, "missing the Battle of Midway has been the greatest disappointment of my life," but then delivered what both the enthusiastic future officers and the entire nation wanted to hear. Halsey concluded by vowing that, "I am going back to the Pacific where I intend personally to have a crack at those yellow-bellied sons of bitches and their carriers."[37]

"BILL HALSEY'S BACK!"

During a meeting in San Francisco with King, Nimitz, and the undersecretary of the Navy, James Forrestal, Halsey learned that all had not unfolded smoothly while he recuperated. American Marines had met stiffer resistance than expected in the Solomon Islands, Army and Navy commanders argued over whether the Army's General Douglas MacArthur or the Navy's Admiral Nimitz should be in overall command in the South Pacific, and Admiral King worried about both the morale and the mental health of the current Commander of the South Pacific, Vice Admiral Robert L. Ghormley. Lacking details of these developments because of his illness, Halsey withheld judgment until he had more facts, but he sensed a disturbing nervousness among the group.

After the meetings ended, Halsey and Nimitz flew to Pearl Harbor on September 11, 1942. Since the *Enterprise* was then undergoing repairs, Nimitz named Halsey as Commander, Air Force, Pacific Fleet (ComAirPac), a temporary post that would enable him to catch up on recent Pacific events before returning to the war zone. Once the *Enter-*

prise was ready for operation, Halsey would board as commander of Task Force 16 and command carrier forces in future encounters. The prospect of controlling such powerful units against the enemy took some of the sting out of missing the past three months of the war.

The next day Halsey accompanied Admiral Nimitz to the *Enterprise,* where the senior officer planned to hand out decorations to the crew. No one outside CinCPac offices knew of Halsey's return, and Nimitz asked Halsey to wait out of sight until called. After the medal ceremony Nimitz stepped closer to the microphone and announced, "Boys, I've got a surprise for you. Bill Halsey's back!" The sight of the admiral caused a momentary silence before the crew erupted in such wild applause that Foster Hailey, a correspondent observing the scene, wrote in the *New York Times* that, "officers and men alike forgot decorum and yelled and cheered and whistled until they were hoarse." Halsey was so touched by the spectacle that he later wrote, "The men's cheers made tears come to my eyes."[38] The love affair between Halsey and his men had not lost a step in his absence.

A correspondent noted that the affection was more than the simple deference shown by sailors to an admiral. This approached an admiration one might find between a student and his mentor, or between a son and a father. "It is the writer's belief that the American sailor is the straightest-shooting, best naval fighting man in the world when he is led by officers in whom he has confidence," wrote the reporter. "Of all the admirals afloat in the Pacific, this correspondent believes, none would be more certain to inspire their loyalty and command their respect than Admiral Halsey. His return to active command is the best news for months."[39]

CHAPTER 5

"A KNUCKLE-SWINGER LIKE HALSEY"

Not since Pearl Harbor had American forces faced such a calamitous situation as the one in October 1942 at Guadalcanal, an island in the Solomon chain 1,100 miles northwest of Australia. Operation Watchtower, as the military designated the August 1942 Guadalcanal landings, suffered a series of setbacks. Meant to halt the Japanese thrust toward Australia and New Zealand and establish a base from which the United States could eventually launch its own offensive, U.S. naval and Marine forces instead scraped for their lives. "It now appears that we are unable to control the sea area in the Guadalcanal area," declared the Greybook for October 15. "The situation is not hopeless, but it is certainly critical."[1]

Pessimism in the United States mirrored the military's uncertainty in the South Pacific. The *New York Times* noted military correspondent Hanson Baldwin stated, "It is as if the Marines held Jones Beach and the rest of Long Island were loosely dominated by the enemy." One Marine at Henderson Field on Guadalcanal later wrote that, practically surrounded as he and his military compatriots were with enemy forces, he now "knew to a certain extent how the boys on Wake and Bataan must have felt."[2] These were two locations at which American defenders eventually had to surrender.

If Nimitz could not halt the enemy at Guadalcanal, Australia would be imperiled, momentum gained from the Doolittle Raid, Midway, and the Coral Sea would be lost, and the war's outcome would be in jeopardy. Something had to be done to infuse life in the forces battling the Japanese in the South Pacific.

"HANGING ON BY A SHOESTRING"

Vice Admiral Ghormley, the commander of the South Pacific, encountered mishaps from the beginning. Vice Admiral Frank Jack Fletcher, in charge of the naval forces off the Solomons, withdrew his carriers less than two days after the initial landings. Without the protection provided by the aircraft carriers, Rear Admiral Richmond Kelly Turner, commander of the amphibious forces, had to pull back the transports, most still jammed with badly needed supplies, leaving the Marines ashore under Major General Alexander A. Vandegrift with barely a four-day stock of ammunition and forcing them to go to reduced rations.

The situation at sea was no better. In the Battle of Savo Island in early August, the U.S. Navy suffered the worst defeat in its history when it lost four cruisers and more than 1,000 dead in one hour to a surprise Japanese night surface engagement. When the Japanese sank the *Wasp* the next month, Nimitz was left with only one operational carrier, *Hornet,* with which to counter the victorious Japanese advance.

Despite the limitations, Vandegrift's Marines managed to maintain a slim hold on Guadalcanal centered around the vital fighter strip at Henderson Field. The crisis came down to who could rush enough men and supplies into Guadalcanal fast enough and keep them there long enough to attain victory.

The head of the Army Air Corps, General "Hap" Arnold, believed that while desperate circumstances existed at Guadalcanal, the answer lay not in supplies but in men. He concluded, "the best shot is getting new leaders who know and understand modern warfare; men who are aggressive and not afraid to fight their ships. So far, I'm afraid it's been the other way around."[3]

The Marine commander pleaded for more men and supplies to alleviate the dire conditions. On October 13 he sent a priority dispatch to Nimitz, Ghormley, and Turner in which he estimated that 10,000 Japanese had landed the previous day. His force of Marines teetered on the brink of collapse as a result of sheer exhaustion from constant combat and debilitating malaria. "They were a salty lot, bronzed and lean, their dungarees practically in shreds," Vandegrift wrote later. "They held the enemy in terrible contempt." He added, "They joked about nearly everything but their humor didn't fool me. They were tired men. I wanted desperately to get them off the island."[4]

He received a boost on October 13 when 2,800 soldiers of the 164th Infantry Regiment of the Army's Americal Division arrived, but the reinforcements only plugged one of numerous holes in his defense. Vandegrift explained to Nimitz and Ghormley that the situation called for "two urgent and immediate steps: take and maintain control of the sea areas adjacent to Cactus [the military code name for Guadalcanal] to prevent further enemy landings and enemy bombardments such as this force has taken for the last three nights; reinforcement of ground forces by at least one division in order that extensive operations may be initiated to destroy hostile forces now on Cactus."[5]

These disturbing events occurred as Nimitz at Pearl Harbor and Admiral King in Washington, D.C., held grave misgivings about Admiral Ghormley's competence. King had never warmed to Ghormley, who incurred King's legendary ire for sending a July message concluding that the oncoming Guadalcanal assault was likely to fail. When King and Nimitz met at San Francisco in early September, the two discussed the state of Ghormley's command skills and health, a situation Nimitz promised to investigate upon his return to the Pacific.

At Pearl Harbor Nimitz asked journalists returning from assignments to Guadalcanal for their thoughts. Hanson Baldwin of the *New York Times* told him Ghormley "was really completely defeatist. He was almost despairing." Baldwin wrote that the poor results came from "overcaution and the defensive complex."[6] Instead of leaving his office for exercise or breaks, the admiral remained in cramped quarters aboard the tender *Argonne,* a vessel so tiny that Ghormley's staff officers nicknamed her the

Agony Maru. Ghormley had not even left the ship for a visit to the front, something Nimitz found shocking.

Reporters had harsh words for the Navy in general, which they accused of suffering from timidity at a time when nerve was required. "It seemed to me that some of our officers thought only of NOT losing more ships," wrote Associated Press correspondent Clark Lee, "and it was in that mood that we undertook our early operations in the Solomons."[7]

After receiving the dismal evaluations, Nimitz decided to investigate conditions himself and on September 28 flew to Nouméa, where he learned that the harsh conclusions were, if anything, understating the case. Eighty cargo vessels waited in the harbor to be unloaded, and Ghormley's ill-kept quarters shocked the commander. Nimitz directed a series of questions at Ghormley and his staff, but no one seemed to have ready answers.

A quick trip to Guadalcanal the next day restored Nimitz's faith that, with the proper leadership, Guadalcanal could be held. Whereas pessimism stifled South Pacific headquarters in Nouméa, an obvious optimism buttressed the weary Marines and their commanders who were slugging it out with the enemy. Vandegrift told his naval counterpart that overcaution gripped too many navy officers. "Out here too many commanders have been far too leery about risking their ships."[8] Vandegrift argued that his men fighting ashore had to see that the Navy did all it could at sea to help them. Vandegrift and his Marines could not last much longer in a situation where Japanese ships shelled Henderson Field with impunity.

Nimitz returned to Pearl Harbor on October 5 convinced that he had to take action. Hap Arnold had come to the same conclusion during his September visit. "My estimate, upon leaving Admiral Ghormley's headquarters, was this: So far, the Navy had taken one hell of a beating and at that time was hanging on by a shoestring. They did not have a logistic setup efficient enough to insure success. The Marines were very tired and would grab at anything as a possible aid—something to restore their confidence."[9]

The Marines did not realize it, but then traveling the Pacific, oblivious to these developments, rested their answer—Halsey.

"THE HOTTEST POTATO THEY EVER HANDED ME!"

On the afternoon of October 15 Nimitz gathered with staff members who had accompanied him to Guadalcanal to discuss Ghormley. They unanimously agreed that what they had witnessed during the visit proved that he could no longer handle the responsibilities. Nimitz directly asked each man if the officer should be replaced. One by one, each answered in the affirmative.

Nimitz and the staff debated a handful of replacements, but all carried drawbacks. Halsey's name generated the most enthusiasm, although some wondered if he might be better used at sea with the carriers rather than behind a desk, which had not been his strong suit. Nimitz adjourned the meeting without making his decision, but by the end of the evening he had made the decision to replace Ghormley with Halsey. He then sent Admiral King a message asking permission for Halsey to step in. He referenced Ghormley's two most recent messages, plus what he had observed during his visit to the South Pacific, as justifications for the move. Halsey, he claimed, "has that rare combination of intellectual capacity and military audacity, and can calculate to a cat's whisker the risk involved."[10] King replied in the affirmative, at which time Nimitz summoned Halsey to Nouméa. Nimitz informed Ghormley of his relief and asked that he remain on the scene to assist Halsey during the transition period.

Unaware of developments, Halsey had embarked on a tour of the South Pacific. He was given command of a carrier task force centered around the *Enterprise,* and used the time before departure to leisurely inspect facilities and installations in the South Pacific and familiarize himself with the developments that had occurred since his illness.

Halsey was two days into his tour when Nimitz ordered him to cancel plans to fly from Canton in the Phoenix Islands to Guadalcanal and instead travel to South Pacific headquarters at Nouméa. He departed on October 18, reading detective novels, napping, and even taking the aircraft's controls to pass the time.

Halsey could never have guessed what awaited him as the aircraft set down in the harbor's waters at Nouméa. The plane's "four propellers had scarcely stopped turning when a whaleboat came alongside," Halsey recalled in his memoirs. "As I stepped aboard, Admiral Ghormley's Flag Lieutenant saluted me and gave me a sealed envelope." When Halsey ripped open the packet, he found a second sealed envelope marked "Secret."

Halsey suspected something out of the ordinary. "It is unusual to deliver a dispatch with such promptness as I would have been on board Admiral Ghormley's flagship in a very short time. I realized the dispatch must be very important and a flash of wonderment passed through my brain."

Halsey tore open the second envelope and read the words that handed him his most important wartime post. "You will take command of the South Pacific Area and South Pacific Forces immediately," stated Nimitz's order. Halsey scanned it a second time before handing the dispatch to his staff intelligence officer, Colonel Julian Brown. "Jesus Christ and General Jackson! This is the hottest potato they ever handed me!"[11] he exclaimed.

Halsey was at first disappointed to be removed from a seagoing command and placed behind a desk, a move the former football player likened to being benched. He knew little about the South Pacific military situation and, more crucially, the roles played by the other branches of the military that he would now command.

He also disliked replacing an old Academy chum and football teammate, but the two handled the awkward moment without acrimony. "This is a tough job they've given you, Bill," Ghormley warned Halsey. "I damn well know it!"[12] Halsey replied. The pair then disappeared into Ghormley's cabin, where Ghormley brought Halsey up to date on the South Pacific. When they re-emerged, the ship's company was called to quarters and Halsey and Ghormley read their orders as stipulated by naval custom.

With that brief ceremony, Halsey passed from the first to the second of his wartime phases. He had previously commanded a task force at sea, but from October 18, 1942, until June 1944, he would do his fighting from behind a desk, rallying the forces on Guadalcanal and supervising the military's response in the Solomons.

From foxholes on Guadalcanal to destroyers prowling the waters, jubilation replaced gloom when the official word arrived that Halsey had taken over. "I'll never forget it!" reported Lieutenant Commander Roger Kent, Air Combat Officer on Guadalcanal. "One minute we were too limp with malaria to crawl out of our foxholes; the next, we were running around whooping like kids. I remember two Marines working up to a brawl. One of them was arguing that getting the Old Man [Halsey] was like getting two battleships and two carriers, and the other was swearing he was worth two battleships and *three* carriers. If morale had been enough, we'd have won the war right there."[13]

The joy extended to the correspondents and military analysts who had grown accustomed to filing disheartening reports of the fighting. "The effect on the men of the fleet and those ashore at Guadalcanal was electric," wrote Gilbert Cant. "Halsey had the reputation of being the fightingest admiral in the Navy."[14]

From his headquarters in the Southwest Pacific, General Douglas MacArthur, a man resistant to extolling others, was effusive in his praise of his naval counterpart. "William Halsey was one of our great sailors." MacArthur added that Halsey was "Blunt, outspoken, dynamic, he had already proven himself to be a battle commander of the highest order. . . . He was of the same aggressive type as John Paul Jones, David Farragut, and George Dewey. His one thought was to close with the enemy and fight him to the death. The bugaboo of many sailors, the fear of losing ships, was completely alien to his conception of sea action. . . . No name rates higher in the annals of our country's naval history."[15]

Civilians back home, already familiar with Halsey's name from his island raids, matched the military's enthusiasm. Decades after the war it is difficult to fully grasp the impact Halsey made across the breadth of the land, but contemporary newspaper and magazine accounts convey the extent to which the public looked to Halsey to remedy what had been seen as a sinking ship. "New South Pacific Chief Aggressive Commander," proclaimed a *Los Angeles Times* headline. The *New York Times* joined in with, "Shift to Offensive Is Seen in Washington Selection of 'Fighting' Admiral Halsey as Commander in the South Pacific," while the *Washington Post* announced, "Admiral Halsey, Unorthodox Fighter, Takes Over Navy's Toughest Command."[16]

"No 'Spit-and-Polish' Officer, He Values Shooting First—His Audacity Stunned Japanese," stated the headline of Foster Hailey's October

25 article in the *New York Times.* Hailey explained that Halsey's takeover "will be hailed with delight by the men of the Pacific Fleet" and that Halsey "is known among Navy men as a rough, tough fighting man who is as quick with his praise as with his blame when it is warranted. He is the sort of a leader men will follow right to hell and back." Hailey added that "Of all the admirals afloat in the Pacific, this correspondent believes, none would be more certain to inspire their loyalty and command their respect than Admiral Halsey. His return to active command is the best news for months."[17]

"THIS WON'T BE ANOTHER BATAAN"

Halsey speedily reinforced his nation's trust by implementing immediate steps to produce a quick turnaround. He wanted the fatigued Marines and sailors to realize that they had a commander who not only believed they could win, but one who would seize every opportunity to engage the enemy. This goal required three tasks—to reinforce the Marines on Guadalcanal, to prevent the enemy from reinforcing their own troops on the island, and to destroy a Japanese Navy that had been to that point dominant in the waters around Guadalcanal.

When he examined the resources at his command, Halsey found the cupboard all but empty. A handful of cruisers and submarines, a task force anchored around the battleship USS *Washington,* and another centered about the carrier *Hornet* steamed at his disposal, but he needed additional ships and planes, especially carriers and their air squadrons, if he were to have a chance. At that time the enemy enjoyed an edge in warships and trained crews, fought with a skill in night fighting that the Americans had yet to match, and effectively employed a deadly long-range torpedo that handily outperformed the torpedoes then available to American warships.

Compounding matters was that Halsey competed with another theater for those precious resources. On the other side of the world, the United States was preparing for its first major assault against Hitler, the massive November invasion of North Africa that siphoned vast quantities of men and war materials to that region. He stated later that if he were to select a symbol representative of those desperate days, "I would have a motif of a rusty nail and a frayed shoestring. It was certainly the way we felt about it in those days and we had very little prospects of getting anything more. There was a great feeling among all hands that the South Pacific Forces were forgotten men." Halsey understood that Roosevelt and Churchill had targeted Hitler as the primary target, but he wished more could have been done. "It is hard to convince those of us . . . why we should not have some of the gravy that is being shipped in great quantities to Europe."[18]

The president did what he could to aid his new commander. Recognizing the gravity of the situation in the South Pacific, on October 24 Roosevelt sent a memo to the Joint Chiefs of Staff stating, "My anxiety about the Southwest Pacific is to make sure that every possible weapon gets into that area to hold Guadalcanal."[19] While this was comforting, Halsey would have to contain the Japanese with what he possessed as those additional supplies would not reach the Solomons for weeks.

In the interim, Halsey's optimism and belligerence substituted for bullets and bombs. When the Roman Catholic chaplain then ministering to the Marines on Guadalcanal, Father Frederick P. Gehring, informed Halsey that many of his Marines worried that Guadalcanal might become another Bataan, the Philippine site of an Allied surrender to the Japanese, Halsey shouted, "This won't be another Bataan, dammit. We're going to win, and you and I will both see Yamamoto in hell!" [20]

Halsey replaced Ghormley's method of command with one that allowed him to focus on the most crucial matters while his staff dealt with everything else. He brought his own staff from the *Enterprise*, including Ashford, Commander Bromfield B. Nichol, Commander Leonard J. Dow, and Captain Ray Thurber to assist him in running the South Pacific, then gave them the autonomy to make their own decisions.

When Ashford first walked into Halsey's office, the admiral sat at his desk reading dispatches. Halsey took a hurried peak at his former flag lieutenant and said, "It's a goddamn mess. Look around and see what's to be done and do it."[21] He briefly outlined the state of affairs on Guadalcanal and told Ashford they could expect a major sea battle in the coming days that could decide victor and vanquished in the South Pacific. His message was clear: take care of the minutiae so that Halsey could be free to run the show at sea.

SINCE EARLY AUGUST, Vandegrift's Marines had borne the brunt of the Japanese offensive, turning away major assaults as their ranks thinned. To obtain a clearer picture of conditions at Guadalcanal, Halsey radioed Vandegrift to report to Nouméa as soon as possible. On October 23 Vandegrift, accompanied by the visiting Marine commandant General Thomas Holcomb, flew to Nouméa to meet with Halsey and other senior officers.

He first asked Vandegrift to describe the situation at Guadalcanal. Vandegrift mentioned sleepless nights, the devastating effects of naval bombardments, the shortage of planes and supplies, the malaria that was decimating his ranks, and the demoralizing effect on his men of observing the nonstop flow of Japanese soldiers and supplies while they had to make do with what they had. "I told him [Halsey] that to hold we simply had to have air and ground reinforcement, that our people were practically worn out," wrote Vandegrift.

When Halsey asked the others for their views, Harmon and Holcomb backed everything Vandegrift said, but Turner focused on the Navy's problems of resupplying the forces ashore. Not only did he claim to possess an inadequate number of transports and escort ships, but the vessels had to operate in Japanese-controlled waters. As he had lost an alarming number of ships and men in the process, Turner urged caution.

Vandegrift waited while Halsey assessed the information for a few moments. "Gray eyebrows bristling, the compactly built Halsey drummed the desk a moment with his fingers. He abruptly turned to me. 'Can you hold?'"

"Yes, I can hold," Vandegrift replied. "But I have to have more active support than I have been getting."

Halsey thought of what both Vandegrift and Turner said before siding with the Marine. "You go on back there, Vandegrift. I promise to get you everything I have."[22]

The Army's 147th Infantry Regiment was then on the way to seizing Ndeni, an island 350 miles east of Guadalcanal in the Santa Cruz group, so that an airfield could be constructed, but Halsey canceled the operation and diverted the troops to Vandegrift. In the coming weeks he transferred the 8th Marine Regiment from Samoa, brought in a specialized Marine battalion called Carlson's Raiders that mounted a famous thirty-day patrol behind enemy lines, found more artillery, and sent in a Seabee (construction battalion) unit.

With this move, Halsey defused the negativism that had prevailed for more than two months under Ghormley and laid the foundation for a dramatic reversal of fortune in the South Pacific. In September and October 1942 Vandegrift's Marines had halted Japanese thrusts, but they could not pursue the enemy into the jungles because Vandegrift lacked sufficient resources. With the forces Halsey now promised, Vandegrift could both strengthen his lines around Henderson and mount his own offenses against the enemy.

Urgency drove Halsey. When one Army division arrived in the South Pacific, its commanding officer visited Halsey and said, "Give me three weeks to unload and then combat load my transports and then I'll be ready to go anywhere." Halsey laughed and remarked, "Your division is leaving for Guadalcanal tomorrow."[23]

"STRIKE, REPEAT, STRIKE"

The Marines, heartened by Halsey's arrival and his promises to do all he could to support them, battled with renewed vigor. On October 23 the enemy staged a multipronged assault. One infantry regiment, buttressed by light tanks, charged across the Matanikau River from the west bank directly into withering Marine gunfire. That attack stalled, but it diverted attention from a stronger advance toward the airfield's southern flank. A battalion commanded by the legendary Lieutenant Colonel Lewis "Chesty" Puller repulsed the Japanese, who unsuccessfully tried to crack through Marine lines again the following night. More than 3,000 enemy dead littered the battle areas from an assault that all but ended their chances to wrest Henderson from American control.

Promising help for Vandegrift's Marines was one step, but Halsey also had to show that he was willing to risk his navy in battle with the Japanese surface fleet. He could not ask the Marines to fight and die while withholding his ships from action.

Cryptanalysts at Pearl Harbor alerted Halsey that ten Japanese submarines and four carriers were headed toward the South Pacific.

Before he had settled in, Halsey faced a Japanese land assault supported, it appeared, by one of the strongest surface forces to arrive in the area. Working with a hybrid staff containing a handful of his regulars supplemented by Ghormley's holdovers, Halsey hurriedly assembled a battle plan to counter the Japanese. He told Vandegrift that although he had little with which to engage the Japanese, he would send every available ship to oppose the enemy sea threat.

Even for Halsey, the promise stretched credulity as four carriers—*Shokaku, Zuikaku, Zuiho,* and *Junyo*—carrying 194 aircraft, accompanied by four battleships, ten cruisers, and twenty-nine destroyers advanced toward Guadalcanal in two groups. So assured were the Japanese that Vice Admiral Matome Ugaki wrote in his diary on the eve of the battle, "Everyone is awaiting tonight's success with bated breath."[24]

Even with the *Enterprise*'s October 23 appearance at Nouméa, Halsey could not hope to match his foe. Against the Japanese, Halsey had two carriers with 137 aircraft, two battleships, nine cruisers, and twenty-four destroyers organized in three groups.

Halsey believed that the Japanese expected the U.S. Navy to react according to the conservative pattern established in recent weeks, but he had a surprise in store for them. "The yellow bastards have been playing us for suckers," he wrote Admiral Nimitz. Instead of holding his ships and carriers south of Guadalcanal out of range of Japanese land-based aircraft, as Ghormley had done, he intended to send the *Hornet,* soon to be accompanied by the *Enterprise,* north around the Santa Cruz Islands to Guadalcanal's east, where they would lie in wait for the enemy ships to appear. Halsey intended to spring another flanking attack on an unsuspecting enemy, much as Spruance had done at Midway, "in the rather vain hope that we would not be detected and that we would be able to get in the first attack."[25] Halsey's plan risked the South Pacific's only two aircraft carriers, but he believed that he had no choice if he were to avoid losing Guadalcanal.

Around 4:00 A.M. on October 26, a Catalina search plane sighted a Japanese unit 300 miles northwest of Rear Admiral Thomas Kinkaid's *Enterprise.* Unfortunately, the pilot failed to include the composition of the force, its course, or its speed. Without that information Kinkaid could only guess whether Japanese carriers were accompanying that group, or whether they were approaching Guadalcanal from a different sector. He could immediately launch his attack planes to achieve the first strike, as Halsey wanted, but he chanced sending them against a target devoid of carriers while leaving the *Enterprise* and *Hornet* vulnerable to an air attack from elsewhere. Kinkaid was not about to risk his carriers without a clearer picture of what lay before him. He chose to hold his attack force and send out scout aircraft to precisely fix the location of the Japanese carriers.

At 6:00 A.M. on October 26 the *Enterprise* launched sixteen aircraft with orders to scout 200 miles out from the carrier. When, at 7:50 A.M., two scout aircraft confirmed the existence of enemy carriers 200 miles distant, Kinkaid finally ordered a launch.

Halsey had been monitoring the same dispatches at Nouméa. At the initial 4:00 A.M. word of enemy ships, he sent a speedy, "Strike, Repeat, Strike" to Kinkaid, then waited impatiently for Kinkaid to take action. As far as Halsey was concerned, Kinkaid's 7:50 launching of the *Hornet*'s aircraft came four hours too late.

Kinkaid's delay handed the Japanese an opening. As the *Hornet*'s aviators winged toward the Japanese carriers, they passed a group of Japanese aircraft approaching the *Enterprise* and the *Hornet* sixty miles out. By 10:00 A.M. smoke from enemy bombs billowed from the damaged *Hornet* and *Enterprise.* Later in the afternoon, with the *Hornet* dead in the water and beyond salvage, Kinkaid ordered the carrier sunk. He radioed Halsey that the *Enterprise* had sustained enough damage that he would have to retire to Nouméa with the only remaining aircraft carrier in the South Pacific.

In the meantime Kinkaid's aviators compensated for the *Hornet*'s loss by inflicting enough damage to force the Japanese Navy to retreat rather than continue toward Guadalcanal. The carriers *Shokaku* and *Zuiho,* nursing damage from American 1,000-pound bombs, set course for home, and Japan lost so many experienced aviators that the carriers had, in effect, been temporarily removed as a factor in the Solomons.

Halsey privately railed against Kinkaid's role in the battle. He believed that Kinkaid had acted too conservatively in launching his strike force, an action that Halsey believed cost him the *Hornet.* The battle produced strained relations between Halsey and his subordinate, which were later aggravated by their roles in the Battle of Leyte Gulf.

Halsey had momentarily halted the Japanese, but he maintained a fragile supply line to Guadalcanal. With the *Hornet*'s sinking, he decided not to risk his carriers by operating them within range of Japanese land-based aircraft until the new *Essex*-class group, then being constructed in U.S. shipyards, arrived to strengthen his navy. In the meantime, three escort carriers were ordered to move from the Atlantic to the South Pacific, and Halsey even asked Nimitz to inquire about the availability of British aircraft carriers.

Because he so badly needed the *Enterprise* at a time when additional Japanese attempts to seize Guadalcanal were expected, Halsey ordered that repairs be completed at Nouméa rather than sending the carrier to distant Pearl Harbor. Labor crews worked around the clock to ready her for battle, and some of the *Hornet*'s air group shifted to the *Enterprise.* Repair parties left untouched the damaged forward elevator, which was fortunately wedged in the up position, from fear that if they lowered the elevator and it stuck in that position, the carrier would effectively be removed as a weapon. As Halsey concluded, a damaged ship was better than no ship.

Despite the drawbacks, Nimitz saw reason for optimism, much of it owing to Halsey's refreshing enthusiasm. "While our situation in the Southern Solomons is far from satisfactory, it is far from hopeless." Nimitz concluded that because of Vandegrift's vigorous defense on land and Halsey's actions at Santa Cruz, "It is now definite that the enemy suffered heavy attrition losses during October, and considerable damage to striking forces on October 25. Thus, they could not continue what seems to have been the start of a grand scale attack on Guadalcanal."[26]

"KEEP ON KILLING JAPS"

Now that he had momentarily checked the Japanese, Halsey turned to another critical issue—morale. His island raids had delivered a needed boost, but morale was low on Guadalcanal and at home because of the Japanese domination of the war's first half-year. "We are not in the least downhearted or upset by our difficulties," he wrote to Nimitz on

October 31, "but obsessed with one idea only, to kill the yellow bastards and we shall do it." More accustomed to scanning Ghormley's dour forecasts, Nimitz scribbled in the letter's margin, "This is the spirit desired."[27]

Halsey tackled both concerns during a November 8 visit to Guadalcanal, something his predecessor had never done. Halsey accompanied Vandegrift to the site of by-now famous encounters, including Edson's Ridge, where an outnumbered group of Marine Raiders had heroically repelled an assault against Henderson Field, and the banks of the Matanikau River, where the enemy had hurled repeated attacks against Marine lines.

Halsey dressed so inconspicuously in a ragged cap and ruffled shirt as he drove about the island in a mud-spattered jeep that his staff feared he would not be recognized. They urged him to be more visible by standing in the vehicle and waving to the Marines, but he vetoed the notion. "It smells of exhibitionism—the hell with it,"[28] he told his staff. He preferred to mingle with the men one-on-one and trade remarks with youngsters fresh from battle so that he could better gauge their mood. Everywhere he stopped, Marines and Army infantry gathered around the admiral, smiles creasing their battle-grimed faces and a sense of pride lighting their eyes. Marines responded to Halsey because they sensed that he was one of the boys. His uninhibited talk, replete with cursing and derogatory remarks against the Japanese, found a receptive home among youths battling along the front lines. In their opinion, he understood the average soldier as few commanders did.

"On November 8 Admiral Halsey flew in like a wonderful breath of fresh air," wrote Vandegrift, who had shepherded his men through the roughest portion of the struggle and who knew he would yet have to ask his men to endure more. "During a tour of the area he showed extreme interest and enthusiasm in all phases of the operation, concurring with my existent positions and future plans. More important, he talked to a large number of Marines, saw their gaunt, malaria-ridden bodies, their faces lined from what seemed a nightmare of years."[29]

After inspecting the perimeter and meeting with the fighting men, Halsey chatted with a group of war correspondents, most of whom had been covering the campaign since the previous August. In many ways

Halsey, who understood the ability of the press to convey his message to the vast readership back home, perfected the sound bite years before television popularized the term. He peppered his remarks with highly quotable phrases that resonated back home, many reflecting the current wartime stereotypes and bigotry. Readers loved his hard-hitting style, which contrasted with the noncommittal utterances from Washington, D.C., and with the abysmal headlines.

When a correspondent asked Halsey his formula for winning the war, he wasted little time coming to the point. Halsey referred to the enemy as "Japtards" and blurted that his recipe was to "kill Japs, kill Japs and keep on killing Japs." Halsey added that although the fighting at Guadalcanal was "fine from our point of view" and pointedly praised the Marines, Army infantry, and aviators, he cautioned that the public would have to prepare for more losses in the immediate future. "You can't make an omelet without breaking eggs," explained Halsey to the cluster of reporters. "You can't fight a war safely or without losing ships."[30]

In an attempt to shatter the wartime myth of the Japanese superman that prevailed after Pearl Harbor, Halsey stated his faith in the Americans under his command. "When we first started out, I held that one of our men was the equal of three Japs," he told the reporters. "I have since increased this to twenty. They are just monkeys, and I say 'monkeys' because I cannot say what I should like to call them. Japan's next move will be to retreat; and they will keep on retreating."[31]

These words, coming as they did after a dismal year of fighting, quenched the American public's thirst for optimism and bombast. They had heard for too long about defeat; they wanted to read about battles that paved the first bricks on the long path leading to Tokyo. Halsey handed it to them on a platter of golden words, using this press conference to reassure his countrymen that all would be well. Halsey spent much of his first month instilling the belief into his fighting forces and on the home front that success was at hand.

The morning after he spoke to the reporters, Halsey decorated thirteen Marine officers and men. Halsey whispered remarks to each as he pinned medals on the young Marines, including eighteen-year-old Private Joseph D. R. Champayne, who earned a Navy Cross for remaining in his foxhole on October 23 when a Japanese tank halted directly over his position. Champayne placed a hand grenade in the tank's caterpillar treads, then raced away before the explosion dismantled the vehicle. "You will undoubtedly be more than a private the next time I come here," Halsey said to the young hero. Once finished with the medals, Halsey said to the thirteen, "I have never been more proud of you in my life. I wish to God that every man, woman and child in our great country could know and see what you are doing here. God bless you."[32] The thirteen heroes rejoined the front lines as soon as the ceremony ended, but they returned with fresh stories of their new commander, a man who cast the spotlight on privates and corporals in an effort to let them know he appreciated their efforts.

On his return trip to Nouméa later that morning, Halsey visited a naval hospital at Efate, where he moved from cot to cot to express his gratitude to the wounded. Like Halsey's tour of the battlefields and the awards ceremony, news of this hospital visit—another action Ghormley had failed to take—bounded about Guadalcanal, helping to fashion the legend Halsey became in the South Pacific.

Halsey would need more than words, however, as he learned upon returning to headquarters in Nouméa. The Japanese were on the prowl.

"THE BEST DEFENSE IS A STRONG OFFENSE"

Back at Nouméa on November 9, Halsey learned that the Japanese assault that was under way surpassed the enemy's previous attempts. Culled from intercepted Japanese radio dispatches by cryptanalysts at Pearl Harbor, the information so alarmed Nimitz that on November 9 he alerted Halsey that a carrier-assisted "grand scale offensive aimed at Guadalcanal [is] to be undertaken by the enemy in the very near future." Nimitz estimated the attack date to be Friday, November 13, and that it was "expected to be a major effort to recapture Guadalcanal." Japanese aircraft would begin pounding the island three days before the arrival of a force expected to contain as many as five aircraft carriers and thirty-six escorting vessels. Nimitz knew the enemy force could outgun Halsey's, but added, "While this looks like a big punch I am confident that you with your forces will take their measure." Upon assessing the high odds and reading Nimitz's statement of support, Halsey said to Browning, with a touch of sarcasm, "It's good to know that the old man has so much confidence in me."[33]

Halsey scraped together every ship that could be brought into play, including the damaged *Enterprise,* to save the men on shore. His captains and unit commanders had one task. There would be no shirking action, even if the battle occurred on Friday, November 13, a day the superstitious Halsey detested. "If I have any principle of warfare that is burned within my brain," Halsey later wrote, "it is that the best defense is a strong offense. Lord Nelson expressed this very well, 'No captain can go wrong who places his ship alongside the enemy's.'"[34]

Halsey later called this period one of the most trying moments of his career. He could not afford to sit back and do nothing, as that would further demoralize the men ashore who would be subjected to yet another vicious naval bombardment, but meager resources narrowed his options. In fulfilling his promise to Vandegrift of complete support, Halsey accepted two risks that Ghormley had avoided. He would send his cruisers and destroyers to engage more-powerful Japanese battleships, which was certain to end in many American deaths, and he would ignore naval doctrine by ordering the ships to operate in the confining waters surrounding Guadalcanal, which would hamper their maneuverability. Halsey ordered every mechanic in Nouméa to work around the clock to get every possible ship battle-ready as "this was a time when even half-ships counted."[35]

In addition to the *Enterprise,* Halsey had two battleships, four heavy cruisers, four light cruisers, and twenty-two destroyers to turn back Yamamoto. Part of the force was already at sea, escorting 6,000 reinforcements to Guadalcanal. He ordered those units, under Rear Admirals Daniel J. Callaghan and Norman Scott, to shepherd the transports into Guadalcanal, unload the troops, escort the transports out of the area no later than twilight on November 12, then return to engage the Japanese. Halsey also detached three ships from Callaghan's command and sent them back as support for Kinkaid and the *Enterprise.*

On November 11 Halsey ordered Kinkaid to leave Nouméa, even though repair crews had not yet completed their work on the *Enter-*

prise. The reliable carrier headed to battle with the inoperable elevator and leaking a trail of oil. He told Kinkaid to take station 200 miles south of San Cristobal, an island fifty miles southeast of Guadalcanal. This, Halsey believed, would bring the carrier's aircraft squadrons into play while keeping the *Enterprise* to the south, away from the restricted waters off Guadalcanal and, hopefully, out of harm's way. Halsey needed that ship until additional carriers arrived from the United States.

While Callaghan and Scott's transports finished unloading, search aircraft spotted a large Japanese force steaming south toward Guadalcanal. Intelligence from Pearl Harbor confirmed the absence of enemy carriers, but Halsey faced the uncomfortable prospect of employing his smaller cruisers against the more powerful battleships. The admirals escorted the transports to safety, then returned to prepare for battle. Admiral Callaghan, in the heavy cruiser USS *San Francisco,* would be in overall command of a unit that included another four cruisers and eight destroyers, while Halsey expected that Kinkaid would have the *Enterprise* task force in place below San Cristobal Island before the Japanese arrived, ready to support Callaghan.

JUST BEFORE 2:00 A.M. on Friday, November 13, Admiral Callaghan led his five cruisers and eight destroyers into Sealark Channel off Guadalcanal from the south as Japanese Vice Admiral Hiroaki Abe's two battleships, one cruiser, and fourteen destroyers approached from the north. Chaos ensued as the opponents intermingled in the narrow channel, firing madly like Western gunslingers at targets that emerged mere hundreds of yards away. For thirty minutes guns thundered with such ferocity that, for one of the few times in the campaign, the troops ashore did not envy their naval brethren. "The battle would have pleased Mars," Vandegrift wrote. "For nearly an hour we watched naval guns belch orange death with such rapid vehemence that the island seemed to shake beneath us."[36]

In Nouméa, Halsey stewed. He had set in motion the men and ships to fight the battle, but he could now do nothing but wait. He paced and sat, stared and thought, a lonely outsider hundreds of miles from the fighting he had incited.

"I must have smoked at least two packs of cigarettes. When the tension became unbearable I skimmed through the trashiest magazine I could find." Each moment proved excruciating for the man who preferred to be in the thick of things: he knew that Academy friends and fellow Navy personnel were sacrificing their lives to execute his orders. "This is the hardest thing an area commander in the rear has to face. Your feeling is one of complete helplessness. You know you have put your men into a fight and you hope you have done everything possible to make that fight successful but you are always searching your mind for something you may have left undone. It is great mental agony."[37]

Halsey's trepidation proved unnecessary as Callaghan and Scott turned back Abe's ships before he could deliver either a bombardment of Henderson Field or additional reinforcements. Shortly after dawn American bombers and torpedo planes jumped on Abe as he fled northward and sank one battleship while tossing his force into disarray.

Callaghan paid a severe price for saving Henderson Field. While sending one Japanese battleship and two destroyers to the bottom, Callaghan lost his own life as well as two cruisers and four destroyers, with two other ships badly damaged. Also among the dead was Admiral Scott, who, with Callaghan, had sacrificed his life in the stirring action to save Halsey's troops on shore.

"As the day ends it seems most probable that while we have suffered severe losses in ships and personnel," concluded Nimitz's Greybook of November 13, "our gallant shipmates have again thwarted the enemy. If so, this may well be the [underline in original] decisive battle of this campaign."[38]

ROUND ONE OF the crucial November naval battle had gone to Halsey, but the Japanese were far from finished. They intended to counter against a weakened Halsey with a nighttime bombardment of Henderson, followed by a second attempt to land the reinforcements. With Callaghan's force no longer available, Halsey and his staff debated possible scenarios. Some cautioned against risking his depleted force, but Halsey brushed aside the advice. He would not disappoint those men on shore by holding back ships that might be able to prevent a devastating bombardment. The battleships then escorting Kinkaid would have to fill in for Callaghan's depleted unit.

A tardy order and subsequent delays prevented Kinkaid from taking part in the battle. At 4:00 P.M. on November 13, Halsey alerted Kinkaid to be prepared to detach a force of battleships and destroyers to check the Japanese bombardment unit, but he inexplicably failed to send the order to execute the plan for another hour. Only at 5:00 P.M. did Kinkaid receive the command to detach his two battleships, USS *South Dakota* and USS *Washington,* accompanied by four destroyers, under the command of Rear Admiral Willis A. Lee Jr., and send them northward.

Halsey assumed Kinkaid was farther north than he actually was that evening. Rather than closing on Guadalcanal as Halsey expected, Kinkaid, wary of losing the South Pacific's only carrier, slowed by the necessity to turn south into the wind for flight operations, and retarded by a series of submarine alerts, stood 360 miles southeast of Ironbottom Sound. Kinkaid realized that neither Lee's detached force nor the *Enterprise* would reach Halsey's desired location in time to be effective, and he informed Halsey he could not arrive until 7:00 A.M. the next morning.

As a result, Vandegrift's forces had to endure another night of shelling. In what had to gall the Marine commander, Halsey dashed off a message informing Vandegrift, "Sorry—Lee cannot comply—too far,"[39] then sat back to await developments. "I literally held my breath,"[40] Halsey said of the night of November 13–14. At 1:25 A.M. on November 14, two Japanese cruisers pounded Henderson Field for thirty minutes with 989 eight-inch shells that shattered aircraft and rattled dugouts. Though significant, the destruction would have been far more severe had Callaghan and Scott not earlier hamstrung their opponent.

At 8:30 A.M. on November 14, Halsey ordered the *Enterprise* to transfer her air group to Guadalcanal where it could assist the overworked aviators at Henderson Field, then withdraw to Nouméa. His carrier might have been absent earlier, but he could at least bolster the Cactus Air Force by adding the carrier's forty aircraft, which more than doubled the number available to repel any reinforcement attempt.

Another threat soon brewed. American search planes launched for the dawn patrol reported that the eleven troop transports packed with more than 10,000 reinforcements, which had been turned back the day before, were now again headed toward the island. The development, following so closely after the bombardment, astonished officials in Washington, D.C., who believed that Callaghan and Scott had successfully halted the enemy attempt to reinforce their troops. Under Secretary of the Navy James Forrestal later wrote that these anxious moments equaled the tension he experienced the night before the monumental June 6, 1944, Normandy landings.

Forrestal's worries proved premature, however. Fighters and bombers raced from Henderson to attack, sinking one cruiser and damaging three others before focusing on the transports. Vandegrift's pilots, aided by Halsey's *Enterprise* aviators, demolished seven of the Japanese vessels, sending crew and reinforcements to watery deaths.

At the news Halsey shouted to his staff, "I believe we have the bastards licked." He added that without the reinforcements, momentum on Guadalcanal would switch to Vandegrift. "A large number of Nips achieved their greatest ambition—they joined their ancestors."[41] The Japanese soldiers on Guadalcanal had been fighting with reduced rations and supplies, which they now would have to share with troops that had brought no additional resources.

Halsey could not celebrate for long. The enemy may have been wounded, but he was far from finished as a third Japanese force had materialized. Halsey ordered Admiral Lee to take his two battleships, *Washington* and *South Dakota,* and their four escorting destroyers—then representing the last of Halsey's surface ships—to meet the onrushing battleship, four cruisers, and nine destroyers under Japanese Vice Admiral Nobutake Kondo.

The thirty-minute slugfest during the night of November 14–15 matched its predecessor's intensity. Kondo sank all four of Lee's destroyers and damaged the *South Dakota,* but not before the monstrous guns of Lee's battleship, *Washington,* landed fifty hits in seven minutes that left the Japanese battleship *Kirishima* and a destroyer in shambles and forced Kondo to flee to the north.

The coup de grâce occurred later that morning when bombers from Henderson and Marine artillery blasted the four surviving transports, which had beached on the island. Artillery shells and bombs ripped into the Japanese, hurling food rations and body parts skyward. Of the 12,000 reinforcements and 10,000 tons of supplies sent to Guadalcanal in the eleven transports, only 2,000 men and 5 tons of matériel reached the front lines at Guadalcanal. Lee's action, coupled with the subsequent destruction of the Japanese transports, according to Halsey, "put a finis to their attempts."[42]

"THE SUN BEGAN TO RISE ON ME"

Halsey gained a clear-cut victory in the three-day Naval Battle of Guadalcanal. Callaghan, Scott, Lee, and their crews stopped the Japanese from significantly reinforcing the troops fighting against Vandegrift while ferrying in more forces for the Marines fighting ashore. At the same time, they saved Henderson Field—the nucleus from which Halsey's subsequent Solomons offensive originated. Though both sides suffered similar losses—Halsey lost two cruisers, seven destroyers, and more than 1,700 men against Yamamoto's two battleships, one cruiser, three destroyers, eleven transports, and almost 1,900 men—the Japanese lacked the ability to match the United States ship for ship and man for man. Tokyo could not long wage a costly war of attrition.

Halsey sensed the importance of this battle. As the reports came in, "it became increasingly apparent that we had inflicted a great defeat on the Japs and prevented all but meager and unsupplied reinforcements reaching his beleagured [sic] troops. The sun began to rise on me." He added in an official report, "The sea and air power of the Japanese in the Guadalcanal area was decisively smashed."[43]

Even after the war, when Halsey gathered material for his autobiography, he declined to temper his judgment. "This battle was a decisive American victory by any standard," he affirmed in 1947. "It was also the third great turning point of the war in the Pacific. Midway stopped the Japanese advance in the Central Pacific; Coral Sea stopped it in the Southwest Pacific; Guadalcanal stopped it in the South Pacific." Halsey contended that had he lost, the Marines on Guadalcanal would have been forced to surrender. "Unobstructed, the enemy would have driven south, cut our supply lines to New Zealand and Australia and enveloped them." He added, "Until then he [Japan] had been advancing at his will. From then on he retreated at ours."[44]

In the aftermath of the battle, Halsey credited the men who most deserved acclaim—the sailors, Marines, and infantry under his command. He sent a message to every ship, base, and unit in the South Pacific heralding their efforts. "Your names have been written in golden letters on the pages of history and you have won the everlasting gratitude of your countrymen. No honor for you could be too great. My pride in you is beyond expression."[45]

Halsey could not be so kind in two cases in which he believed the officers had acted with timidity. On October 23 he replaced Admiral Kinkaid with Rear Admiral Ted Sherman, largely because Halsey believed Kinkaid had commanded his ships too conservatively during the Battle of Santa Cruz and again at the Naval Battle of Guadalcanal. Halsey wrote Nimitz that the war-weary Kinkaid, who had been at sea for almost a year, needed a rest back in the United States. Though Kinkaid went on to serve elsewhere with distinction, ill feelings festered between the two.

The second case proved more controversial. In the first day's fighting, during which Admiral Callaghan sacrificed his life, an enemy submarine sank the cruiser USS *Juneau* as the American ships departed the battle area. The ship erupted with such ferocity that the task group's senior officer, Captain Gilbert C. Hoover aboard the USS *Helena,* assumed nobody had survived. With a Japanese submarine in the area, and possessing only a solitary destroyer as escort for his force, Hoover signaled a circling B–17 bomber pilot to relay word of the loss to Nouméa and exited to protect his remaining ships.

To Hoover's later dismay, about one hundred of the *Juneau*'s crew had survived the horrific blast. By the time rescue craft tardily raced to the scene more than a week later, only ten remained alive. Nearly 700 sailors, including the five Sullivan brothers from Waterloo, Iowa, went down with the ship or died before being rescued.

Halsey discussed the matter with his staff and decided to relieve Hoover. Halsey acted swiftly from a desire to eradicate any thought of timidity in the South Pacific. He wanted men of action, not hesitation, and by taking this action he held Hoover as an example for others. After events cooled and Halsey evaluated matters more calmly, he concluded that he might have acted too hastily and wondered "if I had done an injustice to a man who had had a magnificent combat record." Halsey wrote a second letter requesting that Hoover be restored to command, stating that he would happily agree to have him again serve under him. "I am deeply regretful of this whole incident," Halsey wrote in his memoirs. "I have already acknowledged my mistake to him and to the Navy Department, and here I acknowledge it publicly."[46]

"THE MEN OF CACTUS LIFT THEIR BATTERED HELMETS"

Praise for the admiral and the men fighting in the Solomons rolled in, from the president and military commanders to ensigns and private citizens. Halsey was again the public's number-one hero and the media's darling.

President Roosevelt stated at his regular Tuesday press conference that the fight in the Solomons was "a major victory, to the Navy itself, where outward confidence had been greatly nullified by doubts as to the manner in which the Navy would meet formidable Japanese odds. Those doubts no longer exist." He later claimed, "It would seem that the turning point in this war has at last been reached."[47]

The most appreciative individual may have been General Vandegrift, whose tired Marines, supported by Army infantry, had gallantly maintained control of Henderson Field. Vandegrift's November 16 message to Halsey reiterated his admiration of the man and of his subordinates when he asserted, "To them the men of Cactus lift their battered helmets in deepest admiration."[48]

The nation's press was even more effusive than it had been after Halsey's island raids. *Time* magazine selected him for its November 30 cover, placing an image of Halsey directly above the words, "When an attacker is attacked . . ." In an article titled, "Hit Hard, Hit Fast, Hit Often" six words that aptly summed Halsey's philosophy, the magazine profiled the admiral's recent feats in terms usually reserved for champions like Washington and Lincoln. "On all the ships in the Fleet, the

Halsey battle cry was memorized: Hit hard, hit fast, hit often." The article asserted that, "The few times the Japs had been hit, while reinforcing the Solomons, they had been hit and run from. But this time there was a new spirit in the U.S. task forces. The Americans came in slugging again and yet again."[49]

Headlines in the nation's newspapers hailed Halsey's triumph, not only for halting the Japanese but also for stemming the burgeoning doubts about the country's military. "Admiral Takes Big Chances to Gain Big Victories," "Halsey's Triumph," and "Aggressive Spirit" were the headlines on stories in the *Washington Post* about the three-day battle. The paper compared the action to the crucial World War I clash at Jutland, and said that "Halsey emerged last night even a greater hero in public estimation than when he battered the Japs in the Marshall Islands last January 31 and gave the United States its first notable victory of the war."

A *Post* editorial declared that, "Halsey took a leaf out of Nelson's copybook, one of the maxims of which is: The boldest measures are the safest." Even more crucial, in the *Post*'s view, was the impact on public morale. "The cloud that was hanging this weekend over the Solomons has been dissipated in as spectacular a victory as has ever been recorded in our naval annals," one that removed the anxiety that "has lately been profound." The newspaper emphasized, "The country thus has every reason to be proud of Halsey," who might have helped the nation turn a corner. The editors stated that Halsey's spirit won the battle, and that "the exploit of Halsey will serve as an example of what the aggressive spirit can do to bridge gaps in relative strength in men and ships. We have need of that spirit till we catch up to the Japanese. We shall have need of it even when we can match them ship for ship in the Pacific."

The *Post* wrote that after this battle, "It is the handwriting on the wall for America's enemies," whose luster Halsey had stolen. His Marines and naval forces showed that "Japanese fighting men, with their vaunted suicidal proclivities do not excel ours in audacity and determination, on the sea, in the air, or on the ground."[50]

The *Los Angeles Times* joined in. Under the headline "Leader of Battle at Solomons Refuses to Fight by Rule Book," the article labeled Halsey "a highly unorthodox admiral, who figuratively tosses the rule book out a porthole when he goes to sea." The article reprinted the words Halsey had used after the island raids to summarize his command beliefs: "We get away with it because we violate all the traditional rules of naval warfare. We do the exact opposite of what they expect us to do. We deliberately put ourselves under fire of enemy batteries. We expose ourselves to shore-based planes. We do not stay behind the battle with our carriers. Most important: whatever we do, we do fast."[51]

Halsey even became the subject for a flattering poem written by renowned national columnist H. J. Phillips. This poem was reprinted in hundreds of newspapers.[52]

"YOU ARE A GREAT HERO AT THE MOMENT"

Public reaction to Halsey's victory equaled the official and press jubilation, as generals and ensigns, seamen and civilians directed an avalanche of mail toward the commander. A November 18 letter from John B. Polhemus explained that in 1913, "I had the pleasure of serving under you in the [destroyer] Jarvis." Polhemus could hardly contain his exuberance over knowing the nation's newest hero. "About the time of the Marshall Island raid, when I realized who you were, I began bragging of having once served under you and predicting that you would come out of the war as our outstanding hero. Since my prediction now seems to be coming true, I have increased my bragging, but instead of my friends becoming bored with me, they feel that it is something of an honor to know someone that once knew Admiral Halsey, sort of 'Hand that shook the hand of John L. Sullivan' complex." Polhemus ended his letter by declaring, "our trust and faith in you is unlimited."[53]

Since the letters were not intended to be made public, Halsey felt free to express his emotions without restraint. In a response to Captain Rufus F. Zogbaum, who wrote on November 27 that, "Those Yellow Bastards need a fighting man to teach them manners and the country has found one in you," Halsey composed a blistering reply. While unacceptable in eras that place more premium on political correctness, it conveyed the emotions held by many in the nation in the 1940s. "These yellow bastards are beasts alright and it's not me, but the greatest fighting men this country ever produced that are teaching them their manners." Halsey then promoted what, even in the 1940s, would be considered controversial. "We are trying to keep our swords sharp on these yellow bellied sons of bitches and will continue to give them Hell every time they want it. The day is not in the too distant future when we will be able to go after them and kick them off the face of the earth. In order to save the world, I am going to advocate at the peace table for the few yellow bellies that are left—emasculation for the males and spaying for the females."[54]

President Roosevelt nominated Halsey as a full admiral because of the naval victory. In talking of the elevation, Secretary Frank Knox called Halsey "one of the few great naval leaders in history." When Congress approved his nomination on November 26, Halsey became one of only six men, including King and Nimitz, to be so honored. Even during what was the high point of his naval career, Halsey shifted the praise to the men fighting under his command. "Naturally, I was very proud and happy, but with the full realization that although it was an individual award it was intended for acceptance by me as a recognition of the splendid work that the South Pacific forces had been continuing to do, and I was promoted as the representative of that force."[55]

His colleagues were pleased with Halsey's promotion, which, they thought, relayed the approval of both the president and Congress of the aggressive manner of warfare waged by Halsey. "Allah be praised—Billie Halsey has just been made an admiral!" proclaimed Rear Admiral William L. Calhoun, the Commander Service Squadron, South Pacific Force when he learned of the step. Calhoun ordered the ship's repair shop to craft two sets of four-star pins for Halsey so he could surprise their superior. When Calhoun handed them to Halsey, Halsey declined to wear them until he received official notification. In a touching display toward the men Halsey felt were the true heroes, he removed his two three-star pin clusters and told an officer, "Send one of these to Mrs. Scott and the other to Mrs. Callaghan. Tell them it was their husband's bravery that got me my new ones."[56]

HALSEY HAD REGISTERED an impressive first month in the South Pacific. Dropped into a whirlpool that had already swallowed Ghormley, in thirty remarkable days he adopted five steps to transform a desperate situation into one filled with hope. He brought renewed optimism to the South Pacific, kept his promise to Vandegrift by diverting every available troop to Guadalcanal, checked enemy advances on land, displayed a willingness to toss his ships into battle no matter the odds, and restored American confidence among the frontline forces and at home.

By halting the enemy and removing the immediate threat to Guadalcanal, he gained time during which he implemented additional steps to ensure that complete victory arrived—not just on Guadalcanal but throughout the Solomons.

CHAPTER 6

"I WILL STAY ON THE OFFENSIVE"

For the next two months Halsey consolidated his foothold on Guadalcanal. While he continued to scavenge for additional reinforcements and supplies to bolster Vandegrift's offensive against General Harukichi Hyakutake, he assigned two tasks to his naval units—isolate the Japanese on land by preventing additional troops and supplies from reaching the island, and repulse the Japanese fleet should it make an appearance. While they focused on these assignments, Halsey marshaled his forces to end the fighting on Guadalcanal and begin the nation's first Pacific offensive—an advance up the Solomon Islands chain toward the enemy fortress at Rabaul.

"The First Breathing Spell"

Glimmers of hope foreshadowed good things to come. "Things have been very quiet in this area lately," Halsey wrote Nimitz on November 29. "It is the first breathing spell." He mentioned the stronger force of cruisers standing at Espiritu Santo and even hinted that he considered an air strike against Rabaul, the heart of the Japanese military in the South Pacific. "We are slowly but surely digging our way out from under the difficulties," he wrote Nimitz. "Everyone here is working like a beaver, . . . We shall lick hell out of the yellow bastards every time an opportunity presents. That is a promise. In the meantime we are all happy, cheerful and trying to do a little bit better than our best."[1]

Halsey could not sit still if he were to continue the momentum. He concluded from the October and November naval clashes that he had to instill a more disciplined approach at sea. Typically, American cruisers and battleships steamed into action single file, shielded by destroyers stationed at the column's front and rear. This disposition, though, impeded his destroyers' ability to assemble as a unit upon sighting the enemy and to more fully utilize their strength—the torpedo assault.

In late November Halsey asked Kinkaid, now in command of Task Force 67, which contained all the cruisers then in the South Pacific, to prepare a tactical guide for ships to follow. Kinkaid rearranged the ships into one destroyer and two cruiser groups, each containing at least one ship equipped with radar. When the enemy had been spotted, aircraft would illuminate the area with flares, upon which the destroyers stationed in the van would deliver their torpedo attack, then swerve to the side to allow the cruisers to lay a bombardment on the disorganized enemy from 12,000 yards away.

Kinkaid departed to take command in the Aleutians before he had the chance to test his plan in the Solomons. When search aircraft located another Japanese unit steaming south to deliver supplies, Halsey ordered Kinkaid's successor, Rear Admiral Carleton Wright, to wait off Tassafaronga near Henderson Field, and then follow Kinkaid's new tactics when the Japanese had entered the channel below Savo Island.

Wright, commanding five cruisers and four destroyers, engaged eight Japanese destroyers on the night of November 30 in what became the final major surface battle in the southern Solomons. When one enemy destroyer opened fire, rather than first conduct a torpedo attack Wright directed cruiser salvos onto the illuminated vessel. Though he sank the destroyer and prevented the enemy from reinforcing the troops on land, his premature action allowed the remaining Japanese destroyers to launch their missiles. The Japanese sank the cruiser USS *Northampton* and put three other cruisers out of action in recording a victory over the stronger Wright.

Halsey lauded Wright for his efforts but believed his mishandling of his forces had enabled the enemy to escape with minimal damage while inflicting greater harm on Wright. Wright should have detached his destroyers to launch a torpedo attack before the Japanese had time to do the same. Halsey also contended that, to be effective, a commander must place his flagship closer to the front rather than lag behind as Wright's had.

Halsey would not allow substandard performance to last much longer. During the grim days in the South Pacific, many of the engagements unfolded because of "the way we must throw destroyers and cruisers into action without organization."[2] Now that he faced a lull, and with the enemy being pushed back on land in December, Halsey planned to address the issue.

"Halseyize That Gang Down in Washington"

Halsey's recent exploits had cemented his reputation as one of the most outstanding military leaders in the nation's history. "As for the military men of the U.S., 1942 offered them few opportunities for great achievement," concluded *Time* magazine. However, one name stood out as representative of the attitude the nation required to defeat a ruthless foe. "Outstanding among Americans for accomplishment in battle stood the name of Admiral William Halsey, who, not once but again & again, took his task force into swift encounters against the Japs to deal them telling blows."[3]

Emperor Hirohito looked forward to the next twelve months. In his New Year's Day Imperial Rescript, he told his nation that despite momentary setbacks in the South Pacific, he expected grand accomplishments in the year ahead. "The darkness is very deep but dawn is about to break in the Eastern Sky. Today the finest of the Japanese Army, Navy and Air units are gathering. Sooner or later they will head toward the Solomon Islands where a decisive battle is being fought between Japan and America."[4]

The press-savvy Halsey stole the emperor's thunder with a headline-grabbing press conference that was reprinted in newspapers across the nation. With conditions improving in Guadalcanal, Halsey accepted a long-standing invitation from New Zealand's government to visit that country. On January 2 he flew to Auckland, where he used the occasion to bolster New Zealand's confidence as well as direct another ringing declaration to Americans still uneasy over the war's course.

Halsey found his opening during a press conference when a reporter asked him what he expected Japan's next move would be. To the large gathering assembled at his hotel, Halsey announced in grand fashion, "Japan's next move will be to retreat. A start has been made to make them retreat. They will not be able to stop going back."[5]

When *New York Times* correspondent J. Norman Lodge asked Halsey his prediction for 1943, the admiral answered, "Victory for the United Nations. Complete, absolute defeat for the Axis Powers."

"This year?" said a startled Lodge.

"Yes."

Halsey explained that he based his optimistic outlook on the fighting abilities of the forces then assembled in the South Pacific, which he believed to be more than a match for the Japanese military. He added that his forces had passed to the offensive and "All the Axis is hearing the tolling of the bells. And we are doing 'the rope pulling.'" A broad smile, Lodge noticed, spread across Halsey's face as he uttered his words.

Reporters captured Halsey's every word as he claimed that the Japanese have "apish or bestial instincts . . ." and cautioned Hirohito, "As Emperor and leader of traitorous and brutal Japan during the years of her foul attacks on peaceful peoples, your time is short." More direct with Japan's prime minister Hideki Tojo, Halsey said, "When you unleashed your cowardly attack on Dec. 7 you started something you can't finish. Beneath your thin veneer of civilization lies the dominant instinct to kill. Because of this you have released the greatest instinct to fight in the American people ever in history."

He had harsher words for Japanese citizens, warning them to cease before the United States turned its full force upon them. "That heavy rumbling you hear now will gradually grow into a shock of bursting bombs, the shrieking of shells and the clashing of swords on your own soil. You had better stop now before it is too late."

With that Halsey rose from his chair and departed. "And as abruptly as the interview had begun," wrote Lodge, "it stopped."[6]

As he intended, Halsey's words created a firestorm. Tokyo Rose referred to the special tortures that awaited Halsey once the Japanese had him in chains, remarks that caused Halsey's closest friends in the Navy to pretend to stir a boiling cauldron containing Halsey whenever they saw the admiral.

HALSEY'S OTHER AUDIENCE, the citizens of New Zealand and of the United States, applauded his remarks. The *New Zealand Herald* reported that Halsey's "confidence was clearly immense," and that "It was so great and so obviously no bigger than his conviction that it was infectious, and as statement succeeded statement it became very clear why it is said of Admiral William 'Pudge' Halsey by his officers and men that they would follow him to Hell. He is a man whose confidence could clearly win battles." The newspaper concluded by asserting, "He has the right way of it, for we shall certainly not conquer in 1943 unless we believe we can, and plan and work to do it."[7]

The *Seattle Daily Journal* reflected public opinion in the United States. The January 5 editorial stated that, "Admiral Halsey has a way of speaking his mind that appeals to most Americans." In a comparison sure to find favor with Halsey, the newspaper likened the situation to a football game, where the team has overcome early setbacks and is driving toward the enemy. At that time, "it would be a poor quarterback indeed who would tell his teammates, 'You probably can't click over now, but the game is still young and possibly we can eventually get through.' That isn't the way Admiral Halsey plays the game. He knows the opposition has taken some stiff jolts, and he is merely saying what an exceptionally smart quarterback would say; 'There's the goal. We can smash through right now; they can't stop us! Give it all the horsepower you've got. Here we go!'"[8]

Halsey had again correctly sensed the public's mood and delivered the words it most needed. He connected with the country's majority, men and women who wanted a brutal military response to Japan's opening victory and a speedy end to a war.

In a letter to Halsey, J. I. Faynes of Little Rock, Arkansas, claimed that his declaration to the reporters "was the spark that lit us all up for another 'Go.'" Bertram Jay Gumpert of New York City added, "Perhaps those cautious people who warn, 'this is a long war and we must not be overconfident' are right, but it is good to know that one of our high commanders is willing to assume a public 'we'll-lick-hell-out-of-them-in-damn-short-order' attitude."[9]

M. D. Haire claimed that everyone he knew agreed with Halsey, the admiral who spoke for the common man. "I wish something could be done to Halseyize that gang down in Washington. If they would only halfway adopt your viewpoint it would galvanize this country into such unified action that nothing could stop. . . . Oh, for more men like you in high places."[10]

Despite the near-universal acclaim, Halsey dealt with criticism as well. The Navy Department feared his remarks would solidify Japanese opposition and wondered if the public would be disheartened twelve months distant if the war had not ended. State Department dignitaries who would have to work with Japanese officials after the war to ensure peace objected to Halsey's harsh words toward Hirohito and Tojo, production analysts worried that factory output might plunge, and draft-board supervisors feared a negative public reaction to additional calls for draftees.

Halsey countered by saying that "the correspondents had asked for my opinion, not for my guess at what State hoped it was. So I said what I thought: the Japanese are bastards." He realized the United States lacked the manpower and resources to win the war within a year, but other motives compelled him to speak out. "They accused me of everything from recklessness to drunkenness," he wrote. "God Almighty, I knew we wouldn't be in Tokyo that soon! I knew we wouldn't be there even by the end of 1944. I may be tactless, but I'm not a damned fool!" Halsey could not understand the objections.

Production executives and accountants might be more interested in supply and demand, but "What the civilian bigwigs didn't consider is this: my forces were tired; their morale was low; they were beginning to think that they were abused and forgotten, that they had been fighting too much and too long. Moreover, the new myth of Japanese invincibility had not yet been entirely discredited. Prior to Pearl Harbor, the United States in general had rated Japan as no better than a class-C nation. After that one successful sneak attack, however, panicky eyes saw the monkeymen as supermen. I saw them as nothing of the sort, and I wanted my forces to know how I felt. I stand by the opinion that the Japs are bastards, and I stand by this one, too."[11]

"These Young Fellas Are Full of 'Pee and Ginger'"

Halsey would have preferred a better outcome to kick off the New Year than the events of January, despite opening the month with a pair of successful bombardments. On January 5, 1943, and again on January 24, cruisers commanded by Rear Admiral Walden L. "Pug" Ainsworth shelled the Japanese airfield at Munda north of Guadalcanal. Naval bombardments, especially between land assaults when the destroyers and cruisers were not needed to support invasions, became an effective weapon during Halsey's tenure.

Not so fortunate was the result off Rennell Island 120 miles southeast of Guadalcanal. The action started when American aerial reconnaissance detected indications of a Japanese naval buildup at Rabaul and at Buin on the Solomon island of Bougainville—troop transports and freighters mingled with Japanese destroyers, while Japanese carriers and battleships appeared to be on the prowl. Radio intelligence supported the theory that a Japanese move was imminent. Halsey jumped at the opportunity to inflict a surface defeat on his foe. While amassing troop transports to evacuate the Marines, he would collect his growing naval might and spring a surprise on the Japanese.

Halsey assembled a formidable force of six separate groups. Four transports and four destroyers of Task Group 62.8 carried the replacements that were to land on Guadalcanal, while Task Force 18, a unit of three heavy cruisers, three light cruisers, two escort carriers, and eight destroyers under Rear Admiral Robert C. "Ike" Giffen provided their escort. In the meantime, four groups containing an amalgam of carriers, battleships, cruisers, and destroyers steamed between 250 and 400 miles behind the two forward groups, waiting for an opportunity to engage enemy vessels.

Yamamoto refused to play along with Halsey's wishes. Following the bitter losses at Midway, a reversal in the Coral Sea, and added poundings in the Solomons, Halsey's antagonist could no longer mount a vast naval operation. Instead he sent Lieutenant Commander Joji Higai of the 701st Air Group and thirty-two torpedo bombers to stage one of the war's first nighttime torpedo attacks.

Ike Giffen guided Task Force 18 out of Efate on January 27. A string of mistakes and poor judgment plagued the operation from the start. Because of Giffen's previous experience in the Atlantic, he placed inordinate attention on a possible submarine threat while downplaying the danger from the skies. He also erred in positioning the slower escort carriers with his faster cruisers and destroyers, which restricted the entire group to 18 knots, the maximum speed attainable by the carriers.

Giffen arrived fifty miles north of Rennell Island late in the afternoon of January 29 and stationed his six destroyers in a semicircle two miles ahead. While appropriate for the Atlantic, where the larger threat was from German U-boats, this formation poorly protected Giffen's carriers and cruisers from air attack and exposed the after beams and quarters of his ships to an attack.

Never expecting the Japanese to mount an assault after dark, Giffen declined to order a twilight combat air patrol. The misjudgment handed Higai and his thirty-two torpedo-bombers their opportunity. Japanese scout planes dropped parachutes from which dangled yellow-white flares to illuminate Giffen's cruisers and destroyers. Within moments of the opening salvo, two torpedoes smacked into the USS *Chicago* and stopped the cruiser dead in the water.

The attack ended quickly, with the *Chicago* in danger of sinking. After receiving orders from Admiral Halsey to steam toward Efate, Giffen split Task Force 18 during the afternoon of January 30, taking most of the ships with him while leaving only six destroyers to escort the *Chicago.* Japanese aircraft from Rabaul pursued the *Chicago* and sank her in a subsequent torpedo assault. Giffen's errors of judgment contributed to this American defeat. Nimitz ordered that the cruiser's sinking be withheld from the public and vowed in a staff meeting, with more than an edge of irritation in his voice, that he would sack anyone who divulged the information.

Marine and Army units ashore fared better. The Japanese, worn down from months of combat and suffering from a dearth of food and other key provisions, fought sporadically, mainly in vain attempts to prevent the Americans from seizing more land. "No ground action is reported from Guadalcanal," stated the Greybook summary for December 24. "The troops in that area have been quiet for some time." The next month Halsey related to Nimitz that the Army infantry is "going ahead fast" and that conditions "look very pretty"[12] for a speedy end.

While Army Major General Millard F. Harmon chased the Japanese on land, Halsey used his navy to shield the island. With his cruisers and destroyers, aided by a handful of PT boats, Halsey erected a protective ring about Guadalcanal to give Harmon a sanctuary in which he could wipe out Hyakutake's troops without worrying about facing fresh reinforcements.

In the absence of large surface forces Halsey, who felt a kinship with the Navy's smaller craft, relied on speedy strikes by those weapons to harm the Japanese—nighttime naval bombardments by destroyers, surface raids by PT boats, and submarine forays.

On January 11, 1943, Halsey wrote Nimitz of his intention to station an "offensive destroyer force in the Tulagi [area] in a semi-permanent status" on January 15. "It is the first offensive force that we have had in the South Pacific. I hope it grows larger and larger and that the Yellow Bastards' forces grow smaller and smaller."[13]

Besides a handful of cruisers and destroyers, Halsey relied on submarines based out of Brisbane, Australia, and a few PT boats to keep the Japanese honest. Halsey especially admired the work of the PT boats in countering the Japanese attempts at reinforcement. "These young fellows are full of 'pee and ginger,'" he wrote Nimitz on December 11. Though tiny, they charged the enemy with abandon, much as Halsey imagined himself in one of the destroyers he had commanded earlier in his career. "The PT boats are doing a marvelous job," he added nine days later. "I am immensely proud of them."[14]

The high-speed PT boats and their torpedoes kept the enemy off balance. In speedy runs, the agile craft, with their four torpedo tubes and four .50-caliber machine guns, patrolled the inner waters separating the various Solomon islands, frustrating the Tokyo Express in nightly attacks on Japanese supply barges and destroyers. The small craft, which included the *PT–109* commanded by the young Lieutenant (jg) John F.

Kennedy, sank numerous enemy vessels and handed Halsey one of his most effective tools.

By February Halsey had defeated the Japanese on Guadalcanal. He could now throw 50,000 well-supplied fresh troops at Japan's 35,000 haggard, hungry forces. On January 14 Tokyo informed the Japanese commander that destroyers would sweep into the area and evacuate the men. On the night of February 7–8 the Japanese surprised Halsey by feinting toward Henderson while destroyers evacuated the last of Hyakutake's men from Guadalcanal.

"Total and complete defeat of Japanese forces on Guadalcanal effected 1625 today," Major General Alexander Patch, the commander of ground forces on Guadalcanal, radioed Halsey on February 9. Halsey used a play on words in his jubilant response to his Army cohort: "In sending a Patch to act as tailor for Guadalcanal, I did not expect you to remove the enemy's pants and sew it on quite so quickly. Thanks and congratulations."[15]

"Halsey's Finest Hour"

Under Halsey's leadership, American forces at Guadalcanal had turned an apparent disaster into a stunning triumph. More than 24,000 Japanese perished in the half-year-long campaign to control Guadalcanal, an island they labeled the Isle of Death, and the loss of 892 aircraft and 1,882 irreplaceable trained aviators surpassed the totals registered at the Battle of Midway, the sea fight that Halsey had missed because of his illness.

Halsey's accomplishments in four months at Guadalcanal gained the adulation of observers in 1942 as well as historians years afterward. Correspondent Clark Lee watched the rapid turnaround from gloom to victory and concluded, "I believe the change dated from the appointment of Admiral William F. Halsey as commander in chief of our South Pacific forces. The old idea of 'we can't go there because the Japs are there,' was replaced by Halsey's watchword, 'Attack: Repeat: Attack.'"[16]

Viewing events more than forty years later esteemed Pacific War historian Richard Frank stated that, "Guadalcanal was Halsey's finest hour in the war. His arrival unquestionably bolstered morale at a critical juncture, and no one may underestimate the degree to which morale guides the outcome of any contest. . . . Quite simply, Guadalcanal was the literal turning point of the war in the Pacific."[17]

As Halsey viewed it, the victory resulted from teamwork and a confidence in one's abilities. Those traits produced a dramatic reversal in the war's path, one that set a limit on Tokyo's southeastward expansion. "I am immensely proud of the Guadalcanal campaign," Halsey stated in his memoirs. "It started with a frayed shoe string and little repairs were made to that shoe string during the campaign. The shoe string was tough and it did its job. The Japs were halted in their tracks and thrown from the offensive to the defensive. They never regained the offensive role."[18]

Halsey now turned his focus to the remainder of the Solomon Islands, which were still in Japanese hands. He envisioned those tiny outposts as steps toward his ultimate objective—the neutralization of the fortress of Rabaul and the decimation of Japanese naval and air power in the South Pacific. Over the next sixteen months, he annihilated the enemy in the South Pacific in an offensive reminiscent of the old Western cavalry charges.

With Task One of the three-stage South Pacific strategy accomplished by the seizure of Guadalcanal, Halsey in the South Pacific and Douglas MacArthur in the Southwest Pacific turned to Task Two. While MacArthur advanced northwest along the coast of New Guinea, Halsey moved northward up the Solomons from Guadalcanal. Each would eventually join forces for Task Three—an assault against the Japanese stronghold at Rabaul.

One caveat ruled Halsey's actions—he dared not recklessly use the few carriers he possessed in the narrow waters surrounding the Solomons. In removing carrier air support, Halsey had to amass land-based air power before moving up the Solomon chain. He could thus not send his surface forces beyond the range of fighters and bombers based at Guadalcanal until he possessed additional airfields to Guadalcanal's north; he would then be able to move his operations to the new airfields and expand the area in which his ships could operate northward. He planned to repeat that process until he stood at Rabaul's doorstep.

Rabaul, the crown jewel of Japan's South Pacific defense line, dominated Halsey's thoughts. For over a year every move in the Solomons—every ship, plane, bullet, and bomb—targeted Rabaul 565 miles to the northwest. With its large harbor protected by a frightening array of antiaircraft guns and ships, Rabaul posed a potent challenge. To escape the confines of the South Pacific and steer America's expanding military might toward the Home Islands, Halsey had to remove Rabaul from the equation.

Tentacles stretched from the Japanese Home Islands 2,100 miles southeast to the massive anchorage at Truk in the Caroline Islands. From there supplies flowed either 1,300 miles against MacArthur to the southwest or 1,400 miles southeast against Halsey in the Solomons. Anything reaching the Solomons from Truk first passed through Rabaul. To protect the southern approaches to the island, the Japanese had peppered the Solomons with airfields, thereby encasing Rabaul in layers of air defenses. Before Halsey could threaten Rabaul, he first had to eliminate in succession those enemy airfields resting between Guadalcanal and the island.

Halsey accomplished the task in three leaps, first to New Georgia, then to Vella Lavella, and finally onto Bougainville, in the process staging an offensive to match that of his famous Army cohort on the other side of the world. Sixteen months before General George Patton commenced his vaunted drive across central Europe, Halsey swept up the Solomons, knocking the Japanese from a series of island bastions and exasperating them with a deft combination of land, sea, and air power. Like a quarterback constantly throwing the unexpected at a confused defense, Halsey, blessed with multiple offensive weapons, used every option to keep the perplexed Japanese off balance as he churned up the Solomons in America's first major Pacific offensive. By the time he finished in June 1944, he had shattered Japanese power in the Solomons, killed his antagonist, Yamamoto, and opened the door to Tokyo.

"You Know What to Do"

Before embarking on that offensive, though, Halsey conveyed to his commanders that, no matter what their branch of service, they had his consent to act on their own initiative and to run their task forces or bases in the way they saw best. He would only step in when events dictated a decision from him or when the officer lacked resourcefulness.

"I early placed emphasis on the principle of unity of command," Halsey wrote in an official report. "I insisted that each commander of a task force must have full authority over all components of his force, regardless of service or nationality."[19]

The commanders in the field or at sea appreciated the confidence Halsey displayed in their abilities. Commander Arleigh Burke related the time in 1943 when Halsey alerted him that a squadron of Japanese destroyers steamed toward him. Rather than issue a list of instructions, Halsey simply added, "Proceed. You know what to do." Burke claimed Halsey's faith in him gave a needed shot in the arm. Burke, who smashed the enemy that night, stated that Halsey understood a key principle of command—"give the men the incentive, the opportunity and the information, and they will excel themselves as we had done that night, fighting for a commander whom we respected and loved."[20]

As he had at Guadalcanal, Halsey insisted that his commanders be aggressive. He wrote Nimitz in July 1943 of the need to relieve an officer because of a "lack of initiative in quick action when a submarine appeared in his area." In Halsey's mind, the man committed an unpardonable sin by repeating his tardiness. "On several occasions it was deemed necessary to prod him into action," added Halsey. He explained to Nimitz that while he had known the officer since Academy days, "War is a cruel thing at the best, and individuals must be subordinated for the good of the country."[21]

Lieutenant Ashford recalled the time when a staff member mentioned that, due to a shortage of supplies, the South Pacific might have to go into a defensive mode. "With that Admiral Halsey's eyes blazed and I will never forget his reply, 'As long as I have one plane and one pilot, I will stay on the offensive.'"[22]

Ever the trainer, Halsey made certain that he possessed the best-qualified teams and crews. As his drive headed up the Solomons, he created the forward area, a zone that stood between the front lines and rear areas in which task forces and ships could train together to better meet the enemy and where they could practice for their next assignments.

Halsey built an antiaircraft school at Nouméa to improve ships' crews skill in shooting down enemy aircraft. As a result, Halsey's ships benefited from the skilled antiaircraft gunners who, armed with the new proximity fuse that exploded when it drew within range of a target rather than having to directly strike the target itself, enjoyed greater success in destroying approaching enemy aircraft.

By implementing these moves, Halsey laid the foundations for his assault on Rabaul. In doing so, Halsey showed that, rather than being the one-dimensional sea commander many assumed him to be, he could be effective from behind a desk as well.

"This Is a Team"

A seemingly minor action laid the foundation for the next eighteen months. When Halsey arrived as commander, Navy and Marine officers still had to wear neckties in the steamy South Pacific, while their Army cohorts did not. Halsey ordered that henceforth, not a tie was to be seen in the South Pacific. "Gentlemen, we are the South Pacific Fighting Force," he emphasized to his senior commanders. "I don't want anybody even to be thinking in terms of Army, Navy or Marines. Every man must understand that, and every man will understand it, if I have to take off his uniform and issue coveralls with 'South Pacific Fighting Force' printed on the seat of the pants!"[23] Halsey's relaxation of uniform regulations achieved more than comfort or team unity—it conveyed the impression of a military now rolling up its sleeves and settling down to the hard tasks at hand after a period of indecision under Ghormley. Lest anyone doubt what that task was, Halsey erected a huge sign at the fleet landing at Tulagi, an island immediately across from Guadalcanal, proclaiming in bold letters the message he delivered to the press on November 8, "KILL JAPS, KILL JAPS, KILL MORE JAPS!"

Halsey wanted the home front to understand his motives in the South Pacific as well. When Charles Belnap, the president of Monsanto Chemical Company, wrote a letter criticizing as undignified the shabby hat Halsey wore, Halsey sent a ready explanation. While the hat was "not worth a damn," Halsey stated that "it accomplishes one of my chief aims out here, and that is to make it very difficult to distinguish between the officers of the Army, Navy, and Marines. We go on the principle that this is a team and no time for anything but team play and no service rivalry. It works."[24]

When Commander Harold Hopkins, a regal man who served as the British Royal Navy's liaison officer, first met Halsey, the admiral bounced into the room wearing shorts, a plain khaki shirt, and no socks. Taken somewhat aback, Hopkins waited while the ebullient Halsey mixed drinks for the two.

A thirty-minute discussion dispelled any doubts about Halsey's qualifications. "I remember thinking that he might well have been a parson, a jolly one, an old time farmer, or Long John Silver," said Hopkins in words that Halsey would have loved. "But when I left him and thought of what he had said, I realized that I had been listening to one of the great admirals of the war."[25]

The worldwide war involved scores of nations, but in the South Pacific Halsey created his own realm. The sign at Nouméa greeting fresh arrivals emphasized the attitude.

> Complete with black tie
> You do look terrific,
> But take it off here:
> This is still South Pacific![26]

Not even Halsey's son, *Saratoga* aviation supply officer Lieutenant (jg) William F. Halsey III, received preferential treatment in the team-oriented South Pacific. On August 7, 1943, Halsey's son flew to Nouméa to pick up spare parts for the carrier. The father and son enjoyed a pleasant evening together before Bill departed the next morning in a flight of three torpedo planes. Two days later Captain H. Raymond Thurber, Halsey's operations officer, informed him that the three aircraft were missing at sea and described the rescue efforts in process. Halsey paled visibly at the news, noted Lieutenant Ashford, but refused to allow his high stature to influence the search. "My son is the same as every other son in the combat zone. Look for him just as you'd look for anybody else."[27]

Relief came two days later when a search plane spotted rubber rafts ashore on Eromanga, an island between New Caledonia and Efate. The next day rescue craft picked up Halsey's son and nine other servicemen who had been forced down owing to bad weather.

To make his officers at sea feel a part of his team, Halsey often visited the officers' club, where he shook hands and shared drinks with the men. He invited the commanders of every ship arriving at Nouméa to attend his daily 9:00 A.M. meeting, where they were free to join in whatever was being discussed. Eager to gain information about the fighting, Halsey queried men just back from the combat zone. He asked about the condition of their crews, what weapons worked most effectively or failed most often, the state of their supply situation, and other things to help determine whether the measures adopted at Nouméa had a positive impact in the Solomons.

Unlike Ghormley, who relied strictly on Navy cohorts for advice, Halsey made certain to consult military brethren, whom he fondly called his War Lords, and claimed that much of his success resulted from "the merging of the knowledge and combat experience of all, each commander benefiting from and adding to the combat knowledge gained by his predecessor."[28] Halsey always declared that he could gain more from a friendly chat and a shared bottle of Scotch with generals and admirals than from reading reports.

"My Dear Mrs. Bainbridge"

His son's mishap at sea was only one of many that paired military urgency with familial concerns. Most happened in less dramatic fashion, but they affected Halsey in diverse ways and illustrated the tight bond he enjoyed with the populace back home. In reading letters sent to Halsey during the war by mothers and fathers, schoolchildren and servicemen, one senses that Americans at the time considered Halsey more of a friend or a confidante than a military commander. They admired MacArthur, who amassed a reputation as a genius, but they could not relate to a man who came across as too distant, too unreachable, too formidable. Halsey was more to their liking, a man with whom they could envision sharing a beer and a cigar, slapping each other on the back and laughing over an off-color joke.

The collection of letters, housed at the Library of Congress, shows Halsey at his most human. Congratulations came not only from those he knew, but from strangers who felt the need to connect with the man who did so much to lead the nation into calmer waters. But as quickly as the letters could evoke laughter and momentary relief from the burdens of command for Halsey, they could also remind him of the ultimate effect of his orders. Most troubling for Halsey were the letters sent by grieving mothers seeking details of the death or disappearance of their sons or, worse, those that accused him of needlessly wasting a precious life. Staff members knew whenever Halsey received such a letter, for the admiral spent hours agonizing over its contents.

Unlike some officers who have little trouble issuing commands, Halsey personalized his orders. He sent men and boys, not ships and squadrons, into combat. He received such an enormous volume of mail that he could not personally scan each letter—he had a war to run, after all—but he asked to be handed letters from parents whose sons had died or were missing in action. As difficult as they were for him to read, they reminded Halsey that his decisions exacted a frightening cost, one he chose not to disregard.

Mrs. Bainbridge's letter especially haunted Halsey. Her son, George Frederick Bainbridge, perished when Japanese submarine torpedoes sank the *Juneau* off Guadalcanal in November 1942. Mrs. Bainbridge wrote such a protracted letter filled with anger, disappointment, and angst that Halsey penned his own lengthy reply.

After learning that her son's cruiser had been sunk, Mrs. Bainbridge wrote that "Everything went wrong, our meals were untouched, Thanksgiving was a terribly lonesome day, and Xmas we nearly died. Dad and I were here all alone. Fred always trimed [sic] the tree, this year the corner was a bare wall. . . . We had plenty of heat, but our hearts had grown cold."

Her emotions intensified as Mrs. Bainbridge neared the end. "I want somebody to tell me Fred was a hero. . . . I want my boy back. I only loaned him for a while. He was too nice to be blowed to bites. It is cruel. . . . He hadn't started to live yet, just 23. . . . I loved Fred too much and am brokenhearted now. I can't stand it."

She closed her letter by asking Halsey to recommend Fred for a medal. If he would, "the cross would be a little easier to bear. I could hug the medal and think it was my Fred when I say my prayers at night. I wouldn't be so lonely then. It would bring him nearer to me."

Halsey's reply reveals the struggle he faced to adequately answer. "My dear Mrs. Bainbridge," he opened, "As I begin my answer to it I do so realizing words are of little avail, either in bringing you real help and comfort at this time or in expressing my own feelings when face to face with one of the war's many tragic situations. I know what Frederick's loss means to you and Mr. Bainbridge and I confess that this sad picture of a home mourning for a son missing somewhere in action is perhaps the heaviest burden of one who finds himself in command of so many in time of war."

Halsey ended by appealing to the family's strong religious beliefs. "The fond memories which no one can ever take from you, the knowledge that your son rests now side by side upon the altar of freedom with brave men of all ages, time itself, and above everything the mysterious and all-sufficient care of Him whom Frederick loved and worshipped, these all, I feel sure, will in some day, not too far off, bring comfort and hope to you and Mr. Bainbridge."[29]

As a small way of helping the family grapple with their son's disappearance, Halsey mentioned that he would send a copy of this letter to the senior survivor of the *Juneau* asking the man to write a letter to Mrs. Bainbridge telling whatever he knew about the ship and her son.

"We Were Part of His Team"

A key component of Halsey's success was taking care of the men, not just the admirals and ensigns but also the seamen and privates. Halsey believed that an individual performed more efficiently if he knew that his superior had his back. He took quick action, for instance, when he discovered that mail had not been reaching the Marines. A quick inspection at Nouméa unearthed stacks of mail, many weeks old, piled two stories high in open fields. Disturbed that the units engaging the enemy at the front had been so brusquely swept aside, Halsey made certain the flow of mail from home rushed unimpeded to Guadalcanal.

On November 13, 1942 Halsey ordered the Army's 101st Medical Regiment to the island to improve sanitation and care for the wounded, and later in the month he shipped a large quantity of turkeys to the front so the troops could enjoy a bit of Thanksgiving. He asked for the hurried development and use of night fighters, a weapon the South Pacific then lacked, to combat the nightly nuisance raids the Japanese mounted to disrupt sleep and lower morale.

One look at the cramped conditions aboard the *Argonne*, where Ghormley had stubbornly remained, convinced Halsey that he needed more spacious accommodations. "The people on my staff had to have every possible convenience obtainable," Halsey wrote. "They were under a tremendous strain and worked long and irregular hours. When a man's job allows him only a very few hours sleep at night, I am determined that he shall pass those few hours in comfort."[30]

When the French, who governed New Caledonia, dragged their feet in approving a move into improved quarters, Halsey ordered the Seabees to prepare a building ashore and simply moved headquarters on his own. Once the work space was settled, Halsey moved into a lavish residence formerly used by the Japanese consulate. Situated on a hilltop, the structure offered a breathtaking view of the harbor below as well as providing him the pleasure of enjoying what had once belonged to the enemy. "It gave me deep satisfaction to watch the American flag being raised over this establishment every morning,"[31] he said.

Halsey had Seabees build two Quonset huts to provide accommodations for his staff. The huts, nicknamed Wicky-Wacky Lodge, as well as another residence called Havoc Hall, soon became famous throughout the South Pacific for the amiability they offered. Two Hollywood film personalities, actor Robert Montgomery and movie director Gene Markey, remained from Ghormley's staff to assist Halsey's team, and when the long work hours ended, staff and visitors—every commanding officer made certain to stop by when arriving in port—gathered around the bar and the piano to share lighthearted banter or join in song.

"He had the ability to make each one of us feel that we were part of his team and that he knew exactly what we were doing all the time," stated Lieutenant Commander William R. Smedberg III, commanding officer of the destroyer, USS *Lansdowne* of Halsey. "And every now and then he'd send a message to an individual ship, 'That was a great job you did' at such and such a time. He just made you feel that he knew exactly what you were doing. He would come up and come on board ship now and again—fly up and come out on the ship, say hello to you, and you got the feeling that you knew him and he knew you. He developed a great esprit."[32]

What most struck Carney, Halsey's no-nonsense chief of staff, was his superior's empathy. He felt for his men, understood the conditions they faced and the risks they willingly accepted. "His recollection for names and places till the end of his life was fantastic. His interest in the . . . individual person, around this command of his—which was a big one, we had over a quarter of a million people—was not feigned in the least. It was genuine. It was real."[33]

On November 4, 1943, Halsey visited the light cruiser USS *Montpelier.* Aboard the vessel Seaman First Class James J. Fahey observed the spectacle, and later wrote of what the visit of the theater commander meant to the crew of one of Halsey's ships. "It was the brass himself, the number 1 man, Admiral 'Bull' Halsey. The men would do anything for him. He rates with the greats of all time."

As a PT boat brought Halsey alongside, "Everyone wanted to get a look at the 'Bull.' Halsey is a tough-looking man and looks as if he could take care of one of his namesakes." A bit later as Fahey carried ammunition, he walked directly by Halsey so he could closely assess the man. "As he stood there watching us carry ammunition, I tried to look right through him. I tried to study him and see what he was made of. I left him standing there, with the shell on my shoulder and the knowledge that he came from good stock. It did not take long to draw that conclusion because he had it written all over him. We got the best man in command down here in the 'Bull.'" Fahey added that before Halsey left the ship, "he congratulated everyone for the great job they had done."[34]

To help his men blow off steam between operations, Halsey transformed Nouméa's largest hotel into Club Pacifico, where officers and enlisted men could gather and relax with an alcoholic drink. Halsey knew his units needed more to escape the rigors of combat than the Red Cross offering of soft drinks and cigarettes, and Club Pacifico quickly grew into one of the favorite South Pacific haunts.

Arleigh Burke experienced firsthand Halsey's empathy toward his men. "The first time I came face to face with Bull Halsey, I was literally shaking in my boots," Burke wrote after the war. In early 1942 Burke commanded Destroyer Division 43, a unit that had faced constant, exhausting combat. Both his men and ships badly needed a break, and Burke sent a stream of letters to Halsey's office "raising hell because we weren't getting what we needed." With morale declining, Burke decided to send his destroyers to Sydney for rest and radioed Halsey of it, but Halsey shot back, "Keep them in the Solomons." Burke attempted to arrange a break again, but with the same result.

A boiler on the USS *Saufley* so badly needed maintenance that on his own initiative Burke sent the destroyer to Australia. He collected whatever money he could from his officers and told the *Saufley*'s captain to purchase and bring back beer and whiskey for the squadron. Burke did not inform headquarters until after the destroyer had left.

He soon received a message from Halsey ordering him to stop by the next time Burke steamed into Nouméa. When he did, Burke walked into Halsey's office, where he found the admiral sitting at his desk with his back to Burke. Halsey made him wait a bit, then turned and said, "Oh, Burke," and looked at notes before adding, "*Saufley.*" Halsey sat bolt upright and asked, "Why in God's name did you take it in your own hands to send *Saufley* to Sydney?"

Burke, wondering if he had reached the end of his naval career, decided that honesty best served his purposes. He answered, "Sir, my boys haven't had any beer or whiskey for months. . . ." Halsey interrupted, "You mean, you mean you sent that ship down there for *booze?*" Burke wondered if he should tell Halsey about the defective boiler, but simply said yes.

Halsey thought for a few moments before saying, "All right, Burke. You win. Your boys have been doing a great job, and I can't condemn you for going out on a limb for them." He then pointed a finger at Burke, "If you had told me that you sent *Saufley* for *repairs*, I'd have had your hide."

A relieved Burke stated, "That's when I knew I would follow Admiral William Halsey anywhere in this world, or beyond. And so would thousands of other sailors, from the lowliest apprentice right on up the line."[35] Burke claimed that this thoughtfulness toward him and his crews made them want to fight even harder for Halsey.

An eleven-year-old Halsey strikes an assertive pose with his beloved football for a student photograph at Pingry School in Elizabeth, New Jersey in 1894.
Courtesy of the U.S. Naval Academy Museum

A seventeen-year-old Halsey in 1899 during his first year of medical school at the University of Virginia.
Courtesy of the National Archives

In the summer of 1923 naval attaché Halsey (second row, second from left) stands with other embassy personnel at the U. S. Embassy in Berlin, Germany.
Courtesy of the Naval Historical Center

In rising seas and foul weather, one of Lt. Col. James H. Doolittle's bombers rises from the deck of the USS Hornet *on April 18, 1942. Halsey watched from his perch aboard the USS* Enterprise, *holding his breath until the final B–25 was on its way to bomb Tokyo and other locales in Japan.*
Courtesy of the Naval Historical Center

(left) One of Halsey's commanders erected this sign at the Tulagi fleet landing across from Guadalcanal. The sign perfectly expresses Halsey's sentiments on how best to win the war. Courtesy of the Naval Historical Center

(right) The original caption for this 1942 photo of Halsey on the bridge of his flagship is an example of the Navy's promotion of the war hero at a time when the nation desperately needed heroes. It reads, "A real sea dog is Vice Admiral Halsey, commander of all U.S. Navy aircraft carriers in the Pacific Ocean and the senior admiral at sea." Courtesy of the National Archives

Halsey is here pictured with his staff aboard the USS Enterprise *in early 1942. Standing to Halsey's immediate right is his controversial chief of staff, Miles R. Browning. Courtesy of the National Archives*

A wartime poster uses Halsey's image and aggressive nature to prod factory workers to greater productivity.
Courtesy of the Naval Historical Center

Halsey confers with his superior in the Pacific, Admiral Chester W. Nimitz, at Espiritu Santo, New Hebrides, on January 20, 1943, shortly after the tide had turned at Guadalcanal.
Courtesy of the Naval Historical Center

Wearing his usual South Pacific uniform of shorts and rumpled hat, Halsey is the center of attention as he energetically chats with members of his staff as a barge takes the group to a conference.
Courtesy of the National Archives

Members of the press interview Halsey during an inspection tour of Bougainville in late 1943. Chatting with Halsey are (from left to right) Marine correspondent Lieutenant Sanford Hunt, United Press correspondent Frank Tremaine, Associated Press reporter Fred Hampson, and Marine press relations officer Lieutenant Jonathan Rice.
Courtesy of the National Archives

In this 1944 photograph Halsey poses with family during a brief respite back in the United States. The adults (from left to right) are his daughter, Mrs. Preston Lea Spruance, Halsey, his wife Fan, and his mother, Mrs. Anne Halsey. Three grandchildren (from left to right) Margaret Spruance, age 8, William Halsey Spruance, age 5, and Preston Lea Spruance, Jr., age 10, flank the adults.
Courtesy of the National Archives

President Franklin D. Roosevelt hands Halsey a Gold Star in lieu of a third Distinguished Service Medal at the White House on March 8, 1945. Halsey's wife, Fan, stands next to him.
Courtesy of the National Archives

In this photograph Halsey sits on a white horse presented upon his arrival in Tokyo after war's end. Throughout the war Halsey had vowed to ride Emperor Hirohito's horse once victory had been achieved.
Courtesy of the National Archives

Admiral Chester W. Nimitz signs the surrender document aboard the USS Missouri *on September 2, 1945. Standing directly behind him are (left to right) Gen. Douglas MacArthur, Admiral Halsey, and Rear Adm. Forrest Sherman.*
Courtesy of the Naval Historical Center

The nation handed Halsey a warm welcome upon his return to the United States. He is here receiving the key to San Francisco. More honors followed as Halsey embarked on a triumphant tour of large cities.
Courtesy of the National Archives

Three of the Navy's most powerful officers gather after victory. To Halsey's left is his immediate superior, Admiral Chester W. Nimitz, while Admiral Ernest J. King, Commander-in-Chief, U. S. Fleet and Chief of Naval Operations, looks on from Halsey's right. Secretary of the Navy James V. Forrestal shakes Halsey's hand.
Courtesy of the National Archives

CHAPTER 7

"THE HUNTERS HAD BECOME THE HUNTED"

Guadalcanal became the springboard for an impressive offensive up the Solomons in which Halsey embarked upon a succession of land, sea, and air attacks, bypassing Japanese strongholds to hit lightly defended objectives. At the same time he unleashed an aerial assault that reduced the fortress at Rabaul to a meaningless entity for the war's remainder. Rather than command from a bridge, Halsey worked behind the scenes directing a drive that snatched the Solomons from Japan's control.

"I DON'T GIVE A DAMN WHO KILLS THEM"

While Halsey tried to ease conditions for his men, others made his situation more difficult. He had to work with government officials from Allied nations, especially the French, who had ruled New Caledonia for almost one hundred years. Some French residents opposed an American presence on the island out of fear that it might provoke a Japanese attack, while the official French representatives maintained a cool relationship with the Americans. French business owners closed their stores to American soldiers or ignored them when they walked in, while local citizens viewed Americans almost as an occupation army.

When the island's governor declined a request to install a radio tower to handle the increased traffic, Halsey ordered his Seabees to construct what he needed. A French official complained to Halsey of the alarming number of French girls impregnated by American soldiers and demanded to know what steps Halsey would take to address the situation. "Fighting men are 'frolicking' men, and I'm not going to do a damned thing about it. If you Frenchmen can't keep your daughters out of trouble, don't count on the armed forces of the United States to do it for you."[1]

Though the French posed the largest problem, Halsey also had to contend with anxious government officials from Australia and New Zealand who worried for the fates of their nations, as well as with officials from other Pacific countries. When urged to employ Fiji Islanders in some of his Solomon attacks, Halsey explained to Nimitz that it was almost impossible as the natives from the many different islands were hostile to each other. However, he mentioned that he welcomed their assistance as soon as a solution became apparent, and "when we start rolling the Yellow Sons of Bitches back, I'll denude everything and throw it at 'em. . . . I don't give a damn who kills them as long as they get killed."[2]

Most observers expected sparks to fly when Halsey had to deal with Douglas MacArthur, whose adjoining realm of the Southwest Pacific often brought the two into contact. Some, especially MacArthur's staff, regarded the general with awe, but Halsey wanted none of that. When first arriving in the South Pacific, Halsey ordered his staff to be blunt with their corresponding officers on MacArthur's staff. "I refuse to get into a controversy with him or any other self-advertising Son of a Bitch," Halsey wrote Nimitz of the man he labeled "Little Doug."[3]

Halsey shed those opinions after his April meeting with MacArthur, when the pair discussed the New Georgia operation. On April 15 Halsey flew to Brisbane for a three-day conference with MacArthur. Though each was at first wary of his counterpart, the two quickly warmed to each another. "Five minutes after I reported," Halsey wrote, "I felt as if we were lifelong friends."[4]

Unaccustomed to being around men who spoke their mind, MacArthur welcomed Halsey's opinions, as he knew that Halsey would deliver a candid assessment. In the spring of 1944 Halsey wanted use of the expansive harbor of Manus in the Admiralty Islands as an advance base, but it stood in MacArthur's theater. Nimitz proposed adjusting the boundary lines separating Halsey's from MacArthur's sector, but MacArthur would not yield. Even though Manus provided the perfect location as a staging area for the invasion of the Philippines, MacArthur feared that if he agreed, Nimitz and the Navy would enjoy too much authority over the Philippine operation, an assault he considered his personal mission.

Staff members engaged in a heated debate over the issue, to no avail. Halsey ended the discussion when he told MacArthur, "General, I disagree with you entirely and I'm going one step further and tell you I think you are hampering the war effort by ordering suspension of the Naval base at Manus." When he added that MacArthur placed his personal honor above the welfare of the nation, MacArthur relented. "My God, Bull! You can't mean that? We can't have anything like that."[5]

MacArthur had such high regard for Halsey that near the end of 1943 he offered Halsey command of all his naval forces. The prospect of working for a man like MacArthur, certain to be in the midst of every important Pacific matter until war's end, had to be flattering to Halsey, but he declined. Halsey could never abandon Nimitz and the Navy for personal laurels.

HALSEY FEARED no greater call on his time than the August 1943 South Pacific visit by Eleanor Roosevelt. He had no personal objections, but he worried about taking fighter aircraft from the combat zone to escort the First Lady as she made her way through the theater. With his Solomons offensive heating up, the last thing Halsey needed was to be distracted by a political bigwig, an occasion certain to draw high-ranking figures from both Australia and MacArthur's theater.

Mrs. Roosevelt wore a Red Cross uniform when she arrived at Nouméa on August 25, 1943. She handed Halsey a letter from the president stating that if Halsey considered it safe for Mrs. Roosevelt to travel to Guadalcanal, he had the president's approval, but Halsey politely denied the request. She replied that she was willing to accept the risks in order to visit the men in the forward areas, but Halsey remained adamant. "Guadalcanal is no place for you, Ma'am!" he responded. "I am not worried about the responsibility and I am not worried about the chances you take because I know you take them gladly. What worries me is the heavy fighting that is now going on in and around New Georgia, and I need every fighting plane I can put my fingers on to complete that campaign. If you go to Guadalcanal, it will necessitate a fighter escort for your plane. I can not spare an escort at the moment." The two agreed that she would remain in Nouméa for two days, travel to Australia, then upon her return decide if the fighting had eased sufficiently to arrange a trip to Guadalcanal. Halsey quartered Mrs. Roosevelt in the heavily guarded Wicky-Wacky Lodge, then hosted a reception and dinner that evening, "one of the few occasions when I wore a tie in the South Pacific Area."[6]

The next morning Mrs. Roosevelt began visiting every hospital in Nouméa, stopping at the bed of each wounded serviceman to share a few words and ask if she could do anything for them. Most asked her to contact their families upon returning to the United States, promises that Mrs. Roosevelt faithfully kept by telephoning or writing letters to each family. Halsey, uncertain at first over the value of her trip, watched men pour out their hearts to the First Lady and witnessed the benefit that resulted from a few minutes alone with each man.

"When I say that she inspected those hospitals, I don't mean that she shook hands with the chief medical officer, glanced into a sun-parlor, and left. I mean that she went into every ward, stopped at every bed, and spoke to every patient: What was his name? How did he feel? Was there anything he needed? Could she take a message home for him?" Impressed, Halsey wrote, "I watched the expressions on the faces of the patients, many of whom were grievously wounded. That sight made me change my opinion of the value of her visit immediately. She accomplished more good in less time than any single person or delegation of persons who visited my area during my entire tenure of office in the South Pacific."[7] Following Mrs. Roosevelt's trip to Australia, Halsey judged the situation secure enough to allow her to visit Guadalcanal, where she again made the rounds in every hospital.

By the time she left the South Pacific, Mrs. Roosevelt had gained a new admirer. Halsey saw her off at the plane and told her that "it was impossible for me to express my appreciation of what she had done, and was doing, for my men. I was ashamed of my original surliness. She alone had accomplished more good than any other person, or any group of civilians, who had passed through my area." Mrs. Roosevelt, for her part, was equally moved by Halsey, a man who obviously shared her concern for the men's welfare. "I will never forget Admiral Halsey's hospitality to me, nor how grateful I was for his kindness and thoughtfulness at his headquarters in the South Pacific."[8]

"OKAY, LADS, THAT'S IT"

Halsey's most difficult task in transforming the South Pacific may have been increasing the flow of supplies and reinforcements to Guadalcanal. A lack of shipping and unloading facilities hampered efforts to move the matériel from New Zealand and Nouméa to the front, and the dangers from enemy submarines intensified as the vessels neared the island.

To help remedy the situation, in late October Halsey switched the planned construction of the main fleet base from New Zealand to Nouméa, 1,200 miles closer to Guadalcanal, and two smaller advanced bases at Espiritu Santo and Efate in the New Hebrides 600 miles southeast of Guadalcanal. That reduced the buildup of supplies then at Auckland, as well as provided a haven from enemy submarines and aircraft for his overworked cruisers and destroyers that operated for long stretches in the combat zone.

Each time his forces advanced northward, accompanying engineers and construction battalions (Seabees) speedily transformed the newly acquired jungle into another base. Halsey so appreciated the work performed by his engineers and Seabees, who kept his military machine fueled and running, that he asserted that he could not have compiled his successes without the bulldozer, the Jeep, the Douglas DC–3 transport plane, and other forms of transportation that moved troops and supplies so speedily.

On November 16 Halsey streamlined the haphazard arrangement. Rather than each branch of the service overseeing its own logistics, Halsey placed the entire operation under the control of Army Brigadier General Raymond E. S. Williamson. Within one month the bottleneck so eased that shipments to Guadalcanal increased 40 percent. Ships at Guadalcanal unloaded supplies on only thirteen days during October; improved conditions allowed the military to shuttle in matériel every day in December.

Halsey could achieve so much in a relatively brief time because he assembled a staff in which he not only placed supreme confidence, but also engaged in a freewheeling dialogue during which every member had the chance to propose any idea or question the merits of another's notion. Armed with the latest intelligence updates, he met each day with his close circle in a room bearing the framed quote, "The Lord gave us two ends to use, one to think with and one to sit with. The war depends on which we choose—heads we win, tails we lose."[9] Like a parent watching his sons argue, Halsey presided over heated spats that violated every stipulation found in *Robert's Rules of Order.* He detested tentativeness and alibis. The staff was to have no trepidation in either challenging Halsey or admitting a blunder.

Hunches and instinct were Halsey's guides. He listened carefully to the pros and cons of an issue, but his staff became accustomed to Halsey's complimenting their presentations, then stating that he was following a different course. "It's convincing, but I just have the feeling it's not right. We'll do it my way."[10]

Halsey once listened as his staff debated how to obtain more fuel for the South Pacific's ships and planes. The slow-moving tankers ferrying the commodity from Hawaii or Australia needed destroyers to safeguard them from enemy submarines, but Halsey could only free a handful of ships from their more vital posts in the Solomons. When he asked his staff for notions on how to increase the fuel storage capacity at Nouméa, he remained silent as each staff member posed an obstruction, then said, "You have told me all of the reasons why the project is not feasible. This meeting is now adjourned and will reconvene in fifteen minutes. When you return, I want to hear from you the action you propose to take in order to get the job done."[11]

Halsey delegated as much authority as possible with minor issues and decisions so that he would be free to handle the more serious situations—"Look around, see what it is, and do it" became his favorite dictum—but he knew when to step in and overrule any action he felt unnecessary or wrong. He provided the general picture of what he wanted accomplished then allowed his staff to fill in the details. Captain Ralph E. "Rollo" Wilson, a staff operations officer, claimed that Halsey and his staff worked well together. "Halsey made the ultimate decision," said Wilson, "but in a manner which made each individual present feel he had a part in it. It was the smoothest organization I have ever experienced."[12]

The devilish side emerged in what Halsey and his staff labeled the "Dirty Tricks Department." To confound the enemy, they devised all sorts of measures, such as electronically simulating bombardments and raids, then stationing ships or aircraft to spring an ambush on any Japanese vessels or fighters that emerged to counter the nonexistent threat. If the staff learned of a coming Japanese deployment, they staged fake diversionary operations to keep the enemy guessing as to Halsey's true intentions. The Japanese often halted their plans until they could figure out what Halsey was up to.

Halsey consciously created a casual demeanor not often witnessed on admirals' staffs. If the staff rose when Halsey walked into the mess to eat, he growled, "Sit down, goddammit! How many times do I have to tell you?"[13] His admonitions usually failed to deter them from standing, but it conveyed the relaxed atmosphere Halsey desired. He wanted stimulating conversation in which every man took part.

Halsey liked to surround himself with familiar men, officers with whom he had served and of whose strengths and foibles he was aware. He preferred outgoing, fun-loving individuals, much like himself, and favored Ivy Leaguers, perhaps as a reminder of his collegiate days at the University of Virginia.

Some visitors felt that Halsey maintained too casual a relationship with his staff, one that often included excessive use of alcohol. At one medal award ceremony that contained heavy imbibing, Halsey supposedly had to hold up a drunken sea captain as he awarded him the Navy Cross to prevent him from collapsing.

"There are exceptions, of course," Halsey wrote in his autobiography, sounding like his pirate ancestor, "but as a general rule I never trust a fighting man who doesn't smoke or drink." He enjoyed nightly cocktails, especially a glass or two of Scotch, and loved reciting the toast,

> I've drunk your health in company;
> I've drunk your health alone;
> I've drunk your health so many times,
> I've damned near ruined my own.[14]

Halsey, who could on occasion drink long into the night, get two hours sleep, and awaken fresh and ready for the day's challenges, believed that alcohol was a great morale-booster. His staff had a standing monthly order for seventeen cases of Scotch and six of bourbon, and one staff member described liberties with Halsey as the most fun he had experienced.

Halsey's loyalty sometimes blinded him to shortcomings, particularly when it came to Miles Browning's foul temper and tactlessness. His chief of staff angered fellow staff officers and subordinates, and rumors circulated that a champion Marine boxer had roughed up the chief of staff after finding Browning in bed with his wife, but Halsey trusted the man's ability in aviation matters.

The final straw occurred after Browning behaved embarrassingly during a visit by Secretary Knox. Nimitz and King replaced him with Rear Admiral Robert B. "Mick" Carney and shifted Browning to a different command.

Carney took over on July 26, 1943. Halsey, miffed that Nimitz had removed Browning, at first maintained cool relations with Carney, but the officer's superb administrative talent and his knack for disagreeing without offending others soon overcame Halsey's wariness. Carney streamlined South Pacific operations, eliminating redundant posts and upgrading efficiency, and created an advance headquarters to enable Halsey to move operations more speedily toward the front. Carney so thoroughly reorganized Halsey's operations that, according to the new chief of staff, all Halsey had to do was announce that the tactical headquarters was moving out, "and you could jump in your car and be on your way to the airfield, leaving at the basic headquarters the staff to take care of the long-range planning, the long-range administration of bulk logistics, and things of that sort."[15]

As part of Halsey's routine, before each day's dinner he usually enjoyed a drink or two, typically his favorite, Scotch, but he settled for a martini or whatever else might be available as a substitute. He drank coffee nonstop and smoked two packs of cigarettes throughout days jammed with meetings and dispatches.

As stated in his autobiography, Halsey generally arose at 5:30 A.M., even if duties kept him awake until the early morning hours. Fastidious in his appearance, he never left his quarters without his uniform carefully groomed, shoes sparkling, and each hair combed in place. After a 7:30 breakfast with staff members, Halsey headed to his office to scan the night's dispatches. The daily morning conference commenced promptly at 9:00 with an intelligence briefing, then lasted another half hour to forty-five minutes while Halsey greeted newly arrived officers and caught up on the theater's business. Following the meeting, Halsey worked in his office until noon, writing letters to Nimitz and other commanders and planning his next moves against the Japanese. A one-hour break for lunch preceded afternoons filled with more meetings, at the end of which he either swam or walked for an hour. After dinner, Halsey attended a movie or read periodicals before joining his officers for a few hours of socializing.

Staff became accustomed to Halsey's calling items by their naval appellations. He used fathoms rather than feet and called the rear seats in cars the stern sheets. He preferred the longer "nineteen and forty-three," and despite the image created by the press, did not swear as often as most assumed. Halsey, who realized the benefit of good theater, reserved his most colorful phrasing for the nation's reporters. One staff member stated, "The Old Man can put on a good show when he wants to. He's a seagoing Hamlet."[16]

Halsey needed every possible aid, as he faced pressure-packed tasks that strained men half his age. He had already experienced such situations with his island raids, the Doolittle Raid, and in the perilous weeks at Guadalcanal. He now stared at another monumental task—pushing the enemy out of the Solomons and neutralizing the fortress of Rabaul.

HALSEY'S BLACK HOLE

Much as he would have liked to leapfrog directly to Rabaul, Halsey first had to remove the enemy garrisons standing between him and his ultimate objective. That required landings in the Russell Islands, New Georgia, and Vella Lavella before culminating in a large-scale assault against Bougainville, 240 miles southeast of Rabaul.

The initial step proved simple. In February 1943 an unopposed landing in the Russell Islands, thirty miles northwest of Guadalcanal, enabled Halsey to construct an airfield that could support his second step north, an invasion against the major Japanese airfield at Munda.

Before that assault occurred, though, Halsey's air arm notched a significant triumph. Concerned over the alarming losses in the South Pacific, Admiral Yamamoto implemented the I Operation, an offensive designed to punish Halsey's airfields and knock his Solomon offensive off schedule while gaining time to build Japanese defenses in the northern Solomons. In early April he sent massive carrier strikes against Guadalcanal and Tulagi and against MacArthur's units in New Guinea. When the Japanese pilots returned with highly exaggerated claims of sweeping the skies clean of American aircraft, Yamamoto decided to visit airfields on southern Bougainville to express his thanks.

On April 14 American intelligence intercepted radio messages containing Yamamoto's complete schedule for the April 18 visit. Sent in the same code the United States had broken at Midway, the messages revealed that Yamamoto would depart from Rabaul escorted by six fighter aircraft and fly to Bougainville, and listed the times that Yamamoto would arrive off the island. As those Japanese airfields lay just within range of American fighters out of Henderson, Halsey and Nimitz saw an opportunity.

The military benefits of a mission to kill Yamamoto were obvious. Nimitz believed any commander who succeeded Yamamoto would be less capable than the brilliant admiral, who enjoyed a popularity in Japan second only to that of the emperor. Before proceeding with what amounted to the assassination of a major government official, though, Nimitz consulted Washington. After a quick discussion with his advisers, Roosevelt assented to the operation on the grounds that shortening the war and saving lives morally validated the targeting of one man.

"It's down in Halsey's bailiwick," Nimitz said to one of his intelligence officers at Pearl Harbor. "If there's a way [to shoot down Yamamoto's aircraft], he'll find it."[17] Halsey, who appreciated the irony in killing Yamamoto on the first anniversary of the Doolittle Raid, was more than willing to order the plan.

On April 18, as Yamamoto's bomber neared Bougainville, eighteen Army fighters shot down two aircraft, including the one carrying Admiral Yamamoto. Halsey could not be certain that Yamamoto perished in the crash until May 21, when the Japanese government announced his death in battle. Japanese officials called Yamamoto the face of the Imperial Navy and termed his loss irreparable. Halsey agreed with a fellow commander when he applauded the news, but mused, "I'd hoped to lead that scoundrel up Pennsylvania Avenue in chains, with the rest of you kicking him where it would do the most good."[18]

Halsey followed the death of Yamamoto with an air campaign based on ruthless efficiency and superior weaponry. He brought in gifted aviators to run his air show. Rear Admiral Aubrey W. Fitch, Halsey's commander in charge of air operations throughout the South Pacific, earned his wings as a naval aviator on February 4, 1930. His expertise, which included participating in the Battle of the Coral Sea as Commander Task Group 17.5 consisting of the *Lexington* and *Yorktown,* made him a valuable asset.

To handle air operations strictly in the Solomons, Halsey turned to an old friend, Rear Admiral Marc A. "Pete" Mitscher, who commanded the *Hornet* during the Doolittle Raid. Graduating from the Academy six years after Halsey, Mitscher became one of the pioneers of naval aviation. He participated in the Navy's historic 1919 transatlantic flight, earning a Navy Cross in the process. Like Fitch, Mitscher shared a fondness for hard-hitting tactics. "I knew we'd probably catch hell from the Japs in the air," Halsey explained. "That's why I sent Pete Mitscher up there. Pete was a fighting fool, and I knew it."[19]

Halsey benefited from a solid pool of aviators and an enhanced fighter. The Navy's aviation training system vastly outproduced the Japanese, who saw their number of skilled pilots drop after each battle. Halsey paired his four Marine fighter squadrons with a new fighter aircraft that matched or surpassed in performance the acclaimed Zero, the Chance-Vought F4-U Corsair. With its oversized nose, the plane could fly faster and climb quicker than any Japanese aircraft. Its increased range allowed the plane to escort bombers on raids against distant

Bougainville and its sheath of airfields, to fly close ground support for Army and Marine units, and permitted aviators like Gregory Boyington to pit his famous Black Sheep Squadron in fighter sweeps against the Japanese. Within six months every Marine fighter squadron in the South Pacific flew the Corsair.

"The Corsair was a sweet-flying baby if I ever flew one," wrote Boyington, one of the top aviators in the Pacific War. "No longer would we have to fight the Nip's fight, for we could make our own rules."[20] The plane seemed the perfect match for Halsey's no-nonsense approach—go straight at the enemy with a powerful punch. It proved so efficient that Japanese pilots nicknamed the aircraft "Whistling Death" while U.S. aviators fondly labeled it a widow maker.

To check Halsey's momentum, the Japanese built a series of airstrips between Rabaul and Guadalcanal. Vice Admiral Jinichi Kusaka, commander of the Eleventh Air Fleet at Rabaul, moved quickly after the loss of Guadalcanal to develop bases at Munda in New Georgia and at Vila on Kolombangara. With a fleet of more than 200 fighters and bombers, he planned to hold the Central Solomons and intended to make Halsey pay dearly for each step he took toward Rabaul.

However, Kusaka was working with inadequate planes and pilots. The Japanese rushed inexperienced mechanics to the front to repair damaged aircraft, but in their hands the number of available fighters and bombers steadily decreased. In an effort to replace lost aircraft, the Japanese pressured manufacturers to produce replacements more quickly, with a resulting loss in quality. Captain Takashi Miyazaki, commanding officer of the Fourth Air Group at Rabaul, explained to interrogators after the war that because of a lack of skilled maintenance personnel and faulty manufacturing methods, only half his aircraft were available at any given time.

With his air campaign, Halsey created a black hole that siphoned Japanese air power in the South Pacific. A vicious cycle ensued. As Halsey's aviators decimated Tokyo's air squadrons, Japan dispatched replacement aircraft and personnel, but those, too, disappeared before Halsey's growing air strength. In the process Halsey equaled or surpassed the harm he might have inflicted in one of those major carrier battles he so eagerly sought.

Captain Toshikazu Ohmae, chief of staff, Southeastern Fleet at Rabaul, spoke to postwar interrogators about Halsey's impact in the South Pacific. "First, we lost our best carriers at Midway, then our pilots in the Solomons. Due to our reduction of fuel, we were unable to properly train replacements, even though we were able to produce carriers." Or, as Commander Masataka Okumiya, one of Japan's leading pilots, says of Halsey's efforts, in the Solomons "The hunters had become the hunted."[21]

"KEEP 'EM DYING"

June offered a return to land action. Munda had exasperated Halsey since late November 1942. The airfield on New Georgia's southwest coast, only 175 miles from Henderson Field, placed enemy air power within range of Guadalcanal. The location, an impressive installation with several cleverly concealed runways, became such a threat that Halsey described it to Nimitz as "a thorn in my side." Daily air strikes commencing on December 6 attempted to hamper Japanese operations—"we will give it all the Hell we can from the air"[22] is how Halsey put it—but until he could land Marines and Army infantry on the island, Halsey would never be able to eliminate Munda as a menace.

Because an imposing chain of reefs and rocks made the Munda area of New Georgia difficult to approach, Halsey first seized nearby Rendova Island to place him within artillery range of the Munda airfield. Cruisers and destroyers bombarded Munda for four days prior to Halsey's first major land assault.

On June 21 two companies of Marines landed at Segi Point, forty miles east of Munda to seize land for an airfield. Nine days later Army Major General John Hester's 6,000 troops joined the Marines for a thrust toward Munda through the jungle.

Halsey's hopes for a swift campaign ended in New Georgia's dense jungles. By landing east of Munda, Halsey sidestepped the main enemy defenses, but he forced inexperienced troops to advance through nightmarish terrain. The Army's Forty-third Division, trained in the United States for maneuvering on plains and wide-open spaces, instead encountered vines and bushes so dense the men could at times see no more than a few feet ahead. Unaccustomed to such warfare, jittery soldiers fired at jungle noises in the night and imagined enemy infiltrators in every shadow.

Major General Oscar W. Griswold, Hester's superior, investigated conditions and concluded that the Forty-third Division suffered from inadequate training, inferior leadership, and unfamiliarity with Japanese jungle tactics. Griswold urged Halsey to dispatch additional forces to buttress the men ashore. Halsey rushed another 35,000 Army and Marine infantry to New Georgia—the only reserve he had—and sent Major General Millard Harmon to the scene with orders to spur the troops on to Munda.

On July 15 Harmon relieved Hester and turned command over to Griswold. Halsey described the performance on New Georgia to Nimitz as "disappointing." He explained that Hester spent too much time in rear areas rather than closer to the front "and had lost immediate intimate touch with his division." Halsey added that Hester appeared fragile, as if he were "traveling on his nerve," but that Griswold had done well "and things have been moving ever since he took over."[23]

Griswold made rapid gains. By the end of July, his ground troops had forced the Japanese off New Georgia to nearby islands, including Kolombangara, allowing Griswold to radio Halsey on August 5 that the island had been secured. Halsey now possessed another airfield to house fighters and bombers for his drive toward Rabaul. With the Russells and New Georgia in hand, he turned to the next rung on the ladder, Vella Lavella.

WHILE HALSEY'S land forces secured New Georgia, his navy engaged the enemy three times in July and August. The first battle unfolded on the night of July 5–6 and showed that, while Halsey had begun assembling an effective fleet, his commanders had much to learn tactically before they matched their opponents' skills. Based on painful lessons culled from the disastrous night engagements off Guadalcanal, Pug Ainsworth's plan for the Battle of Kula Gulf between New Georgia and Kolombangara proved sound. Upon visual contact with the enemy, the destroyers stationed in the van would launch a torpedo assault as Ainsworth's cruisers fired on the enemy column. After attacking, all ships would execute a speedy turn to avoid the deadly torpedoes the Japanese were certain to launch.

Unfortunately, Ainsworth diverged from his plans. When he spotted ten destroyers under Rear Admiral Teruo Akiyama carrying 2,600 troops and supplies in Kula Gulf twelve miles away, he failed to detach his destroyers and delayed firing until he closed the range to 7,000 yards. Instead of opening with a torpedo launch, Ainsworth's large guns took the honors, but in the process divulged Ainsworth's position before his destroyers could mount an attack. Ainsworth's cruisers sank Akimaya's flagship, damaged three destroyers, and prevented two-thirds of the Japanese troops from reaching shore, but Ainsworth lost the cruiser USS *Helena* in the process. Halsey declined to censure his commander, as he had at least halted the enemy, but he believed Ainsworth could have inflicted a more decisive defeat had he properly followed his battle plan.

Ainsworth received a second chance the following week, when Rear Admiral Shunji Izaki brought four destroyer-transports escorted by five destroyers and the light cruiser *Jintsu* into the same area. In the Battle of Kolombangara on July 12–13, the Japanese launched their torpedoes one minute before Ainsworth fired his. While Ainsworth's guns dispatched the enemy cruiser, Japanese torpedoes sank one of Ainsworth's destroyers, damaged two cruisers, and landed badly needed reinforcements.

Ainsworth had again drawn too close before beginning his attack, thereby handing Izaki time to launch his torpedoes first. However, Halsey liked Ainsworth's spirit. He had sunk ships that Japan could ill afford to lose. Though Halsey wished for better results, in Ainsworth he found a man with the aggressiveness Halsey wanted in his commanders.

Nimitz congratulated Halsey on the two encounters, then added words that foreshadowed events the next year off the Philippines. In his July 13 letter Nimitz stated that such actions as Ainsworth's were justified "if we thereby inflict equal or greater damage on [the enemy] than he does on us." Nimitz concluded that "the policy of calculated risk is the principle factor"[24] in determining the viability of a response.

Halsey's emphasis on training combined with his concept of granting his destroyer commanders the freedom to develop new tactics produced greater results in the next sea clash. Benefiting from improved radar and the development of the Combat Information Center (CIC) aboard each ship to collect and evaluate fresh information, Captain Arleigh A. Burke and Commander Frederick Moosbrugger devised enhanced night fighting tactics. Instead of restricting the destroyers to escorting cruisers, the pair planned to have two columns of destroyers lead attacks from a forward position. Under the cover of darkness one column would close on the Japanese, launch their torpedoes, and swerve out of the way. When the Japanese targeted that unit, the second column would reply from a different direction. If the Japanese focused on the second group, the first would shell the enemy from a new position. Halsey approved the tactics, which reminded him of his destroyer days when he and Spruance had experimented in Pacific waters.

Moosbrugger put theory into practice the night of August 6–7 in the Battle of Vella Gulf. Remaining close to the Kolombangara coastline to mask the movements of his six destroyers, Moosbrugger surprised four Japanese destroyers running 1,000 reinforcements into Kolombangara. Following his new doctrine, Moosbrugger split his ships into two columns, one to launch its torpedoes while the other waited for the explosions to guide its fire on the Japanese. Moosbrugger unleashed his torpedoes near midnight and executed a fast turn to the side, waiting in the darkness to learn if his missiles had hit their mark.

Deafening explosions so fiercely rent the night that American sailors thirty miles away assumed a volcano had erupted. Once he had crippled the enemy, Moosbrugger directed a cascade of fire that sank three of the four enemy destroyers, killing 900 while suffering no casualties.

The next week Halsey's land forces once again took center stage. Halsey had first planned to invade Kolombangara, an island across Kula Gulf ten miles northwest of New Georgia, but when intelligence divulged the presence of 12,000 enemy soldiers there, he paused. Hoping to avoid another protracted bloodbath similar to Guadalcanal and Munda, Halsey decided to bypass Kolombangara and seize lightly defended Vella Lavella fourteen miles to the northwest. Vella Lavella offered better land for an airfield and placed Halsey closer to Rabaul.

Bypassing, or leapfrogging, a heavily defended position to hit the enemy in a more vulnerable spot had been utilized to great effect in the war. The Japanese included it in their 1942 Philippines offensive, and the United States employed the tactic to avert Japanese defenses in the Aleutian Islands. Halsey effectively used the tactic in his drive up the Solomon chain. After the war Japanese prime minister General Hideki Tojo named leapfrogging as one of the three factors most contributing to defeat for his nation, American submarines and fast carrier task forces being the other two.

Against light opposition, Halsey opened his assault against Vella Lavella on August 15, landing almost 5,000 men in half a day. Now outflanked, the Japanese on Kolombangara executed a hurried retreat to the north, using barges, canoes, and any other floatable device to escape Halsey's clutches. The admiral diverted aircraft, PT boats, and destroyers to the area, where his men had, as Halsey termed it, "a field day. There were many more Nips that fulfilled their ambition and joined their ancestors."[25]

"CHANGE THE NAME OF RABAUL TO RUBBLE"

By seizing Vella Lavella Halsey had advanced almost 300 miles closer to Rabaul, but he now faced his toughest obstacle in Bougainville, the largest and northernmost Solomon island 150 miles to Rabaul's south. Planning for a last-ditch stand on the island closest to Rabaul, Japan placed a seaplane base and five airfields on or near the island, including the main base at Kahili, so sturdily defended that American pilots grimly joked that while bold pilots attacked Kahili, few lasted long enough to become old pilots.

Bougainville's importance rose when the Combined Chiefs of Staff decided in August 1943 to isolate Rabaul instead of trying to take it. Rather than risk thousands of lives in a costly invasion, Army and Marine aviators would neutralize it with frequent air raids. Possession of airfields on Bougainville would move Halsey within fighter range of Rabaul and enable his pilots to escort the bombers that kept Hirohito's troops and aircraft hemmed in.

First intending to strike in Bougainville's southern region, Halsey altered the plans when aerial reconnaissance divulged the presence of strong Japanese forces stationed in the south. Hoping to find a less costly route, Halsey selected Cape Torokina in Empress Augusta Bay, halfway up the island's western coast, where he could land in a more favorable position, build his airfield, and let the enemy come to him. Reconnaissance showed that fewer than 1,000 Japanese soldiers defended the area, and the existence of thick jungle standing between the Japanese to the south and Cape Torokina would force the enemy to move through the jungle canopy, a costly process Halsey had experienced at Munda.

Risks came with the move as Halsey knew little about Bougainville. The few maps he possessed contained numerous "unexplored" regions, producing uncertainty over whether Cape Torokina's terrain was firm enough to support his vehicles and forces. Recent aerial surveys placed the island as much as eight miles farther north and east of the old charts, meaning that his ship commanders would have to navigate unfamiliar waters that might shelter underwater obstacles. Though strategists preferred a three-to-one advantage in land assaults from the sea, Halsey only possessed 34,000 troops to invade Bougainville against an expected 33,000 Japanese troops.

He also fought with a reduced fleet. The struggle to hold Guadalcanal and move northward had cost many destroyers and other vital ships. Halsey would have to rely on one carrier group, a cruiser division, and three destroyer squadrons to deflect any Japanese surface force. Should the enemy send a powerful naval unit to strike Bougainville, Halsey would be at a disadvantage.

On November 1, Task Force 39, containing the carriers *Princeton* and *Saratoga,* attacked Bougainville airfields and installations while Halsey's land units rushed ashore at Cape Torokina. Against strong opposition, by nightfall 14,000 troops had been landed.

Halsey established airfields on Bougainville from which he mounted his triple offensive. While his air arm struck Rabaul, his land forces contained the enemy on Bougainville, allowing them to control the eastern end of the island until war's end. At the same time, his naval units registered their most significant victories in two surface battles and two risky carrier strikes against Rabaul.

A threatening situation developed when four cruisers and six destroyers under Vice Admiral Sentaro Omori raced from Rabaul to challenge the November 1, 1943, American landings. As Nimitz had committed most of his navy to the assault at Tarawa in the Central Pacific, Halsey collected the few ships at his disposal—Rear Admiral Aaron S. "Tip" Merrill's Task Force 39, consisting of four light cruisers escorted by Arleigh Burke's eight destroyers of Destroyer Squadron 23—to counter the foray. Aided by superb intelligence, on the night of November 1–2 Halsey placed Merrill in optimal position in Empress Augusta Bay to ambush Omori. When Omori approached in two columns, Merrill's ships surprised him with a thundering torpedo and gun attack that routed the Japanese. Halsey's willingness to toss outnumbered forces into the fray, combined with Merrill and Burke's audacity, prevented the Japanese from disrupting the Bougainville landings.

The Navy added another victory later that month when intelligence informed Halsey that the enemy planned to station 900 soldiers on an island north of Bougainville. On November 24 Halsey turned to his most capable destroyer commander, Arleigh Burke, and ordered him to place his squadron in position to block the attempt. Again utilizing the tactics he and Moosbrugger had developed, Burke split his unit in half, waited at the western end of St. George Channel for the enemy to appear, and sank three destroyers while losing none in turning back the enemy.

More stirring were two spectacular November 1943 carrier strikes against Rabaul. In an effort to stop Halsey's invasion of Bougainville, the Japanese diverted seven heavy cruisers, one light cruiser, and four destroyers under Vice Admiral Takeo Kurita from Truk to Rabaul, with orders to refuel and steam south to Bougainville to strike troop transports and bombard the beachhead.

When search aircraft spotted the Japanese force on November 4, Halsey faced a dilemma. He had to meet the enemy to protect his invasion forces, but all he possessed was Rear Admiral Frederick C. Sherman's Task Force 38, consisting of the carriers *Saratoga* and *Princeton* and escorting vessels. "This was the most desperate emergency that confronted me in my entire term as COMSOPAC,"[26] stated Halsey afterward, faced with the need to hit the Japanese before they reached Bougainville and disrupted his landings, but lacking the resources.

Rather than wait for the enemy to come to him, Halsey mounted an attack directly against Rabaul to catch Kurita's ships as they refueled.

The daring plan entailed risks. Both carriers would steam within range of enemy land-based aircraft, which Halsey had purposely avoided throughout the Solomons. Japanese aircraft would outnumber Sherman's one hundred planes, the carrier aircraft would have to fly directly into the frightening rings of antiaircraft guns that guarded Rabaul's approaches, and the carriers would be caught without aircraft should the enemy mount a strike against the ships while the American aircraft hit Rabaul.

According to members of his staff, the raid would undoubtedly produce alarming casualties. Occupied with the Gilbert assault then unfolding in the Central Pacific, Nimitz could send no immediate help, so Halsey was left on his own. "We did not believe before the attack that there would be much of the *Saratoga* and *Princeton*'s air group left and we fully expected heavy damage to both ships," Halsey wrote in his memoirs. "I tried not to remember that my son was serving on board the *Saratoga*."[27]

Halsey examined every possibility in hopes of finding a way to avoid ordering the strike, "and he couldn't," Carney recalled. "He finally signed that order, and he was crying . . . because he knew he was signing the death warrant of a hell of a lot of people." Carney added, "Every one of us knew what was going through the Admiral's mind. It showed in his face, which suddenly looked 150 years old. Halsey reflected for a short time, then said, 'Let 'er go!'"[28]

Luck ran Halsey's way when the thick clouds and rain that hid his carriers from enemy observation cleared over Rabaul. Taking advantage of the opening, on November 5 pilots from the two carriers descended through antiaircraft fire to damage six cruisers and two destroyers, a punch that badly impaired Kurita's ability to attack Bougainville.

Six days later, aided by the aircraft of three carriers under Rear Admiral Alfred E. Montgomery that had recently arrived in Halsey's area, Halsey sent a second strike against Rabaul. While Sherman targeted Rabaul from the north, Montgomery blasted airfields and ships from the south in an action Halsey claimed "ought to change the name of Rabaul to Rubble."[29]

Halsey concluded that because of the damage inflicted by the two successful raids, the Japanese "were forced to beat a hasty retreat back to their stronghold at Truk." They would no longer threaten Halsey's South Pacific drive; for the remainder of the war no large Japanese ships entered Rabaul. "It is real music to me and opens the stops for a funeral dirge for Tojo's Rabaul."[30] Had Kurita succeeded in disrupting Halsey's invasion of Bougainville, he could have delayed the war for months while the Americans regrouped in the South Pacific.

Another bold move by Halsey had paid off.

SINCE POSSESSION OF Bougainville airfields placed Rabaul within fighter range, Halsey could now mount constant air assaults on the fortress. Army bombers departed from airfields to the south and joined with fighter escorts operating out of Bougainville to target Japanese shipping and airfields in and near Rabaul.

In addition to the bombing attacks, Halsey resorted to the fighter sweep, a tactic in which a group of American fighters, rather than being strictly tied to escorting bombers, purposely sought to engage enemy aircraft in aerial dogfights. The tactic allowed Halsey's aviators like Major Gregory Boyington and his Black Sheep Squadron to more suitably utilize the assets provided by the F4U Corsair and other improved aircraft. Boyington suggested that fighters should head out as independent groups and, after clearing the path for the slower bombers behind, linger in the area to challenge enemy aircraft that rose to meet the bombers.

The tactic produced immediate results. Commencing with a large December 17 raid and continuing during the ensuing weeks, American aviators engaged enemy pilots in medieval fashion, charging each other with guns blazing. Inexperienced Japanese aviators became fodder for Halsey's fliers. During Christmas week of 1943, they knocked down seventy-four Japanese aircraft over Rabaul's skies. Halsey's air campaign depleted enemy resources and put the Japanese on notice that they could no longer rely on Rabaul to be an anchor for her forces in the South and Southwest Pacific. For every aviator he lost, Halsey had another waiting, but the Japanese could not replace any man lost, in effect turning the war into a macabre numbers game.

"The days passed in a blur," stated Commander Masataka Okumiya of the deteriorating situation at Rabaul. "Not for a moment did the Americans ease their relentless pressure. Day and night the bombers came to pound Rabaul, to smash at the airfield and shipping in the harbor, while the fighters screamed low on daring strafing passes, shooting up anything they considered worth-while target [sic]." He explained that, "even our most successful interceptions failed to affect adversely the air offensive of the Americans. They threw in more and more replacements, and the ratio of enemy planes to ours widened steadily."[31]

As Rabaul's air power weakened, Halsey's surface vessels operated closer to its shores. Rabaul lost so much of its mystique that *Time* magazine boasted in February 1944, "once mighty Rabaul suffered the indignity of being shelled by destroyers' 5-in. guns."[32] Seeing no alternatives, Japanese officials in Tokyo began planning on a general withdrawal to their inner line of defenses in the Pacific and leaving Rabaul to its fate.

Halsey completed Rabaul's encirclement with two land assaults. On February 15, 1944, he seized Green Island forty miles to Bougainville's north. The move gave him an airfield from which fighters could operate against Rabaul, as well as a PT boat base from which those craft could patrol the New Ireland area.

On March 14 the Joint Chiefs of Staff directed Halsey to take Emirau. Six days later the Fourth Marine Regiment occupied the island unopposed, thereby completing the encirclement of Rabaul and neutralizing what had been one of Japan's most feared bastions. In a startling contrast from his first days on Guadalcanal, when from necessity he lost men and ships with alacrity, he absorbed not one casualty in this final assault, one that illustrated the transformation Halsey crafted in the South Pacific.

In the eighteen months from the date Halsey assumed command in the South Pacific, the officer more accustomed to wizardry at sea had worked wonders on land. He shoved the Japanese out of the Solomons, a chain of islands extending across 700 miles of ocean. In the process he forced the Japanese Navy to abandon the region and so thoroughly decimated Japanese air power that only tattered remnants remained. "Control of the land, the sea, and the air was ours," Halsey asserted in his autobiography. "The South Pacific campaign was finished."[33]

"WE BROKE THEIR BACKS"

Halsey officially remained in command until June 1944, but little remained to accomplish. In an April 20 letter thanking Eleanor Roosevelt for a box of candy, he added, "Life varies little hereabouts, except we have about run out of a war, and things are dull." Realizing, as he put it, that "I had almost fought myself out of a job and that it would soon be necessary for me to move on,"[34] he discussed his options with Nimitz, who informed him that he would soon abdicate his responsibilities in the South Pacific to take command of the Third Fleet. Halsey welcomed the news, which meant that he would once more return to the sea.

Before embarking on his third phase in the Pacific War, in May 1944 Halsey again returned to the United States. He met with Nimitz and King in San Francisco, where he learned that King had reorganized the Pacific Fleet into three divisions. He designated the naval forces under MacArthur as the Seventh Fleet, while under Nimitz both Spruance and Halsey commanded essentially the same ships and men, labeled the Fifth Fleet when Spruance took charge and the Third Fleet with Halsey. While Spruance went to sea during one assault, Halsey remained at Pearl Harbor planning the subsequent attack. When Spruance finished, the two reversed and Halsey took command of the same vessels, the Third Fleet. "Instead of the stagecoach system of keeping the drivers and changing the horses," explained Halsey, "we changed drivers and kept the horses."[35] This arrangement not only maintained the pressure on the enemy, but kept them guessing as to how many different American fleets they faced in the Pacific.

Halsey returned to the Pacific to begin a final tour of bases and airfields. His trip produced undeniable evidence of the vast alterations accomplished by his actions in the South Pacific. Where battlefields and dense jungles had existed earlier, sparkling air bases, fleets of ships, and scores of fighter squadrons now stood. "The old battlefields were already disappearing into the jungle or under neat, new buildings," he recalled. "Where 500 men had lost their lives in a night attack a few months before, eighteen men were now playing baseball. Where a Jap pillbox had crouched, a movie projector stood. Where a hand grenade had wiped out a foxhole, a storekeeper was serving cokes. Only the cemeteries were left."[36]

Halsey would be missed. General MacArthur had grown fond of "The Bull" as he liked to call Halsey. "With deepest regret we see you and your splendid staff go," MacArthur stated in a farewell message. "You leave behind you the unforgettable memory of a great sailor, a determined commander, and a loyal comrade."[37]

On June 15, 1944, twenty months after stepping into one of the war's most desperate situations, Halsey turned over command of the South Pacific to Vice Admiral John Henry Newton. Halsey delivered an emotional speech to his staff, saying of the trying days at Guadalcanal that, "If there is ever a design for a shoulder patch for all those who served in the South Pacific, I would recommend that they show on this patch three things—a piece of string, a can of beans and a rusty nail."[38]

The next day he left Nouméa for Pearl Harbor, again trying unsuccessfully to mask the emotions that overwhelmed him. Testimony to his triumph lay not as much in the flattering words of MacArthur or the honors bestowed by Allied governments, but in the honest outpouring of affection given their commander by the sailors and chief petty officers, the lieutenants and ensigns. "Troops lined the way to the fleet landing," Halsey remembered of the touching moment. "I was given such a rousing goodbye the tears stood in my eyes and all service personnel were there with bands playing." Before departing, Halsey admonished his men to, " . . . Carry on the smashing South Pacific tradition . . . and may we join up again farther along the road to Tokyo."[39]

Time magazine, whose correspondent witnessed the touching display, concluded that, "Headlong 'Bull' Halsey had forged a powerful weapon in the Solomons, had wielded it with skill, daring, many sulfurous asides (a public-relations officer had finally been assigned to clean up his bullish predictions, screen his football-field bombast)." Speaking of his next post with the Fleet, the magazine added, "Now once again he would have a chance to forge a weapon, drive it to the heart of the Japanese empire."[40]

With the three-fold military weapon he fashioned from his ground, sea, and air forces, Halsey stymied the Japanese advance at Guadalcanal and coordinated America's first major Pacific offensive. Relying on capable commanders and tossing into the fray whatever lay at his disposal, Halsey recorded his greatest achievement of the war. More than his island raids and the Doolittle bombing, in the South Pacific Halsey checked the enemy's forward-moving offensive and started Japan on its inevitable retreat back to the Home Islands. Much fighting and dying remained, but Halsey had charted an ineradicable path leading to America's victory and Japan's defeat.

Halsey delivered his judgment in a letter to Ashford. "Let no one ever tell you differently," he cautioned Ashford. "It was in the South Pacific where we broke their backs."[41]

Halsey might not have experienced the surface engagement with the enemy's naval forces that he desired, but in the South Pacific he found the fight for which he had been searching since December 7, 1941.

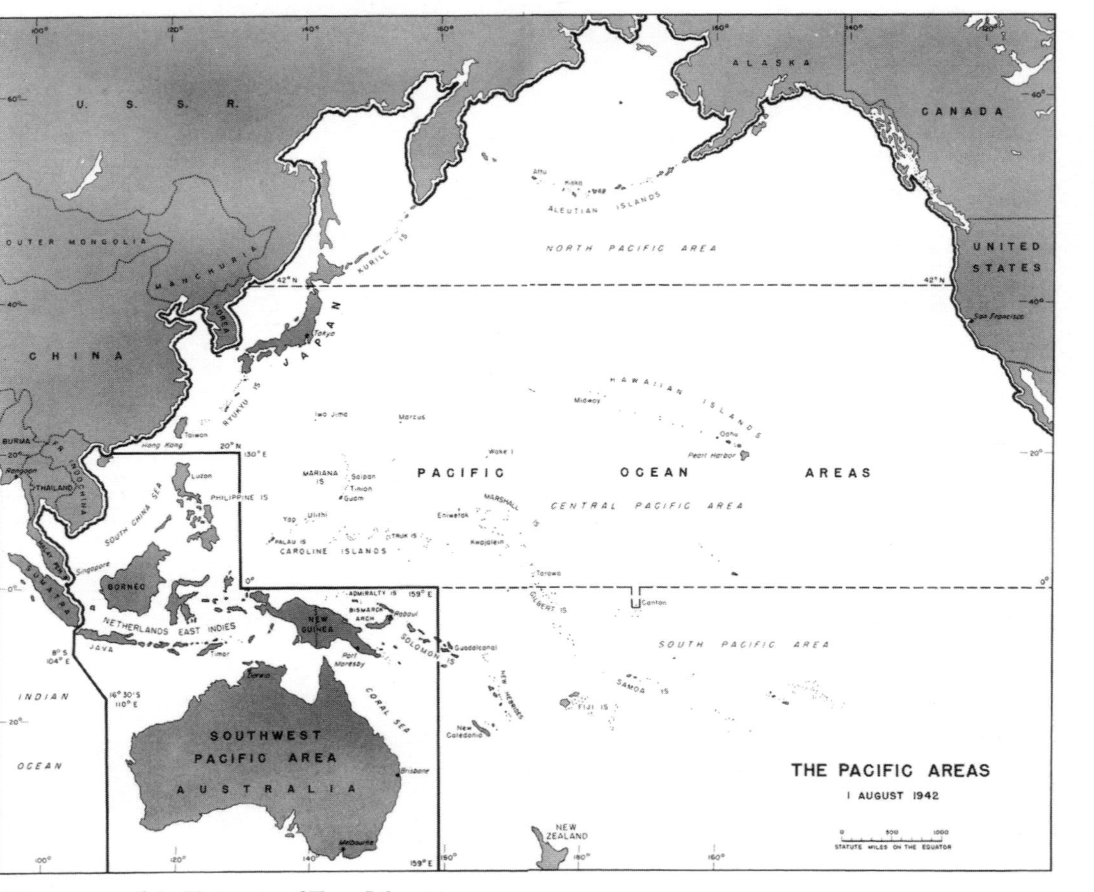

Map courtesy of the University of Texas Libraries.

CHAPTER 8

"DESTRUCTION OF THE ENEMY FLEET IS THE PRINCIPAL TASK"

Halsey had few regrets about leaving the South Pacific. He had performed a yeoman's job transforming a catastrophic situation at Guadalcanal and the Solomons. It was time for him to return to the type of warfare he loved best. In his absence, however, sea combat had experienced dramatic alterations.

"IT IS NOT PLEASANT TO THINK"

The fundamental changes in the Navy he had guided during the island raids of 1942 were evident with one glance at the vast conglomeration Spruance handed to him. "I hadn't been with the fleet for more than two years; I wanted to see what the new carriers and planes looked like,"[1] he said, conveying his ignorance of the transformations that had occurred while he fought the war from behind a desk. Four carrier groups, massed in separate circular formations spreading to the horizon, dwarfed the hundreds of escorting cruisers and destroyers protecting their flanks. When operating together, Task Force 38 occupied a stretch of ocean forty miles long by nine miles wide. A navy that possessed just over 1,000 ships in 1940 had quadrupled in size, boasting 70 new aircraft carriers, 35,000 aircraft, and hundreds of landing craft.

The arrival of the new *Essex*-class fast carrier transformed the nature of sea warfare in the Pacific. Supported by an elaborate seaborne supply line, the sleek new carriers could transport naval air groups to any point in the Pacific. Sea warfare in 1944 had overshadowed that of 1942, in numbers, tactics, and complexity of organization. Naval combat had all but passed Halsey by in his absence.

Whereas in 1942 Halsey had operated with a single aircraft carrier, individual circular formations, in which four carriers operated as an entity, now joined with up to three additional similar circular formations. Spheres of escorting battleships, cruisers, and destroyers shielded the carriers from enemy aircraft with their concentric rings of antiaircraft fire.

This convoluted, layered naval warfare demanded more from a commander than navigation of a single carrier, but Halsey remained stuck in the one-dimensional mode that had worked successfully in the war's desperate months. Those days, though, disappeared when America's factories disgorged ships and planes on a massive scale. The Pacific conflict had turned into an entrepreneur's conflict, one demanding a rigid structure more identifiable with commercial concerns than with Halsey's Annapolis-bred navy.

More than ever, war demanded the correct blend of fighter and thinker, a person who understood his place in an overall strategy where events in Europe and elsewhere in the Pacific affected his options. Halsey could no longer act in a vacuum as he had in 1942, when only two admirals—he and Spruance—accompanied Colonel Doolittle's bombers. So many new admirals had joined the Pacific Fleet that by the time of the Okinawa assault in 1945, forty-four admirals participated in that one landing alone.

Halsey's war career had been built upon instinct and gut feelings over intellectual analysis—the island raids, the Doolittle attack, and much of the drive up the Solomon Islands chain relied upon improvisation and feel. "It is not a pleasant occupation to sit around and think,"[2] Halsey declared to Nimitz in a June 1943 letter.

That attitude placed Halsey at variance with the admiral with whom he alternated command—the contemplative, taciturn Raymond Spruance. The two, although lifelong friends, could hardly have been more dissimilar—Halsey offering a haphazard, almost chaotic style in contrast to Spruance's immaculately organized system. More of an intellectual than Halsey, Spruance evaluated matters before announcing his decisions while Halsey reacted swiftly.

A staff officer stated that with Halsey "you never knew what you were going to do in the next five minutes or how you were going to do it," mainly because Halsey did not know. Instead of rigidly following an overall operations plan, Halsey fired off dispatches to subordinates as events dictated, which often served only to confuse his task force commanders. "My feeling was one of confidence when Spruance was there," stated an officer who worked for both Halsey and Spruance, "and one of concern when Halsey was there."[3]

Halsey returned to the sea at a time when he lacked an understanding of recent tactical innovations and the evolution of the organizational war. He commanded the most powerful collection of naval air assembled, yet he intended to operate the fleet in the same bold manner in which he had commanded his destroyers before the war and his task forces in 1942.

Deficiency of knowledge, however, only partly explains Halsey's role in the war's final year as the warhorse was blinded by his obsession to engage enemy carriers. In 1942–1943 Halsey had fashioned an image that home-front followers loved—a man who would relentlessly seek and ultimately destroy the enemy. In painting that portrait, however, Halsey became a victim of his own press. The public and his men expected him to pursue the enemy, therefore he would. He and his staff frequently stood at the game board on his flagship, USS *New Jersey*, devising different strategies to corner the Japanese fleet.

His chances seemed to be running out. In June 1944, the same month he left the South Pacific, Spruance again met enemy carriers off Saipan in the Battle of the Philippine Sea, where his fighter pilots triumphed over their Japanese foes. It seemed that every sea commander had had his opportunity except Halsey, the man whose forceful reaction to Pearl Harbor buoyed the Navy in its most desperate hour. Who more than he, Halsey wondered, deserved a shot at those targets?

Whenever his chance came, he would not delay as had Spruance, who was criticized for being overly cautious, first during the Battle of

Midway, and again in the Battle of the Philippine Sea. Some top officers, especially aviators, censured Spruance for remaining close to the Saipan invasion beachhead instead of turning to sea and actively seeking the Japanese carriers. In doing so, they said, Spruance had allowed the enemy fleet to live to fight another day. There would be no criticism about over-caution with Halsey in command if he had anything to say about it.

"MY NECK IS WAY OUT"

Halsey faced two tasks in the latter half of 1944—he was to plan and support the invasion of the Palau Island group southeast of the Philippines and neutralize Japanese air power in the Philippines as part of General MacArthur's massive assault on that crucial location. He relished neither opportunity, for he viewed the former as unnecessary and the latter as an inefficient use of his carrier air strength.

The Palaus operation especially bothered him. Halsey was to seize three islands in the Palau group—Peleliu, Angaur, and Babelthuap—as well as the island of Yap 280 miles northeast and Ulithi Atoll, another 120 miles distant. Halsey studied the map and concluded that only the valuable anchorage at Ulithi offered benefits. He believed that other than an airfield or two, Peleliu yielded no advantage, and he thought that the Japanese would fortify and defend the island so sturdily that the costs would not warrant the effort. He thought he could simply leap beyond the Palaus as he had earlier done in the Solomons, when he bypassed Kolombangara to strike Vella Lavella. He cautioned Nimitz about assaulting Peleliu "because I envisioned another Guadalcanal," and urged "that these points be by-passed and the Philippines be invaded at a central position."[4] Nimitz agreed to drop Babelthuap but ordered Halsey to hit Angaur and Peleliu on September 15 and Yap and Ulithi the following month.

On August 24, 1944, almost two years after arriving in the South Pacific, Halsey returned to sea when, aboard his flagship, the sparkling battleship USS *New Jersey,* he left Pearl Harbor accompanied by three destroyers. Halsey preferred to operate from a carrier, but as carriers were more vulnerable during an attack than battleships, which threatened to isolate him from his command at crucial moments, he opted for the modern battleship.

Halsey was once again where he belonged. "I do not have to assure you that it is a grand and glorious feeling to be at sea again," he wrote Nimitz on September 9. "I and my staff have been drilling ourselves daily in Flag CIC, using strategic and tactical battle problems, and we are all hoping that we will be fully prepared to take the maximum advantage of any opportunities the Japs leave lying around."[5]

As much as possible, Halsey maintained a routine at sea that was similar to his routine when he labored on land. After awakening around 5:00 A.M., he headed to Flag Plot, the nerve center for Third Fleet operations one deck above his quarters, for updates, then engaged in light banter at breakfast with staff members. Daily morning meetings ensued, during which Halsey and his staff, who affectionately called him Admiral Bill, planned future operations and discussed recent war developments.

In his few moments of relaxation Halsey read from *The Police Gazette* or played deck tennis with his chief medical officer, Captain Carnes Weeks. Halsey had met Weeks at a cocktail party in Hawaii and was so impressed that he made Weeks his medical officer, with additional responsibilities for maintaining the admiral's liquor supply. Most evenings Weeks handed Halsey a shot or two at bedtime to calm the admiral's nerves and allow him a decent night's rest.

After watching the nightly movie, Halsey met with his Dirty Tricks Department to see what his staff had up their sleeves. "Their job was to think of new and unusual forms of punishment to inflict on the Jap," Halsey wrote. They "kept a burr under the Japs' tails." Carney said that Halsey was constantly asking them about any new plots to fool the Japanese, and if none was in the offing, inquiring why. "And he was always riding my tail—'What'll we do now? What's the best next thing? Get your boys together, let's have an idea, don't sit on your ass, let's have an idea!'"[6]

HALSEY STOPPED AT Manus north of New Guinea on September 4 for a meeting with Vice Admiral Thomas C. Kinkaid, commander of the Seventh Fleet operating with MacArthur, to coordinate their fleets for the coming tasks. After agreeable discussions, Halsey departed the next day to be in position to launch air strikes against the Palaus, where he embarked upon three days of attacks against Japanese airfields.

After striking the Palaus' airfields, Halsey moved toward the island of Mindanao in the Southern Philippines. He was to first neutralize Japanese air power in the Philippines, then advance north and concentrate on airfields on Formosa, Okinawa, and other airstrips north of the Philippines. Eliminating the Japanese from these islands would block the enemy's shipping routes to crucial natural resources in Southeast Asia and the East Indies, as well as hand the United States an excellent staging area for an eventual assault against islands to the north and the Home Islands.

Halsey's carrier aircraft struck targets on Mindanao in two massive raids on September 9–10, while a cruiser-destroyer raid off the southern Philippine coast wiped out a convoy of thirty-two small vessels and twenty sampans bringing supplies to the forces on Mindanao. Some officers remarked about the ease with which both the carrier planes and the raiding ships completed their tasks, leading Halsey to question the enemy's strength on Mindanao. The outcome prodded Halsey to expand his bombing raids to Leyte and other locales in the Central Philippines. He ordered three of his four carrier groups to move north while Rear Admiral Ralph E. Davison remained with Task Group 38.4 to support the Palau operation.

Nearly 3,000 carrier sorties struck the Central Philippines in three large raids from September 12 to 14. Aviators shot down 200 enemy aircraft and destroyed another 300 on the ground, while sinking 59 Japanese ships. As before, Halsey's pilots flew against surprisingly ineffective opposition. "The Japanese apparently completely caught off their guard offered only meager resistance and the Yankee flyers had a field day as they trip-hammered the Nip installations, burned the neatly lined up Jap planes, and proceeded to raise havoc with Japanese shipping,"[7] summed the Third Fleet War Diary for September 12.

Information supplied by Ensign Thomas C. Tillar from the *Hornet* convinced Halsey that the enemy's feeble resistance in the Philippines provided an opening. Armed with this information, Halsey saw a chance to advance the war's schedule. "I came to the conclusion that the Central

Philippines were vulnerable and that the most effective means of shortening the war was to invade immediately."[8]

Halsey discussed the matter with his chief of staff, Mick Carney, and his flag secretary, Harold Stassen. He then sat down in a corner of the bridge for quiet reflection. Urging such a dramatic alteration in plans would undoubtedly irritate some, but the benefits seemed too enticing. "Such a recommendation, in addition to being none of my business, would upset a great many applecarts, possibly all the way up to Mr. Roosevelt and Mr. Churchill," he later wrote. "On the other hand, it looked sound, it ought to save thousands of lives, and it might cut months off the war by hurrying the Nips and keeping them off-balance."[9]

After pondering the issue for a few moments, Halsey informed Carney and Stassen that he intended to recommend a cancellation of the operations against Mindanao, Yap, and the Palaus and the advancement of the scheduled Leyte assault by two months. "I remember very well saying on the bridge when I dictated the dispatch recommending the change in plans, 'Here is where my neck is way out and my head will probably be rolling in a basket tomorrow morning.'"[10] Halsey radioed the message to Nimitz who, even though he opposed canceling the Palau operation at such a late hour, agreed to forward the recommendation to the Joint Chiefs of Staff, then meeting in Québec.

Admiral King interrupted his dinner to confer with his colleagues on the Joint Chiefs of Staff. They concurred that Halsey's recommendation, though risky, made sense, and agreed to take the information to Roosevelt and Churchill, who were also in Québec. The heads of state quickly assented, and within ninety minutes of receiving Halsey's message, the Joint Chiefs radioed an approval. Though retaining the Palau operation, they canceled the Mindanao invasion and moved up the Leyte assault to October 20, two months earlier than scheduled.

A Halsey suggestion had once again aided the war effort. By advancing the war two months, Halsey's recommendation saved thousands of lives that would have been lost in a needless attack into Mindanao or assaulting sturdier defenses that the Japanese would have had time to construct at island locations along the way to Tokyo during that two-month span. On a par with his daring recommendation that he be replaced by non-aviator Raymond Spruance in the hours before Midway, Halsey's prod to the Joint Chiefs benefited the Allied cause, brought the war's end nearer, and saved untold numbers of casualties.

As knowledgeable a man as President Roosevelt admitted as much. On January 6, 1945, during his State of the Union address, Roosevelt went out of his way to praise Admiral Halsey for the recommendation he had forwarded, which the Joint Chiefs of Staff had examined and approved in rapid order. "Thus, within the space of twenty-four hours, a major change of plans was accomplished which involved Army and Navy forces from two different theaters of operations—a change which hastened the liberation of the Philippines and the final day of victory—a change which saved lives which would have been expended in the capture of islands which are now neutralized far behind our lines."[11]

"WE WERE FOXY DEVILS"

On September 15, 1944, the U.S. Marines seized Angaur and Ulithi against minimal opposition, but the Japanese took advantage of Peleliu's many caves to delay the American advance with more than two months of savage fighting. Marines relied on the tested methods of assault to finally take the island—hundreds of attacks by small units against stubborn Japanese defenders fighting from pillboxes and cave complexes. To save Americans, Halsey advocated a remedy most considered illegal and immoral. "It is a question of slow progress in digging the rats out," he said of the Peleliu combat. "Poison gas is indicated as an economical weapon."[12]

Final resistance on Peleliu did not cease until November 25, at the cost of nearly 10,000 American casualties. "They were finally blasted and burned out of this stronghold in an almost foot by foot advance," Halsey wrote of the campaign. "I am a stubborn animal and I certainly think I was right about that [bypassing Peleliu] and I believe the cost in lives very greatly outweighed the advantage we accrued from the seizure of Peleliu and Angaur."[13]

As the Peleliu attack raged, Halsey supervised continued carrier air strikes against Japanese airfields and installations in the Philippines. On September 21 his aviators hit Manila, an important objective for both strategic and morale purposes. Tongue in cheek, Halsey's War Diary concluded, "The Japanese, caught with their flaps down, were unable to launch an airplane until after ten minutes of irreplaceable damage."[14]

Halsey's most effective move was to destroy enemy air strength at its source before the Japanese had the chance to harm MacArthur's forces ashore. He opened with strikes against Okinawa airfields, 1,100 miles northeast of Manila, on October 10, again catching the enemy by surprise. Moving unseen behind a weather front, Task Force 38 blasted Okinawa installations with 1,400 sorties that sank 19 vessels and destroyed 100 aircraft while losing 21 American planes. Halsey immediately turned his carriers southwest for additional strikes against Formosa, off the Chinese coast. He first dispatched an air raid against fields in Luzon in the Philippines as a diversion, then turned at high speed toward Formosa.

The Luzon bombings alerted the Japanese to Halsey's presence, but despite the heightened state of alert, 1,000 fighters and bombers from Task Force 38 ripped into the airfields with impunity on October 12–15, destroying more than 500 aircraft in 1,400 sorties that shattered Tokyo's air strength on the island. Halsey and Task Force 38 operated in the region with such freedom that he considered pulling away from the Philippines entirely, but on October 15 MacArthur ordered him to continue his support of his land operations.

After neutralizing Formosa, Halsey again switched focus to the Philippines, striking the Manila area and Luzon on October 15–19 in preparation for MacArthur's landings. The strikes produced such welcome results that Halsey began planning to rotate his four task groups to Ulithi for rest and replenishment. Three would remain on station while a fourth steamed away.

He had much of which to be proud as Third Fleet aviators overwhelmed the air opposition. In two weeks of strikes, Halsey's air groups sank or damaged almost 400 ships and destroyed 1,200 aircraft while losing fewer than 100 planes. President Roosevelt signaled his pleasure by sending a congratulatory message to Halsey. "It is with pride that the country has followed your fleet's magnificent sweep into enemy waters. In addition to the gallant fighting of your fliers, we appreciate the endurance and superseamanship of your forces."[15]

The largest assemblage of naval might in history steamed Philippine waters in the days before MacArthur's landings. Halsey's Task Force 38 operated in conjunction with MacArthur's Seventh Fleet, an array of 738 ships commanded by Halsey's associate from Guadalcanal days, Admiral Kinkaid.

Combining two such monstrous fleets should have guaranteed success for the Philippine invasion, but an awkward system of divided command hampered their effectiveness. As neither Nimitz nor MacArthur wanted to yield control to the other, the Joint Chiefs of Staff arranged an awkward compromise that gave both men autonomy over their naval forces while asking them to work together. While Halsey answered to Nimitz, Kinkaid answered to MacArthur.

The unwieldy situation might not have proven so catastrophic had there been open lines of communications between Halsey and Kinkaid. MacArthur, however, maintained a tight grip on incoming and outgoing communications with his subordinate commanders. Should Kinkaid wish to contact Halsey, he first had to send the dispatch to MacArthur's radio station at Manus in the Admiralties for approval, and it would then be relayed to Halsey. This inefficient process retarded communications between the two surface commanders and presented a flaw that the enemy could exploit.

Confusion was inevitable, a result Nimitz compounded by giving Halsey an additional mission. While Kinkaid focused on landing the assault force, Halsey was to keep the Japanese fleet off his back. However, while Nimitz's Operation Plan 8–44, signed on September 27, ordered Halsey to "destroy enemy naval and air forces in or threatening the Philippine area," Nimitz added a separate directive giving him the discretion to leave his assigned areas and pursue the enemy should the opportunity arise to destroy the Japanese fleet. If that occurred, presenting what Halsey believed to be a solid prospect for annihilating those ships, "such destruction becomes the primary task." Halsey, who had missed every major carrier clash to date, viewed this directive as a blank check to leave Kinkaid and chase the enemy. Though Nimitz never intended that Halsey should abandon Kinkaid, he failed to make that clear. As far as Halsey was concerned, the order's wording left no doubt that the Japanese fleet, not Kinkaid, was his "primary task."[16]

Armed with Nimitz's free pass, an impatient Halsey was primed to locate the Japanese. He stated as much in a letter to Nimitz the day after his superior signed the order. "In all of my recommended operations," Halsey wrote on September 28, "I aim to achieve superiority at the point of contact through weight of numbers, surprise, superior performance, stratagem, or some other device, and I also am always prepared to change schedules if I see a situation which permits me to capitalize on a momentary enemy weakness." He added that, "Inasmuch as the destruction of the enemy fleet is the principal task, every weapon should be brought into play and the general coordination of those weapons should be in the hands of the tactical commander responsible for the outcome of the battle."[17]

Nimitz cautioned him on October 8 to be aware of developments involving all arms of the invasion, but he might as well have shouted into the wind. With consent to pursue the Japanese, Halsey had his foot to the pedal, ready to accelerate if the enemy carriers appeared.

Halsey's obsession with a surface engagement caused him to abandon his usual regard for his troops. He learned on October 14 that Japanese torpedoes had damaged the cruiser *Canberra* ninety miles east of Formosa, close to Japanese bases. The heavy cruiser USS *Wichita,* accompanied by escorting ships, took the *Canberra* under tow at four knots, a slow speed that exposed both vessels to attack. Halsey could either allow the ships to proceed to Ulithi 1,300 miles distant or sink the *Canberra* and extricate the other ships from harm's way. "We were squarely in the Jap dragon's jaws, and the dragon knew it,"[18] Halsey wrote.

Halsey initially favored sinking the cruiser but his staff, seeing another opportunity for the Dirty Tricks Department, argued otherwise. As Radio Tokyo had already announced that Japanese ships were in pursuit, Carney suggested that Halsey use the *Canberra* group as bait to draw out the enemy fleet, which could then be attacked by aircraft from carriers waiting on the flanks. Halsey agreed and issued orders directing the eight carriers of Rear Admiral Gerald Bogan's 38.2 and Rear Admiral Frederick Sherman's 38.3 east of the *Canberra-Wichita* unit, out of range of Japanese patrol planes, while the other two task groups hit Luzon airfields to keep those planes out of the action.

Halsey formed Task Group 30.3 to accompany the two cruisers, callously nicknamed by Halsey's staff as BaitDiv or CripDiv (for Crippled

Division). While the names may have amused a few members of Halsey's staff, they gained no favor among the crews aboard the stricken ships. Despite Halsey's precautions, Japanese aircraft punched through his defenses and damaged the *Houston,* leaving Halsey with two impaired cruisers. Now more concerned, Halsey scanned the charts that plotted the unit's progress every fifteen minutes to see how much closer to safety the ships had advanced.

Officials in Japan sent a cruiser-destroyer force from the Inland Sea. They enjoyed the chance to thrash Halsey, a man whose coarse comments about the Japanese earned "the proud title (to me) for Public Enemy Number one." A zookeeper in Tokyo, in response to Halsey's repeated depictions of the Japanese as monkeys, expressed his hopes that the fleet returned Halsey alive to Japan, as "I have a special cage in the monkey house where I want to put him."[19] Halsey laughed at the remark and declared his intention to visit that zoo after the war and look up the zookeeper. Japanese officers at the Ofuna prison camp outside Tokyo told the incarcerated Marine aviator Gregory Boyington that they planned to hang the three most hated U.S. officials—Roosevelt, MacArthur, and Halsey.

The plot unraveled when Japanese land-based planes spotted Halsey's task groups and warned the cruiser-destroyer force to retreat. Once more, Tokyo pulled the ships back and announced that they had annihilated Halsey's unit. Halsey, mocking this and other Japanese declarations of his demise, radioed Nimitz that he was ready for more. "The Third Fleet's sunken and damaged ships have been salvaged and are retiring at high speed toward the enemy."[20]

Though disappointed, Halsey could now ease a nagging conscience over using sailors to bait the enemy. "I am very glad I was persuaded to make the decision that I did, but it put a lot of gray hairs in my head," he wrote. "Watching them limp across the ocean took years off my life, but every time I commiserate with myself, I realize how infinitely more agonizing was the strain on the men aboard the cripples. It took guts to spend day after day in the center of a bull's-eye," and that the experience "must have been hell."[21]

He had a right to his guilt. Halsey had crafted an entire career based in part upon a strong allegiance to the men under his command. Here, however, faced with the possibility of engaging the enemy, he abandoned his principles for personal glory. The uncharacteristic move illustrated how badly Halsey wanted to meet the enemy in sea combat at this stage of the war.

"THE THIRD FLEET PROWLED THE OCEAN"

The Japanese counted on that same Halsey obsession with enemy carriers in formulating their response to MacArthur's invasion, which posed the most serious threat to the empire to date. Should the United States seize the Philippines, Japanese supply routes to valuable resources in the East Indies, particularly oil to fuel her ships, would be severed. The fleet would have to remain in either home waters, cut off from its fuel supply, or in the South China Sea, isolated from the ammunition and aircraft produced by Japanese factories. It made no sense for Japan to preserve her fleet while losing the Philippines.

To defend the Philippines, Admiral Soemu Toyoda, commander in chief of the Combined Fleet, devised an intricate plan, called Sho–1, based on deception and daring. Three separate fleets would converge on MacArthur in a widespread pincer action intent on puncturing through the U.S. fleet and disrupting the landings. The plan's success hinged in large measure on one unit drawing Halsey's Third Fleet away from Leyte Gulf so that the other two Japanese surface elements could charge in and smash Kinkaid's exposed Seventh Fleet.

Knowing Halsey's penchant for engaging carriers, Toyoda dangled irresistible bait. Under the command of Vice Admiral Jisaburo Ozawa, the Northern Force of four aircraft carriers and escorting ships would steam south from the Home Islands to lure Halsey from his post off Samar due north of Leyte Gulf. The carriers lacked most of their aircraft, which had been destroyed in recent aerial contests with American forces, but Toyoda hoped the mere presence of aircraft carriers would distract Halsey from his task of shielding Kinkaid.

While Ozawa enticed the Third Fleet, Vice Admiral Shoji Nishimura's Force C of two battleships, one heavy cruiser, and four destroyers would leave Lingga Roads near Singapore, cross the Sulu and Mindanao seas, and steam through Surigao Strait at the southern entrance of Leyte Gulf.

Vice Admiral Kiyohide Shima's Second Striking Force of two heavy cruisers, one light cruiser, and four destroyers would join him along the way. Combined, these two would attack Kinkaid from the south.

The real punch would emerge north of Leyte Gulf, appearing in the area from which Halsey would be lured. Vice Admiral Takeo Kurita's First Striking Force of twenty battleships and cruisers and their escorting destroyers packed a powerful punch, including the world's two newest, most destructive battleships, *Yamato* and *Musashi.* While Ozawa drew Halsey to the north and Nishimura and Shima approached Leyte from the south, Kurita would steam across the Sibuyan Sea, rush through San Bernardino Strait to Leyte's north, emerge from what would hopefully be an unguarded exit, and descend upon Kinkaid from the north while Nishimura and Shima closed from the south.

The wide-ranging plan presented risks, but Toyoda believed he had no choice but to challenge the U.S. fleet no matter the cost. Ozawa expected to lose his entire force, while Kurita predicted that he would return with fewer than half his ships. Toyoda understood that for their miracle to occur, they needed help from Halsey.

The Japanese pincer inched forward on October 18, when Kurita sortied from Lingga Roads and veered northeast toward Brunei Bay in North Borneo. After refueling, he departed on October 22 and steamed north to swing around the northern coast of the Palawan Passage before turning toward the Philippines. Seven hours later, Nishimura guided Force C out of Brunei, headed to the south of the Palawan Passage, then east toward Surigao Strait.

The other two components left the Home Islands. Admiral Shima debouched from the Inland Sea on October 22 in support of Nishimura, while Ozawa guided his decoy force out of Japan on October 20. He made certain to adopt a course that placed him outside the range of American search craft from Saipan in the Marianas so that he would not be discovered too soon and come under attack from other American units. Ozawa had to distract Halsey long enough to sneak Kurita through the San Bernardino Strait.

Oblivious of the fact that the enemy was then descending on the Philippines, on October 20, the first day of MacArthur's landings, Halsey's carrier air groups took position northeast of Leyte Gulf in support of the general's forces. Halsey believed that the opportunity he had long anticipated lay days away at most. He guessed the Japanese could not allow the Philippines to be seized without a fight, and that among their responses would be the carriers. While keeping one eye on San Bernardino Strait and other locations north of Leyte Gulf, the other roamed the waters, searching for the enemy carriers.

On October 21 Halsey asked Kinkaid whether San Bernardino Strait had been swept clean of mines. If the Japanese remained west of the Philippines, he intended to charge through San Bernardino Strait and engage them in the Sibuyan Sea, a risky move into the confining waters of an inland sea. Nimitz, alarmed that his top commander might abandon his eastern post, sent a speedy reminder to Halsey that he was to cover MacArthur, not pursue the Japanese.

Nimitz might have fired off his reminder, but Halsey gave it scant notice. "The Third Fleet was offensive; it prowled the ocean, striking at will with its new battleships and fast carriers," he remarked. As one officer related, Halsey remained focused on enemy carriers, telling his staff that "if a situation arises or can be created for the defeat of the Japanese fleet, that will become the major objective. In other words, the hell with everything else."[22]

Before the battle even began, Halsey prematurely decided that if the Japanese carriers appeared, he would pursue them. Rather than wait and examine each event for what it truly was and adjust his actions accordingly, Halsey molded events to a predetermined pattern. Carriers, not protecting MacArthur's beachhead, occupied Halsey's mind—precisely what Toyoda counted on.

Seeing little evidence that the Japanese were yet coming out to fight, on October 22 Halsey rotated his four carrier groups for reprovisioning at Ulithi. He ordered Vice Admiral John S. McCain back to Ulithi, with Davison's group following the next day. Once those two returned, Halsey would send Bogan's and Sherman's units.

Expectations heightened in the pre-dawn minutes of October 23 when the submarine USS *Darter* radioed that a group of ships had been sighted steaming into the southern entrance to the Palawan Passage 350 miles west of Leyte Gulf. Halsey immediately canceled Davison's departure and ordered his three task groups to refuel and move closer to the

Philippine coast to reduce the flight time westward to the Sibuyan Sea. Halsey guessed that the earliest the Japanese could attack was the next day, and that their assault would include carriers moving down from the north.

While the *Darter* and her companion submarine, USS *Dace*, attacked and sank two cruisers and damaged three other ships, Halsey's carrier forces steamed into position the night of October 23. Rear Admiral Frederick C. Sherman's Task Group 38.3 took station off the Polillo Islands east of Luzon in the northern Philippines. To the southeast, 140 miles distant, Rear Admiral Gerald F. Bogan posted Task Group 38.2 (which included Admiral Halsey) off San Bernardino Strait, while Davison occupied the southernmost position off Leyte Gulf 120 miles southeast of Bogan.

Halsey ordered an exhaustive examination of the western approaches to the Philippines. He assigned each carrier group a search arc extending 300 miles, with teams of one Helldiver bomber and two Hellcat fighters assigned to cover each 10° of arc. As backup, Halsey also stationed additional fighters at 100-mile intervals to relay messages from the search planes to the carriers. In his flagship, the carrier *Essex*, Admiral Sherman worried that this excessive deployment of fighters might hamper his ability to defend himself, but he followed the orders without stating his objections.

All search planes lifted off at daybreak. At 8:20 A.M., one of Bogan's pilots spotted Kurita's five battleships, nine cruisers, and thirteen destroyers south of Mindoro Island steaming into the Sibuyan Sea. At 8:37 Halsey issued the order, "Strike! Repeat: Strike! Good luck!"[23] Nine minutes later he ordered McCain, then 600 miles distant, to reverse course and return to the Philippines.

By sending these orders directly to his carrier task group commanders rather than issuing them first to Mitscher and allowing him to pass it along to his subordinates, Halsey bypassed Mitscher's authority and assumed tactical command, a responsibility that normally would have fallen to Mitscher. Thus shunted to the side while Halsey directed matters, Mitscher became a neutered commander for the duration of the battle. Over the next two crucial days Halsey failed to benefit from Mitscher's expertise as an airman and aviator commander, and the wise counsel he could have provided went unheard.

Believing that Kinkaid's battleships could readily handle any threat that developed to the south, Halsey focused on the Center Force then rushing through the Sibuyan Sea. Because of the unwieldy communications, though, Halsey's change failed to reach Kinkaid. In the absence of word to the contrary, the Seventh Fleet commander assumed that Halsey's aircraft were watching his back.

"BLIND MAN'S BLUFF"

The first action involving Halsey's forces was hardly what he expected. In the north, Admiral Sherman had just turned his carriers into the wind to launch his strike when radar operators picked up four incoming enemy formations of more than 200 aircraft. Sherman, whose fears that he lacked enough fighter strength had materialized, canceled his offensive strike so that his fighters could intercept the oncoming enemy.

Sherman's aviators mounted a stiff defense, but they could not be everywhere. At 9:39 A.M. a Japanese bomber dropped a 550-pound bomb that plunged through the middle of the *Princeton*'s flight deck forward of the elevator. When ammunition stored in lockers started exploding, Captain William H. Buracker issued orders to abandon the ship. Later in the day the cruiser USS *Reno* fired two torpedoes into the carrier that sent her to the bottom.

While Admiral Sherman repelled the Japanese air attack, Bogan and Davison launched their strikes against Kurita. For five hours, from midmorning into the afternoon, American carrier planes hit Kurita's forces steaming across the Sibuyan Sea on the Philippines' western side five separate times. In 259 sorties Halsey's pilots landed 17 bomb and 19 torpedo hits and sank the giant battleship *Musashi*, damaged the battleships *Yamato, Haruna*, and *Nagato*, and forced the cruiser *Myoko* back to Brunei for repairs.

In their after-action reports the aviators reported more damage than actually inflicted. Exaggerated claims led Halsey to believe that Kurita commanded a shattered force, which now could be discounted in favor of searching for a more tempting quarry—enemy carriers. Mitscher, who received similar reports in talking to his aviators, doubted their veracity, but as Halsey had taken over tactical command, said nothing to his superior.

His advice could have been valuable, for Halsey too quickly dismissed Kurita as a threat. Despite his losses, Kurita retained sufficient strength to badly sting the Americans should luck turn his way.

Kurita's staff, fearing that additional American air attacks would annihilate the force, urged the admiral to regroup. When American search planes spotted Kurita's force reversing course in late afternoon, Halsey falsely concluded that Kurita was retiring, when in fact he was only reorganizing for a second approach.

At 5:14 P.M. Kurita turned back toward the Philippines and sent Toyoda a message stating, "Braving any loss and damage we may suffer, the First Striking Force will break into Leyte Gulf and fight to the last man."[24] The first phase of the Battle of Leyte Gulf concluded with Kurita barreling toward the San Bernardino Strait just as Halsey diverted his attention north to locate the Japanese carriers.

Had Halsey ordered more air attacks than the five that occurred, he would have known that Kurita was again advancing toward the Philippines. Halsey could have waited off San Bernardino and allowed Kurita to steam straight into his grasp. "If he had done so, a night engagement against our exhausted force would undoubtedly have been disastrous for us," Kurita's chief of staff, Tomiji Koyanagi wrote. He added, "Thus the enemy missed an opportunity to annihilate the Japanese fleet through his failure to maintain contact in the evening of 24 October."[25]

At 3:12 P.M. Halsey sent a preparatory message to Mitscher, his battleship commander Vice Admiral Willis A. Lee, and his task group commanders stating that he would form Task Force 34, consisting of four battleships, including Halsey's flagship *New Jersey*, two heavy cruisers, three light cruisers, and fourteen destroyers under Lee's command, should it be needed to prevent Kurita from emerging from the strait. To make certain that his commanders understood that he had not yet activated Task Force 34 and that he was only alerting them to the possibility, Halsey later sent a second message via TBS—the short-range Talk Between Ships. Directed to Bogan and Davison, from whose units the new task force would be drawn, the message stated, "If the enemy sorties, TF

34 will be formed *when directed by me* [italics Halsey's]."[26] Until that time the Third Fleet would continue operating as a unit.

Halsey sent these messages only to his subordinates, but as was the custom, Nimitz at Pearl Harbor and Kinkaid at Leyte intercepted and read the first. Both assumed—the first of many assumptions that marred the next twenty-four hours—from reading the plan that Halsey had actually formed Task Force 34 and that it stood off San Bernardino Strait, ready to block Kurita's path toward Leyte Gulf. Unfortunately, neither man could intercept the second message to Bogan and Davison since Halsey transmitted it over the short-range TBS. On the eve of battle the major participants operated on diverse assumptions—Nimitz and Kinkaid assumed that Halsey had blocked the strait's exit, while Halsey assumed they knew otherwise. Kinkaid turned his attention to Nishimura's approaching Southern Force while Halsey looked north to locate the enemy carriers. In the middle lay an unprotected San Bernardino Strait, the avenue toward which Kurita then was heading.

Unaware of the confusion, Halsey scoured the area to his north. The carriers had last been detected in the Inland Sea, indicating their likely approach from the north, but search planes had since reported nothing. According to Halsey his air operations officer, Doug Moulton, "must have said at least 25 to 50 times that day, 'Where in hell are those goddam Nip carriers?'"[27]

It was not for a lack of effort on the part of Ozawa, who sailed with the cruelest orders a commander can receive—to purposely sacrifice his force. He hoped that his strike against Sherman in late morning would draw Halsey toward him, but Halsey assumed that those planes came from one of the Philippine airfields. Ozawa next sent radio transmissions intended for Halsey's interception and dispatched search aircraft meant to be spotted by his opponent, but neither attracted attention. Frustrated, he ordered two hybrid carriers to steam south until they made contact with Halsey.

At 4:40 P.M. American search planes finally spotted Ozawa's main force 200 miles east of Cape Engano at the Philippines' northern tip and 300 miles to Halsey's north. Halsey charted a course toward that surface engagement he had wanted since leaving the Academy in 1904. "This ended my game of blind man's bluff."[28]

CHAPTER 9

"ATTACK WAS HIS WATCHWORD"

"MICK, START THEM NORTH"

With Ozawa's carriers steaming north, at 7:58 P.M. Halsey discussed the alternatives with his staff. In less than half an hour the issue had been settled.

Halsey faced three options. He could keep his entire force off San Bernardino Strait and wait for Kurita to steam toward him while allowing Ozawa to advance. Halsey discounted this step as a passive measure that gave the initiative to the enemy and exposed his fleet to the disadvantage of being struck first.

The second option—leaving Task Force 34 off San Bernardino Strait while taking the rest of the Third Fleet north to engage Ozawa—proved no more alluring to Halsey. Naval doctrine had long emphasized force integrity, and this would divide his unit just as the enemy appeared. Halsey feared that this move would so weaken his two groups that Ozawa in the north and Kurita in the center might be able to "inflict far more damage on my half-fleets separately than they could inflict on the fleet intact."[1]

That left the final option, the one Halsey had intended to adopt all along—taking every ship north to knock out those carriers. This maintained force integrity, and even if a weakened Kurita should emerge from San Bernardino Strait, he believed Kinkaid's three escort carrier groups and battleships possessed enough might to halt a Japanese Center Force that had been mauled by Halsey's aviators the day before. Besides, Kinkaid's search planes were certain to spot Kurita in the strait long before he could do any damage. Halsey would have plenty of time to deal with him if he needed to.

Halsey committed one of the most basic errors a commander can make—he determined ahead of time what he wanted to do, then fit events into his prearranged scheme to conform to his wishes. He was familiar with the Japanese reliance on decoy as a tactic and should have prepared a countermeasure. On March 31 Filipino guerrillas extracted from two crashed Japanese planes copies of Admiral Mineichi Koga's plans for future operations. Koga, who had assumed command after Yamamoto's death, intended to utilize carriers devoid of aircraft to lure American carriers while other units attacked the main objective. Nimitz sent copies of the plan to every Pacific fleet commander, including Halsey. Partly because he feared a decoy would expose the landing elements to Japanese attack, Admiral Spruance kept his carriers close to the Saipan beachhead rather than allow them to pursue enemy surface forces.

But caution was not part of Halsey's makeup. Caution had not guided his actions as a destroyer commander. Caution had not impeded his island raids. Caution had not taken him close to Japan to launch Doolittle's bombers.

Halsey had one other option. He could have taken the entire Third Fleet north, dispatched Ozawa's forces in a dawn engagement, then raced back to San Bernardino Strait in time to block Kurita. That, however, left little time to execute either task thoroughly and staked success on a razor-thin margin that called for expertise in major unit formations, a skill that Halsey lacked as a fleet commander.

Shortly after 8:00 P.M. Halsey walked into Flag Plot, placed his finger on the Northern Force's reported position 300 miles distant, and said to his chief of staff, "Here's where we're going. Mick, start them north."[2]

"HALSEY LEFT US BARE-ASSED!"

At 8:06 P.M., moments after telling Carney to take the Third Fleet north, Halsey learned from a search plane that the Center Force had turned eastward at twelve knots toward San Bernardino Strait. Assuming Kinkaid could handle the development, Halsey declined to modify his orders. Sixteen minutes later, at 8:22, Halsey sent a dispatch to Kinkaid stating that the Center Force had been badly damaged by his aviators the previous day, and that he was "proceeding north with 3 groups to attack carrier force at dawn."[3] He ordered Bogan and Davison to join Sherman's group off Luzon for the run to the north—giving Halsey eleven fast carriers, six fast battleships, nine cruisers, and forty-four destroyers—and told McCain to stop refueling and return to his post off the Philippines. Having enjoyed little rest during the previous forty-eight hours, Halsey then retired to the emergency cabin for a nap.

He drifted off oblivious to the misconception then harbored by Nimitz and Kinkaid. Both assumed from reading Halsey's message that the Third Fleet commander had sent three carrier groups north while retaining Task Force 34 off San Bernardino Strait, but what they failed to take into account was both the message's precise wording and their compatriot's personality. A closer inspection would have divulged that Halsey had said that *he* was proceeding north with the carriers. As his flagship *New Jersey* was part of Lee's battleship unit, that indicated he had taken not just the carriers, but Task Force 34 with him, leaving the strait unguarded. Kinkaid should have realized as well that Halsey would never leave Lee's battleships behind without air cover. Since the message indicated that he had taken all carrier groups then in the area with him, Kinkaid should have concluded that Halsey had left the strait. Kinkaid's misconceptions were understandable, as he was then involved in directing his own engagement with Japanese forces in Surigao Strait, but Nimitz's headquarters had no such excuse. Both Nimitz and Kinkaid knew from long association that Halsey would never send his carriers into a battle from which he would exclude himself. At this late stage of the war Halsey would not be content to watch from the sidelines, as he had been forced to do at Midway, while his carriers engaged the enemy.

AS THE SHIPS churned their way northward and their commander rested, other Third Fleet officers struggled with Halsey's decision. When Admiral Bogan learned that Kurita had reversed course toward San Bernardino Strait, he personally contacted the flagship and urged Halsey to reconsider, but Halsey's staff dismissed him with a curt, "Yes,

yes, we have that information." Though he believed Halsey "was making one hell of a mistake," and felt confident Halsey could handle both the Northern and Center Forces by splitting his Third Fleet, Bogan concluded that further argument with Halsey's staff was futile. "I doubt very much if it would have had any effect," Bogan said after the war, "because Admiral Halsey talked to me time after time and justified his decision to go north."[4]

Captain James S. Russell, Davison's chief of staff, later claimed that, "Halsey's action [in heading north] was such an obvious mistake to Admiral Davison and me. Davison said, 'Jim, this doesn't look right to me.' I asked him if he wanted to say anything to Mitscher, but he replied no, that Mitscher would have more information." Russell then emphasized, "Halsey erred, but he wanted to get those carriers."[5]

Admiral Lee shared with Halsey's staff his unease over the developments, but received nothing but a simple acknowledgement. Admiral Mitscher thought Halsey was wrong but, having been nudged to the sidelines while Halsey grabbed tactical control, declined to bother his superior. When Mitscher's chief of staff, Captain Arleigh Burke, pressed him to urge Halsey to retain Task Force 34 and a group of carriers at the strait while sending the rest northward, Mitscher refused to take the matter to Halsey. "Well, I think you're right," answered Mitscher, "but I don't know you're right." Adding that Halsey was busy and had enough on his mind, Mitscher then headed to his quarters for some rest.

Later in the night Captain Burke and Commander James Flatley, the operations officer, awakened Mitscher with the information that Kurita had reversed course. "Does Admiral Halsey have that report?" asked the annoyed admiral. When Burke replied in the affirmative, Mitscher, showing his irritation with Halsey's abdication of what Mitscher saw as his responsibility, added, "If he wants my advice, he'll ask for it."[6]

Mitscher, who had more experience handling fast carriers than Halsey, erred by remaining silent. Other officers doubted Halsey's moves that night, but none carried the weight of the high-ranking, respected Mitscher. Had he been more forceful, Mitscher might have tempered Halsey's impulsiveness and convinced Halsey to station Lee off San

Bernardino. His inaction removed a voice of reason when it was most needed.

When so many subordinates disagree with their commander's action, it indicates either that the commander sees something none of the others notice, or that the commander is committing a monumental blunder. By allowing his emotions to overrule his reason, Halsey fell into the latter category. The leader cheered by Marines on Guadalcanal and elevated to hero status by an adoring press was not about to let the Japanese fleet slip away, the fleet that had steamed just beyond his grasp on December 7, at the Battle of the Coral Sea, at Midway, and at Saipan. Halsey, the admiral the American public most associated with carrier air power and who posed as a Pacific counterpart to General George Patton, could accept criticism as long as it originated from being overaggressive rather than from timidity. Faced with guarding a static strait or pursuing enemy carriers, Halsey never hesitated. Halsey and his air power thus headed away from San Bernardino Strait just as Kurita steamed toward it, precisely what the Japanese had hoped. As Halsey neared the carrier battle he had long wanted, the door to Leyte Gulf lay wide open to the Center Force.

While Halsey slept, Kurita prepared for battle as his twenty-three warships neared the eastern end of San Bernardino Strait. Rushing out into the open waters of the Philippine Sea thirty-five minutes after midnight, officers and crew aboard each ship stared into the darkness, expecting at any moment a cascade of American shells, but only silence and light winds greeted them. Nothing but water, it appeared, stood between them and MacArthur's transports inside Leyte Gulf. Through a combination of overconfidence, reliance on exaggerated battle reports, and faulty assumptions, Halsey had been lured away. Kurita had drawn within sight of his goal.

Somewhat refreshed from his brief rest, Halsey returned to Flag Plot to check on recent developments. Around 1:00 A.M. on October 25, he ordered his ships to lower their speed to less than twenty-five knots so that they would not mistakenly steam by the enemy in the dark or become involved in one of those night battles for which the Japanese were so famous. Anticipation rose that the surface action lay just ahead.

At 2:05 Halsey's aircraft spotted Japanese ships eighty miles to Halsey's north. Wanting to avoid a night attack, Halsey delayed launching. He preferred to close the distance between him and the enemy and hit Ozawa with a powerful dawn strike.

At 6:30 Halsey launched his first strike of 180 aircraft. Forty minutes later, he received the report that the enemy force included at least four aircraft carriers. Halsey now had in his sights Japan's most valued naval commodity. If he could crush them, he believed he could terminate Japan's naval power in the Pacific and open the road to Tokyo.

At 6:48, as Halsey's planes winged toward Ozawa, 250 miles to the south Kurita's ships steamed within view of Taffy 3, an outgunned collection of six escort carriers and seven escorting vessels then guarding the northern approach to Leyte Gulf. Rear Admiral Ziggy Sprague, commander of Taffy 3, could hardly believe that an enemy surface force had suddenly appeared on his flank. Fewer than forty-eight hours earlier one of Sprague's pilots had flown over Halsey's Third Fleet and claimed that he "felt well-protected because this huge group was nearby."[7] Somehow, the Japanese had punched through and placed Sprague's tiny ships in their sites.

"It's impossible! It can't be, it can't be!" Sprague shouted in consternation, yet his eyes did not deceive him. Then, his voice rising loud enough to be heard above the bridge by Lieutenant Vernon D. Hipchings Jr., Sprague's visual fighter-director officer, Sprague screeched, "That son-of-a-bitch Halsey has left us bare-assed!"[8]

"I HATE TO LET GO"

A frenzied period now unfolded that included heroics on Sprague's part and a series of messages that ricocheted from Halsey to Kinkaid to Sprague to Nimitz to King. From 6:48 A.M. until 10:00 A.M., overworked radio operators aboard the *New Jersey* inundated Flag Plot with messages that altered Halsey's mood from anticipation to shock, then surprise, numbness, and anger. The 3-hour 12-minute span so vexed Halsey that, years later in his autobiography, he still proclaimed of the time, "Now I come to the part of this narrative that I can hardly bring myself to write, so painfully does it rankle still."[9]

The drama actually commenced around 4:00 A.M. when Admiral Kinkaid met with his staff. After concluding matters, he asked if anything else remained. His operations officer, Captain Richard H. Cruzen, reminded him that while they assumed Halsey had left Task Force 34 behind at San Bernardino Strait, they had never directly asked Halsey if he had done so. Kinkaid later stated that he had no reason to think Halsey had done otherwise, as stationing ships at the exit seemed the logical step, but he agreed that the assumption should be confirmed.

At 4:12 King dispatched the question that, if asked a few hours earlier, might have led to a different outcome. "Our surface forces now engaged enemy surface forces Surigao Strait entrance to Leyte Gulf," began the message. Kinkaid then came to the crux of the issue. "Question. Is TF 34 guarding San Bernardino Strait?"[10]

Divided command now muddled the issue. Since Kinkaid functioned under MacArthur's supervision, he first had to send the coded message to a radio station at Manus in MacArthur's domain, where operators decoded the message and relayed it to Halsey. Kinkaid marked the dispatch as urgent, but with events off the Philippines accelerating, many messages bore that label. Manus operators stacked the dispatches in the order in which they arrived or simply grabbed one they thought looked important. Messages piled up, delays lasting hours occurred, and dispatches were forwarded to Halsey out of sequence. Halsey and Kinkaid consequently were rarely on the same page as to events and based judgments on faulty observations. Kinkaid's 4:12 dispatch did not arrive at Halsey's flagship until 6:48, more than two and one half hours later. At that same moment, Kurita already had his gun sites on Sprague's escort carriers.

Officers in the *New Jersey* Flag Plot considered Kinkaid's query as an irritant that distracted their focus on more important matters to the north. Lieutenant Solberg, then watching the messages come in, recalled that after reading the dispatch Halsey's staff responded "with almost a 'Why do you ask?' air. . ."[11] Halsey wondered why Kinkaid even sent the message, as he thought he had earlier made it clear that he had taken every ship north. At 7:05, almost three hours after Kinkaid needed the information, Halsey replied that Task Force 34 was then with the Third Fleet attacking the Japanese carriers.

According to Solberg, the pace of events quickened over the next hour as "a flurry of messages filled Flag Plot."[12] Anxieties dimmed at 8:02 when Halsey received Kinkaid's message—sent at 6:23—that his ships were then pursuing the Japanese Southern Force after successfully repelling them at Surigao Strait 200 miles south of San Bernardino Strait. Relief turned to elation the next minute when the first of Halsey's carrier aviators' reports flooded into Flag Plot that they had begun their attack on Ozawa's carriers. Halsey could soon expect to enjoy a ringside seat at that elusive surface engagement that so many of his comrades had enjoyed.

His jubilation lasted only twenty minutes when a third message, sent in plain English by Admiral Sprague to both speed the process and underscore the severity of the situation, informed Halsey that enemy battleships and cruisers were firing on his unit. Kinkaid, still waiting for Halsey's reply to his message inquiring about Task Force 34, now realized for the first time that Halsey had left the strait unguarded. With shells splashing about Sprague's tiny ships, Kinkaid concluded, "At this point, the situation appeared very critical."[13]

Halsey stared at the information. How, he wondered, had Kinkaid allowed the Japanese to approach? Halsey concluded that Kinkaid's eighteen escort carriers could hold off Kurita long enough for Kinkaid to rush help to the area, but with his gaze fixed on Ozawa's carriers, Halsey overlooked crucial details. Sprague's carriers were little more than patrol and resupply vessels, not combatant ships, and they possessed few guns with which to impede Kurita. He also ignored the fact that Kinkaid's battleships could not reach Sprague for three hours.

The same ships Halsey thought he had destroyed one day earlier were now firing on American vessels. Halsey felt pulled in opposite directions—Ozawa's carriers bobbed temptingly close to the north, while Kinkaid needed help to the south.

Lieutenant John Marshall, an officer in Flag Plot, observed Halsey sitting quietly on his transom, pondering the crisis. One time he blurted to no one in particular, as if expressing a thought to himself, "When I get my teeth into something, I hate to let go." He then lapsed into silence again.

After musing for a time, Halsey remained convinced that Kurita lacked sufficient power to shoot his way into Leyte Gulf. His aviators had inflicted too much damage the day before, and too much naval might stood between Kurita and the gulf. He thus chose to retain Lee's battleships for the impending battle against Ozawa.

"'Attack Repeat Attack' had been Halsey's message from Nouméa to the carriers back in the dark days of 1942 when the Japanese threatened to force us out of Guadalcanal," wrote Solberg. "And attack was his watchword now."[14]

At 8:30 A.M., eight minutes after receiving that dispatch, Halsey received Kinkaid's fourth message, another request for assistance. "Fast battleships are urgently needed immediately at Leyte Gulf,"[15] Kinkaid relayed. Solberg compared the mood in Flag Plot to a yo-yo, and Halsey could not imagine that the Seventh Fleet commander would ask Halsey to abandon his mission and rush to Kinkaid's aid.

Halsey's eagerness to meet Ozawa increased at 8:50 when the aviators from his first air strike against the Northern Force reported they had sunk one of the four enemy carriers and damaged two others. Halsey immediately ordered Lee to increase his speed to twenty-five knots so he could attack Ozawa's hamstrung force. Halsey figured that by noon at the latest, a little more than three hours away, he would be an eyewitness to Ozawa's dismantling.

Just as he was about to grasp the moment for which he had waited since his Academy days, at 9:00 Halsey received Kinkaid's fifth message, this one conveying more urgency than its predecessors. "Enemy force attacked our CVEs [escort carriers] composed of 4 bbs [battleships] 8 cruisers and other ships. Request Lee proceed top speed to cover Leyte. Request immediate strike by fast carriers."[16]

Halsey could hardly ignore such a blatant plea for help. He ordered McCain's Task Group 38.1, then fueling far to the east, to start back toward Leyte Gulf. Halsey knew McCain could not arrive in time to make much difference for Sprague's escort carriers, but it was all he could do, or was willing to do, at this point.

Aboard the fast carrier USS *Franklin,* Rear Admiral Davison and his chief of staff, Captain James S. Russell, gave Sprague little chance to escape Kurita's mighty guns. "When we got Ziggy's [Sprague's] message," explained Russell, "we knew he was in a bad spot because we thought Lee should have been detached. Admiral Davison and I almost had the feeling toward Halsey, 'What the hell, we told you so!'"[17]

Lieutenant Robb White, the CinCPac public relations staff member observing the events off Samar from an escort carrier, later wrote that the officers and men aboard the carrier "are wishing that aid would come and knowing that it will not . . . the great and famous Task Force 38 [Halsey's force] is far to the north. No help is coming."[18]

"WHERE IS TASK FORCE THIRTY-FOUR?"

Halsey chafed at his post aboard the *New Jersey,* but his reaction to the messages so far was calm compared to what next unfolded. At 9:22 A.M. Kinkaid again requested an immediate air and battleship strike against Kurita, but what startled Halsey were the message's last five words. "My OBBs [battleships] low in ammunition."[19] The information indicated that even if Kinkaid's battleships arrived in time to help Sprague, they had little with which to impede Kurita's progress toward the gulf.

Halsey admitted that until this message he had assumed Kinkaid could deal with the events. "Low on ammunition! Here was a new factor," Halsey wrote, "so astonishing that I could hardly accept it. Why hadn't Kinkaid let me know before?"[20] Halsey then noticed the date-time of the dispatch and saw that Kinkaid had sent it at 7:25, almost two hours earlier. By the time he had all the facts, Halsey was too far north to play any significant role in assisting Kinkaid. Halsey replied to Kinkaid that he was then engaging the Japanese carriers, but that McCain and his five carriers had been ordered to their assistance.

"Here I was on the brink of a critical battle," Halsey stated, "and my kid brother was yelling for help around the corner." He felt as if someone tugged at his sleeve from behind while he faced a different task in front. "There was nothing else I could do, except become angrier."[21] Halsey overlooked one key fact—his desire to engage enemy carriers, a longing inflamed by Nimitz's dictum to pursue the fleet, had blinded him to the fact that protecting his kid brothers, in this case Kinkaid and Sprague, was precisely his mission.

That message, however disturbing, was merely an appetizer to the two that followed simultaneously. At 10:00 A.M. the seventh dispatch from Kinkaid painted a dire picture about events to the south. "My situation is critical," Kinkaid transmitted. "Fast battleships and support by air strike may be able to prevent enemy from destroying CVEs and entering Leyte."[22]

At Pearl Harbor, a nervous Nimitz told his assistant chief of staff, Captain Bernard Austin, that he was worried because nothing in Halsey's dispatches indicated that he had stationed a unit off San Bernardino Strait. Austin suggested querying Halsey about the matter, but Nimitz held back out of fear that he might be interfering with the commander on the scene. Standing beside Nimitz, Admiral Spruance pointed to a spot on the charts due east of the strait and muttered that if he were in command, he would station his ships at that location to block the strait's exit.

After more anxious moments, Nimitz decided to send a message to Halsey, more as a reminder as to where Task Force 34 should be than a direct order or comment. Austin dictated the dispatch to his yeoman who, sensing urgency, added "RPT" to the dispatch before walking the message to the communications department at Pearl Harbor, where an ensign added padding—unrelated words to confuse the enemy should they crack the coded dispatch—at the front and back ends. The ensign inserted "Turkey trots to water" to the front, while "The world wonders" ended the missive. The dispatch, "Where is Rpt Where is Task Force Thirty-four RR the world wonders"[23] shot from Nimitz's headquarters to Halsey's communications center.

Communicators aboard the *New Jersey* understood that if they received any message marked urgent, they were to rush it to Halsey without wasting time typing it into the proper dispatch form. The ensign in the ship's communications room removed the initial padding, but whereas communicators in every other ship removed the last words, he retained the tail padding. He feared it might be part of the message, even though the double consonant "rr"—the common method of denoting nonsense words—separated the phrase from the other words. The dispatch, including "The world wonders," continued on to Halsey.

Halsey reacted to the message as if he had been jolted by an electric current. "I was stunned as if I had been struck in the face," he recalled. "The paper rattled in my hands. I snatched off my cap, threw it on the deck, and shouted something that I am ashamed to remember." All talking ceased in Flag Plot, while Lieutenant Solberg watched Halsey's face turn red as he tossed the dispatch to the floor and stomped on it. "What right has Chester [Nimitz] to send me a goddamn message like that?"[24] he shouted.

Mick Carney, who had never seen his superior act in such a manner, rushed over, grabbed Halsey's arm, and shouted, "Stop it! What the hell's the matter with you? Pull yourself together!"[25] With Carney in pursuit, Halsey stormed down the ladder to his quarters, where for an hour the chief of staff tried to calm his commander and determine a response. Halsey berated Nimitz for what he then saw as a clear insult and claimed Nimitz and Kinkaid had erred in assuming the location of Task Force 34.

Halsey's vituperative reaction indicates the two thoughts running through his mind—how badly he longed to participate in a surface action against the enemy, and his guilt, conscious or not, that he placed a higher priority on locating the carriers than on shielding Leyte Gulf. Someone with a clear conscience does not typically react with such vehemence as Halsey did that morning, but his bitter response underscores his uncertainty over the correctness of dashing to the north. Again, just as he was about to attain his lifelong goal, he lost it, as if someone were cruelly yanking it away each time he drew close.

At 11:15 A.M., with Task Force 38 only forty-two miles from a crippled Ozawa, Halsey issued the order that finally redirected his ships south—and ended his chances to engage the enemy in a surface action. "I turned my back on the opportunity I had dreamed of since my days as a cadet"[26] at the Naval Academy, Halsey wrote after the war about his bitterest moment.

Halsey formed Task Force 34.5, consisting of his two fast battleships, including the *New Jersey,* escorted by three light cruisers and eight destroyers, with orders to prepare for a night engagement with the Center Force at San Bernardino Strait. As he sped away from the Japanese Northern Force, four waves of Halsey's carrier aircraft hit Ozawa's near-helpless carriers, sinking the *Chitose*, Pearl Harbor veteran *Zuikaku*, and *Zuiho* while a cruiser dispatched the burning *Chiyoda*.

Halsey arrived at San Bernardino Strait too late to battle Kurita who, assuming that Sprague's Taffy 3 was more potent than it was and acting more hesitant after the previous day's pummeling administered by Halsey's aviators, had fled westward through the strait two hours before Halsey appeared. A lone Japanese destroyer searching for survivors was all that remained for Halsey's big guns. His hopes of participating in that major encounter, so high only hours earlier, had crumbled to witnessing his vessels dispatch an outgunned destroyer. "I was able to watch the action from the *New Jersey*'s bridge," wrote Halsey later, "the first and only surface action I saw during my entire career."[27] Halsey had steamed 300 miles north, then raced back 300 miles south, only to miss the enemy at both points.

Search operations for sailors forced to abandon Sprague's sinking escort carriers and destroyers occupied most of the morning on October 26. As Halsey's ships sliced through the waters, crew came upon numerous Japanese survivors clinging to wreckage waiting to be rescued, but no one was sure what to do. Halsey's aide, William Kitchell, hurried to Halsey's cabin for directions. "My God almighty, Admiral. The little bastards are all over the water! Are you going to stop and pick them up?"

"Hell no," Halsey replied. "I have other things to do."

He ordered their locations plotted on charts and wind and tide data recorded to help locate the Japanese later, but for now he intended to focus on rescuing American sailors and aviators. Later in the day, when his force had time to search for enemy survivors, Halsey added a proviso. "Bring in cooperative swimmers. See that others who refuse to cooperate do not reach the beach where they would be potential reinforcements to the garrison there."[28]

Halsey's crews retrieved only six Japanese from the waters. With his orders to shoot "uncooperative" Japanese in the aftermath of a battle in which sailors had lost friends, Halsey handed his men a license to kill on October 26. He unapologetically included the information in his action report, declaring that six survivors had been picked up while "numerous other uncooperative swimmers were observed."[29] The seemingly innocuous phrase glossed over the killings of defenseless Japanese.

Despite Halsey's consternation over his mad October 25 pursuit, the different phases of what is called the Battle of Leyte Gulf terminated the Japanese Navy as a threat for the remainder of the war. American ships and aviators sank four enemy carriers, three battleships, ten cruisers, and nine destroyers against the loss of one light carrier, two escort carriers, two destroyers, and one destroyer escort.[30]

He had almost been the goat. Because of Kurita's timidity in turning away from Sprague's overmatched ships, Halsey escaped the scathing indictments that would have followed had serious damage occurred to American forces inside the gulf.

"LEAVE THE BULL ALONE"

Sensitive about his actions, Halsey issued two messages before the end of the day on which he had upstaged his fellow commanders and broadcast the information as if his had been the directing hand. At 9:26 on October 25 Halsey radioed Nimitz, "It can be announced with assurance that the Japanese navy has been beaten and routed and broken by the Third and Seventh Fleets."[31]

Nimitz forwarded the message to the Navy Department. King planned to withhold the information from the press until a more thorough review of the battle could be completed, but when MacArthur released his own victory bulletin, King followed suit. At 6:00 P.M. Washington time on October 25, President Roosevelt assembled the White House reporters and read Halsey's message, mentioning only the Third Fleet commander by name.

Congratulations from officials and fellow commanders heaped more praise on Halsey. "The Third Fleet has done it again," Secretary of Navy Forrestal wrote Halsey. "My congratulations to you and all hands. The nation and the whole Navy are very proud." George Marshall called the battle, "A splendid and historic victory. The Army owes you a debt of thanks." General MacArthur radioed Halsey, "We have cooperated with you so long that we expect your brilliant successes. Everyone here has a feeling of complete confidence and inspiration when you go into action in our support." Newspaper headlines heralded Halsey's accomplishment. "Main Fleet Broken," declared the

New York Times on October 27. "Halsey Force Inflicts a Staggering Defeat on Enemy off Formosa."[32]

Home-front readers concluded that Halsey, acting on his own, had routed the enemy. His was the name the American public first associated with the victory, not Kinkaid's or Sprague's. A home front accustomed to Halsey's wartime heroics again fell to his spell.

Within an hour of sending his victory announcement, Halsey wired a top-secret dispatch to Nimitz and King attempting to explain his actions on October 25. In the opening phrase of a message Lieutenant Solberg labeled "a don't-tread-on-me dispatch," Halsey declared his clear intention "So that there be no misunderstanding concerning recent operations of the Third Fleet."[33] Halsey then defended his actions and asserted that as Kurita presented no serious menace to Kinkaid because of the damage his aviators had inflicted in the Sibuyan Sea, he was justified in leaving San Bernardino Strait.

That Halsey felt compelled to send such a self-serving message in the immediate hours following the battle indicates the doubts he harbored. Had he possessed more confidence in the appropriateness of his actions, Halsey would not have felt the need to so forcefully defend himself.

Halsey did not stop there. In an action report written on November 14, Halsey pointedly included a statement of his mission. In detailing the Palau operation and Philippine air strikes, the report stated that, "The primary mission of Task Force 38 still remained the seizure of all opportunities, presented or created, to destroy a major portion of the Japanese Fleet."[34]

In a private letter to Nimitz on November 4, Halsey placed blame for any confusion on divided command. He wrote that the "employment of the Seventh Fleet in conjunction with, but separate and independent from the Pacific Fleet has all the elements of confusion if not disaster." Halsey repeated his words in a November 9 letter to Nimitz, and in a November 13 action report labeled the command organization at Leyte "unsound."[35]

In that same November 13 action report Halsey stated that through the combined efforts of the Third and Seventh Fleets, the Japanese had been halted in their attempt to stop MacArthur's landings, and that the

Japanese Fleet had suffered a "crushing defeat" that eliminated it as a "serious naval threat to our operations for many months, if not forever."[36] The clever addition buttressed Halsey's case. In light of what he had accomplished off the Philippines, how could anyone be upset?

Nimitz recognized the potential for a disruptive debate over tactics at Leyte Gulf and never openly criticized Halsey or any other commander. He wrestled with the issue for three days before sending King a letter marked "PERSONAL" and "TOP SECRET" in which he concluded that Halsey's dispatch to him in the battle's aftermath showed the commander's sensitivity to his actions. He believed that Halsey should have left Lee's battleships behind at the strait, and wrote King, "It never occurred to me that Halsey, knowing the composition of the ships in the Sibuyan Sea, would leave San Bernardino Strait unguarded, even though the Jap detachments in the Sibuyan Sea had been reported seriously damaged." Nimitz ended by attributing success at Samar to "special dispensation from the Lord Almighty."[37] However, he also asked his staff to investigate whether Kinkaid had been tardy in sending search planes over the strait.

Nimitz hoped to forestall a debate that could rend the Navy and divert attention from its prime goal of defeating Japan. While attending the Academy at the turn of the century Nimitz had witnessed the debilitating effects of the Sampson-Schley controversy that mired the Navy in divisive squabbles after the Spanish-American War. He vowed that if a similar event occurred when he commanded forces, he would stifle the debate before it had a chance to harm the Navy. Nimitz not only refused to allow public criticism of Halsey, Kinkaid, or anyone else involved, but moved speedily to eliminate harsh judgments from official records that one day would be made public. When the head of his analytical section, Captain Ralph C. Parker, sharply condemned Halsey in the first official CinCPac report of Leyte Gulf, Nimitz rejected it and ordered Parker to craft a second, less critical version. Nimitz wrote across the report's cover page, "What are you trying to do, Parker, start another Sampson-Schley controversy? Tone this down."[38]

Nimitz and King considered the future of naval aviation in any controversy. Sentiment for a separate Air Force encompassing all aspects of aviation, including the Navy's, had gained momentum in Washington.

King and every other naval aviator vehemently argued against removing carrier air power from the Navy. Anything that cast the Navy in a poor light—as a controversy over Leyte Gulf most assuredly would—was avoided or swept under the rug.

After examining the battle reports, King suggested to Nimitz the next month that Halsey needed a rest, but he tempered his opinion by January. When Halsey visited King in Washington that month, King told him Halsey had his approval for everything he did off Samar.

Kinkaid, understandably, castigated Halsey for allowing Kurita to slip through the strait undetected while Clifton Sprague, the valiant commander of Taffy 3, explained that he, along with Kinkaid and Nimitz, had assumed Halsey had remained on station to his north rather than leaving him unprotected. Other commanders were kinder. When MacArthur heard his staff criticizing Halsey at dinner, he pounded the table to get everyone's attention. "That's enough. Leave the Bull alone. He's still a fighting admiral in my book."[39] Raymond Spruance, the man Halsey believed had too cautiously commanded at Saipan, wrote his wife, Margaret, that what happened at Samar did not surprise him, but that he would not condemn Halsey for his actions. Like few others in the country, Spruance knew the pressures and demands made of commanders in battle, and whatever one's conclusions, Halsey had contributed to a decisive victory at Leyte Gulf.

In December Congress authorized the elevation of four generals and four admirals to five-star rank in an effort to match Britain's posts of field marshal and admiral of the fleet. Halsey expected to receive one of the four Navy nods, but after the Navy Department chose King, Nimitz, and Roosevelt's chief of staff, Admiral William D. Leahy, the final spot remained open until after the war as debate raged over whether Halsey or Spruance should receive it. Halsey eventually became a fleet admiral, but some considered the delay as a sign that the Navy blamed Halsey for the near-debacle off the Philippines.

More than anything, Nimitz and King recognized that the Navy and the American public needed Halsey on the front lines. Who else in the Pacific possessed Halsey's charisma or had his touch with the press? Few admirals better served their country than Nimitz and Spruance, but they consciously shunned the limelight. Halsey's utterances, on the other hand, made banner headlines. In the Pacific, where MacArthur dominated news coverage, Halsey kept the Navy on the front pages.

Not only now, but twice more in the coming months when Halsey tangled with typhoons, King toyed with the idea of removing Halsey, but opted not to sack the popular admiral. "He is the greatest leader of men that we have," King told staff members. "The men are crazy about him, and they will follow him anywhere." In speaking to Carney, King termed Halsey "a national asset" and said that he would support him "as long as Halsey could stay at sea and fight. King considered that he must be one of the combat leaders as long as his spirit, his determination, and his health held up." King also could not dispute that, even though Halsey's actions drew criticism, they had been made while taking the offensive. One of King's staff claimed that King retained Halsey for the same reasons Lincoln kept Grant in command. "I'll keep him. He fights."[40]

Nimitz never forgot the aid Halsey gave him after Pearl Harbor. When Nimitz, newly named to succeed Kimmel, proposed an aggressive reaction to December 7, Halsey supported him against vigorous opposition from Kimmel's staff. Halsey's carrier experience lent credibility to Nimitz's plans, and now that Halsey was under fire, Nimitz declined to lead the posse. "Bill Halsey came to my support and offered to lead the attack. I'll not be a party to any enterprise that can hurt the reputation of a man like that."[41]

For the rest of his life Halsey believed he had acted properly by going north at Samar, even though at times he admitted to a few doubts. He mentioned in his action report that he "regrets the loss of a long-awaited opportunity to slug it out with guns against the guns of the enemy, . . ."[42] but also gloomily suggested that it might have been better if he had commanded at Saipan and Spruance been in command at Samar.

"IT'S YOUR FAULT"

It appears that neither King nor Nimitz realized how fatigued Halsey was. He had been in almost continuous command since December 7,

1941, carrying enormous responsibilities that weighed on men half his age. Halsey consequently did not enter the fight at Leyte Gulf, according to Spruance biographer Thomas Buell, with as firm a grasp on matters. The confusion and lightning pace of events, combined with his exhaustion, produced more than Halsey could then handle.

At the same time, Halsey declined to take advantage of the carrier commanders serving under him. Mitscher, Bogan, and Sherman had knowledge and experience that could have benefited Halsey, but he largely ignored them. At times Halsey commanded from the *New Jersey* as if he existed in a cocoon, shielded from the outside by his Third Fleet staff.

Thus insulated, and driven by his craving to engage enemy carriers, Halsey saw events off Samar as he wanted to see them, not as they actually unfolded. Instead of evaluating events with an open mind, he relied on assumptions that buttressed his predisposed intentions. He assumed that his aviators' exaggerated reports were accurate and that Kurita, badly mauled in the Sibuyan Sea, would never think of returning toward San Bernardino Strait. When Kurita reversed course, Halsey assumed Kinkaid possessed enough power to handle the threat.

A fairly simple solution existed—Halsey only needed to leave a detachment behind to guard the strait while he took the bulk of his forces north. As he chased Ozawa with his carrier air arm, Halsey's detached unit could lie off San Bernardino and pick off Kurita's ships in piecemeal fashion as they exited the strait. But, again following the dictates learned at the Naval War College in the 1930s, and longing to command the strongest force possible, Halsey refused to split his forces.

The words and deeds of the 1942 Halsey trapped the 1944 version. The public had fallen in love with the heroic actions and outrageous words of the "Bull." He built a reputation based on aggression and offense at a time when the Japanese seemed to have a monopoly on such traits, and blessed with a devoted home-front following, Halsey could hardly do less in 1944. Delighted with his raids and with his litany of quotable phrases, home-front audiences grew to expect the same from Halsey—attack. When faced with events at Samar, Halsey could hardly do otherwise. His nation expected it, so he would pursue the carriers.

Though criticism remained focused on Halsey, a number of individuals and factors contributed to the near-disaster off Samar. Divided command caused confusion when clarity was needed. Had one man been in charge, whether MacArthur or Nimitz, a direct line of communications might have avoided the chaos that marked the fighting. Nimitz, however, deserves most of the blame for the confusion at Leyte. Halsey was, after all, being Halsey. Fully cognizant of his subordinate's demeanor, Nimitz muddied the waters by issuing his added directive, an order he knew Halsey would follow should the opportunity arise. He gave Halsey his consent to chase after the carriers, an action at variance with the orders under which Kinkaid and Sprague operated. Handing Halsey such an order and then expecting him not to follow it was naïve at best, foolish at worst. Everyone, including Nimitz, knew that when given the choice between carriers and a strait, Halsey would attack the carriers. Nimitz stumbled in giving Halsey free rein at Leyte. Halsey could not help being Halsey, but Nimitz could have better guided his subordinate.

Nimitz's son, submarine officer Lieutenant Commander. Chester W. Nimitz, Jr., recognized the error. On the evening of October 25, with the battle only a few hours concluded, the two shared cocktails. In front of other high-ranking officers, the son quizzed his father about the day's events. The son told his father that he had given Halsey too much freedom with the added directive, and said of the near-calamity that unfolded, "it's your fault." Admiral Nimitz looked stiffly toward his son and curtly ended the discussion with, "That's your opinion."[43]

Another factor paints a kind picture. Though he shares the blame for leaving San Bernardino Strait open, an action that helped lead to the loss of four ships and hundreds of Taffy 3 men, as E. B. Potter stated in his biography, Halsey compensated with his recommendation to forego the Mindanao assault and move directly to Leyte. Had the Leyte operation occurred as previously scheduled, the Japanese would have enjoyed more time to fortify their positions in the Philippines, resupply Ozawa's carriers, and train his aviators. With the stronger defense, Japan could have inflicted greater casualties on the invaders and lengthened the war. Potter contends, somewhat generously, that Halsey's contribution in hastening the pace of the war offsets the tactical failures on October 25.

Even Halsey might have had difficulty accepting Potter's munificence. When he bumped into Clifton Sprague at Ulithi the next year, the first time he encountered the Taffy 3 commander since the battle, a sheepish Halsey said, "Zeegee [Sprague's nickname], I didn't know whether you would speak to me or not." Sprague, who had castigated Halsey in a private letter to his wife, Annabel, as "The gentleman who failed to keep his appointment last October," replied that he bore no anger toward him. Halsey answered, "I want you to know I think you wrote the most glorious page in American Naval History that day" and continued to praise Sprague so effusively that Sprague called it "embarrasing [sic]."[44] Halsey's roundabout way of apologizing revealed his doubts over what he had done at Samar.

CHAPTER 10

"A WHOLLY FRIGHTENING SITUATION"

"A WEAPON FAR AHEAD OF ITS TIME"

In the aftermath of Leyte Gulf, Halsey hoped to provide a break at Ulithi for his exhausted crews, after which he planned to lead his carriers within striking range of the Home Islands for the first direct assaults against Japan since the Doolittle Raid. Unforeseen torrential rains that retarded the development of air bases in the Philippines, and stiff Japanese resistance, forced him to instead remain off the Philippines to provide air support for MacArthur.

From November 5 until November 25 Halsey's Task Force 38 aircraft mounted seven major strikes against Luzon in which they bombed installations, destroyed nearly 800 Japanese aircraft, and wiped out five enemy transports carrying 10,000 Japanese soldiers and their three escorting destroyers. He so efficiently neutralized enemy opposition that on November 18 he cancelled plans for additional strikes. "Bull Halsey's 3rd Fleet has been doing quite a job on the Japs on Luzon," observed Seaman First Class James J. Fahey aboard the light cruiser USS *Montpelier.* "Old Bull would rather do that than eat."[1]

Halsey was eager to sever the cords with MacArthur, as each day that he operated near the Philippines further exposed his ships to kamikazes.

From late October 1944 until January 1945, suicide aircraft smashed into Third Fleet ships with terrifying frequency, taxing the nerves of men already frayed from long stretches at sea. Halsey, facing a stiff test in the coming months against targets close to and in the Home Islands, needed rest for his crews, but he could not extricate them from combat conditions until MacArthur's land-based air arm could operate effectively on its own.

On October 29, for instance, Halsey could do little but watch from the *New Jersey* as a kamikaze struck the carrier *Intrepid* one half mile away, killing six and wounding ten. The attacks, which made every member of Halsey's Third Fleet, from Halsey to the lowest-rated sailor, feel as if he were standing on a floating bull's-eye, confounded Halsey, who could not conceive how an individual could so willingly embrace death to inflict harm on another. "The psychology behind it was too alien to ours; Americans, who fight to live, find it hard to realize that another people will fight to die." At the same time, he concluded that the kamikazes were "a direct sign of weakness and desperation on the part of the Japanese" and believed "that the beginning crack in the Japanese armor had become apparent."[2]

Halsey had barely regrouped from the day's encounter when six suicide planes struck the next day. They damaged the *Enterprise,* placed a forty-foot hole in the *Franklin*'s flight deck, and opened a large gap in the *Belleau Wood*'s flight deck, in the process killing more than 100 officers and enlisted, wounding 165, and destroying 65 aircraft. "Suffice to say," the *Enterprise* report stated, "'suicide' attack must have been the order of the day for the Jap pilots."[3]

The attacks continued the next month. On November 25 kamikazes struck four carriers as the admiral watched from the *New Jersey* only 900 yards away. Smoke and flames billowed upward more than 1,000 feet, at times completely blocking Halsey's view of the ships.

The November 25 attack goaded Halsey to find improved tactics for dealing with kamikazes. Normal defensive procedure relied on a thick antiaircraft fire curtain, but that allowed the Japanese plane to draw close to the formation. Receiving superb advice and aid from McCain and an officer on McCain's staff, Captain John Thach, Halsey issued new instructions to deal with the threat.

In an attempt to stifle the menace at its source, Halsey started to pin down the Japanese before they lifted off by sending his carrier fighters over Japanese airfields. This step, combined with maintaining a twenty-four-hour combat air patrol over the Third Fleet, required more fighters than his carriers possessed, so he obtained Nimitz's approval to alter their complement. Halsey dropped the number of bombers and torpedo planes to fifteen each while increasing the fighters to seventy-three. He also requested and received two large carriers containing air groups trained in night flying.

Since kamikazes had sometimes followed American aircraft back to their carriers, Halsey stationed picket destroyers at fifty and fifteen miles away from the task force. He ordered his aviators to approach at specified bearings and circle the picket destroyers in a predetermined manner. Any plane not following procedure was assumed to be enemy and would be splashed.

Halsey mounted his combat air patrols at various altitudes and distances from the fleet to counter suicide pilots who skimmed the water in hopes of evading radar, and he stationed fighters at each of the four cardinal points around each task group. Should any kamikaze plane burst through these initial defensive measures, the fleet's antiaircraft guns would hopefully halt the intruder.

Exhaustion magnified the problems plaguing Halsey and lowered his men's efficiency. Many of his sailors had not set foot on shore in almost three months, a condition that inevitably led to slower reactions and inferior work. In late October the *Wasp*'s air group surgeon reported that only 30 of 113 pilots were fit for combat. Though Halsey denied his request for immediate relief, stating that aviators aboard every carrier were weary, he received additional alarms shortly afterward when reports arrived of poor performance and morale among the pilots aboard the *Lexington*.

Lieutenant Solberg wrote that Halsey paced the bridge trying to figure out how to aid his pilots but could not remove them from combat at such a crucial moment. Finally, "he blurted out to no one in particular but just thinking out loud, 'Damn it all, I know they're tired and need a rest. So do all the other carriers. I'd like to give it to them but I can't—the morale of the whole fleet would be gone.'" Solberg added that Halsey "was a tough old salt but he had a heart and it hurt him to deny the rest they deserved."[4]

Halsey finally obtained his break when MacArthur pushed back his planned December 5 assault against Mindoro to December 15. Halsey and the Third Fleet could return to Ulithi for a sorely needed ten days of rest and fun.

Halsey took full advantage of his time at Ulithi, hosting parties that became legendary for their consumption of alcohol and the presence of nurses who worked on the atoll's hospital ships. A young signal officer aboard another vessel, Jerome H. King Jr., recalled reading signals from the *New Jersey* stating, "Send 20 nurses to flagship." According to Evan Thomas's book, *Sea of Thunder,* Halsey arranged for female companionship whenever possible. Halsey's physician, Dr. Carnes Weeks, who carried the extra duties of supervising the ship's liquor supply as well as obtaining nurses for Halsey's parties, wrote his wife in November, "I am running a little party for the Admiral and getting some nurses from a hospital ship—God help them, the nurses I mean!"[5]

"WE WERE COMPLETELY AT ITS MERCY"

On December 11 Halsey led the Third Fleet, now down to three task groups owing to damage from kamikazes, from Ulithi and steered toward Luzon in the northern Philippines. By previous arrangement with MacArthur, Halsey's carriers would suppress Japan's air power in Luzon north of Manila while MacArthur's air general, George C. Kenney—at long last up and operating—handled enemy air south of Manila.

From December 14 to 16 Halsey mounted what his staff called the Big Blue Blanket over Luzon airfields. His carrier aviators bombed and strafed targets around the clock, keeping the enemy's aircraft on the runways and preventing them from striking MacArthur's land forces, which were then commencing the Mindoro attack. Halsey executed his mission so well that not one Luzon-based aircraft threatened the invasion convoy or the assault forces. In the process, his air units destroyed almost 300 enemy aircraft and sank more than 30 ships.

Unfortunately, one of those sunken ships happened to be a transport containing American prisoners of war being shuttled to camps in

China and Japan. Halsey had no way of knowing what the ship carried, but he learned of the tragedy later from two prisoners who had swum ashore from the sinking transport.

Months later Halsey received a letter from the distraught mother of one of the prisoners who died. "Even the detestable Germans occasionally stop and pick up people, whereas you run off and leave them," the mother wrote. "You ought to be hung as a war criminal!"

Halsey empathized with the mother's emotions, but agonized over the letter. "It made him miserable," William Kitchell, Halsey's aide, recounted. "He kept referring to it for days: 'Doesn't she realize that these things are bound to happen in a war?' And he asked us over and over, 'How could our pilots have known?'"[6]

His consternation would soon worsen. On December 17 Halsey steamed to a refueling location 500 miles east of Luzon, specifically selected because it rested outside the range of Japanese land-based aircraft. Though it also placed him inside an area infamous for its December typhoons, Pacific Fleet aerologists spotted nothing alarming.

A 20–30 knot wind buffeted the ships as the refueling started. Halsey had just sat down to eat lunch in his flag mess and could see through an open door the mast of the destroyer USS *Spence* dipping and rolling as the smaller vessel drank fuel from the hoses attached to the *New Jersey*. With the weather intensifying, Halsey worried that the destroyer might collide with the battleship.

Halsey hurriedly ate his lunch so he could stay on top of the matter, and at 12:51 P.M. the concerned commander ceased all refueling and ordered his ships to head on a new course for a rendezvous with an oil tanker 200 miles northwest. In the first of many miscalculations that marred the next twenty-four hours, his staff aerologist informed Halsey that a tropical disturbance had formed 500 miles to the east heading north-northwest, but assured the admiral that along the way it would come upon a cold front and be deflected northeast out of Halsey's track.

The aerologist misjudged the data. Unfortunately, the storm was less than 200 miles from Halsey's ships, gaining speed and strength as it churned directly toward the Third Fleet. Oblivious to this development, Halsey continued refueling so his ships would be prepared for a planned

December 19 air strike against Luzon, a commitment to MacArthur that he intended to keep.

Just to be safe, with the seas rising and fueling again difficult, at 3:33 P.M. Halsey ordered a third course change to the southwest, into what Halsey believed would be calmer waters. Based on his aerologist's conclusions, he thought this would take his ships away from the expanding storm; instead, it set them on a parallel course with the storm.

Worsening seas impeded the Third Fleet as Halsey steamed on his new course. Though the winds had risen to 28 knots by 10:00 P.M., Halsey believed the storm was still hundreds of miles distant.

At 5:00 A.M. on December 18, still seeking calmer waters, Halsey ordered his ships to turn due south, a directive that instead took the Third Fleet directly towards the storm's path. His smaller vessels especially needed fuel, both for air operations against Luzon and for maintaining stability in the worsening waters. The higher a ship rides, as one does when low on fuel, the greater the risk from high winds and waves. A deadly storm would toss destroyers with near-empty tanks as if they were toys.

Halsey resumed fueling at 7:00 A.M. Even his aircraft carriers, the largest ships in his fleet, reported being lashed by pounding seas. By 8:03 A.M. with 43-knot winds and visibility dropping to 500 yards, Halsey canceled refueling, ordered his ships to continue heading south, and notified MacArthur he would have to abort the next day's strikes.

Halsey did not become aware of the storm's full fury until the morning of December 18. Instead of heading on the northeast course predicted by Halsey's aerologist the typhoon dipped south and then continued westward as if it were pursuing Halsey. Caught by nature, all Halsey could do was hope his ships could pass in front of the typhoon's center into the comparatively calmer waters of the navigable semicircle.

Halsey grew more numb as he read the rush of messages calling for help or reporting damage to ship and crew. At 9:07 A.M. the aircraft carrier *Independence* reported a man overboard; four minutes later, planes on the *Monterey*'s hangar deck broke loose and caught fire. In the next thirty minutes the *Independence* lost two additional men overboard and two ships lost their steering. With winds raging at 55 knots, one carrier reported a dangerous 35° roll to both sides. Halsey ordered all ships to adopt whatever course offered the best hope for safety.

Instruments aboard Halsey's *New Jersey* recorded winds of 66 knots at 1:00 P.M. Ten minutes later they soared to 83 knots, with gusts reaching 93 knots. Halsey radioed Nimitz that he was beset by "heavy confused seas, ragged ceiling, heavy rains" and declared that the typhoon, whose full fury had now fallen on the *New Jersey* and Third Fleet, was "of increasing intensity."[7]

Halsey was both fascinated and repelled by the storm's malevolent power. "No one who has not been through a typhoon can conceive its fury," he recalled. "The 70-foot seas smash you from all sides." The *New Jersey* was constructed to withstand strikes from 5-inch shells, said Halsey, "yet this typhoon tossed our enormous ship as if she were a canoe. . . . we could not hear our own voices above the uproar." He thought of those tiny destroyers assailed by the same winds and wondered how they survived. "What it was like on a destroyer one-twentieth the *New Jersey*'s size, I can only imagine."[8]

As the typhoon's center passed within twenty miles of the flagship, Carney held his breath whenever the *New Jersey* lurched to one side or the other. Just as he thought the ship might overturn, the *New Jersey* would halt its maddening flop, remain suspended for a few moments, then swerve in the other direction. Whenever the ship plunged into a trough in the high seas, Halsey and Carney could look upward from the bridge at the waves that threatened to entomb them.

The aircraft carrier *Hancock*'s flight deck, normally standing fifty-seven feet above her waterline, dipped below the waves. The executive officer on one destroyer said, "The wind was howling all through the ship—we were rolling probably 40 degrees—some men were doing their job in a matter of fact way—others were praying or sitting off by themselves, their faces white with fear." As the crew battled to remain on their feet, the wind "howled, whined and finally got back to shrieking again." He added, "We were completely at its mercy wallowing in the trough."[9]

Such fierce winds smacked the carrier *Independence* that twenty-five tons of bombs "roll[ed] around the bomb magazine like beer kegs," and aircraft aboard the *San Jacinto* broke from their restraints and "smashed into other aircraft likewise moored, and tore them loose, ripping out the deck eye-bolts in many instances." The *Independence* action report added that the raging seas "created a wholly frightening situation."[10]

An officer aboard the *Monterey* lost his footing and almost slid overboard when a 70-foot wave rolled the ship 25° to port. As he was about to be swept over the side, he grabbed a 2-inch steel ridge around the carrier's edge and twisted himself onto a catwalk below. Lieutenant (jg) Gerald R. Ford, later to become the thirty-eighth president of the United States, regrouped and led a fire team below decks to extinguish a fire that threatened to rage out of control.

By 2:00 P.M. Halsey noticed a diminishing of the storm. Decreasing winds of 35 knots by 4:00 calmed the seas, enabling ships to better navigate through the waves. With his ships scattered across 2,500 square miles of ocean, Halsey would not soon learn which ships had weathered the ordeal and how many sailors he lost.

"AN INGLORIOUS HOUR FOR OUR ADMIRAL"

At 6:48 P.M., as soon as the storm abated, Halsey directed every ship to search the waters through which the fleet had passed and ordered planes to carry additional life rafts to drop into the water. Halsey extended the search for the next two days, but few survivors were located.

The storm had badly damaged seven ships and destroyed nearly 200 aircraft. Worst, though, were the missing crews. Three destroyers that had not had time to ballast their empty fuel tanks with seawater, the *Hull, Spence,* and *Monaghan,* sank. Of more than 800 crew from the three vessels, only 74 survived, including just 6 from *Monaghan.* In losing nearly 800 men to the typhoon, Halsey absorbed as much damage as if he had been in a major surface engagement with the Imperial Japanese Fleet.

"It was the Navy's greatest uncompensated loss since the Battle of Savo Island," Halsey concluded in comparing his December 1944 ordeal to the crushing August 1942 American defeat in the waters off Guadalcanal. "The losses and damage far exceeded any the enemy had been able to inflict." Lieutenant Solberg summed up the mood of Halsey and his staff by admitting the encounter had been "an inglorious hour for our admiral."[11]

On December 22 Halsey ordered the Third Fleet to Ulithi for repairs. Almost as soon as Halsey dropped anchor, Nimitz stepped aboard to confer with his colleague about the typhoon. Afterward, Nimitz ordered a court of inquiry to determine the facts and to assess blame for the mishap.

On December 26 the Court of Inquiry convened aboard the destroyer USS *Cascade* in Ulithi Lagoon. Chaired by Vice Admiral John H. Hoover, working with Vice Admiral George D. Murray and Rear Admiral Glenn B. Davis, the court called numerous officers and other survivors of the typhoon, including Halsey, McCain, and Bogan.

Bogan's testimony was typical. He contended that Halsey could have avoided most of the damage had he set a southerly course sooner than he did, a recommendation he had sent to McCain on December 17. Bogan said later that Halsey had declined to take the measure out of a desire to support MacArthur's operations in the Philippines. That, Bogan contended, blinded Halsey to the facts.

Halsey appeared before the court on December 28. Knowing that his actions during the typhoon had created a controversy, Halsey came out swinging. When the court asked if he believed he had had a timely warning about the storm's approach, he answered, "I did not have timely warning. I'll put it another way. I had no warning."

Halsey defended his decision to linger in the area rather than steam south as Bogan suggested. He told the court that he had operated under two dictates. "I was under obligation to make a strike on Luzon, but of course a strike could not be made until the fleet was fueled. I was also obligated to avoid by that time what I considered a storm the magnitude of which I did not know." With these words he acknowledged his responsibility to keep his fleet safe from nature, but said that his duties to MacArthur took priority, especially when no signs of a dangerous storm had then appeared.

Halsey argued that the only report mentioning a typhoon came from the *Chandeleur,* and it arrived ten to twelve hours late. It was not until the forenoon of December 18 that he became aware "that we were very close to a violent disturbance of some kind, which I believed was a typhoon. We were completely cornered and in the dangerous semicircle. The consideration then was the fastest way to get out of the dangerous semicircle and get to a position where our destroyers could be fueled."[12]

Halsey then repeated the motivation that guided his actions for much of the time—his duty to aid MacArthur. "That thought of striking Luzon was uppermost in our heads right up to the last minute." Had he been aware of the storm's ferocity, he could have adjusted his orders accordingly, but inadequate weather reporting kept him in the dark. "It was nonexistent," he said of the weather service. "That's the only way I can express it."[13]

He admitted that his aerologist felt the typhoon would hit a high-pressure area coming down from the China coast and be deflected northward and eastward. His aerologist, in fact, had studied December typhoons and concluded that three out of every four curved northward and eastward. Halsey claimed that, owing to the lack of definite knowledge of this storm, he was governed by the aerologist's information and conclusions; left unspoken was Halsey's dismissal of the fact that he might possibly have encountered that treacherous fourth typhoon.

After listening to the testimony, the court assigned blame for the mishap to Halsey. The court stated that Halsey should have issued clearer instructions to his ship commanders about the course they should adopt and that he too long ignored advice from others about the storm's path. While listing these defects, the court determined that Halsey had shown no negligence, but had acted out of a commendable desire to lend support to MacArthur. An inadequate Pacific weather reporting service hamstrung his ability to make informative decisions, and the fast-developing storm sent few indications that it was strengthening into a full-blown typhoon. The court urged the Navy to adopt measures improving ship stability and to open additional weather stations to track typhoons.

In his endorsement to the court's ruling, Nimitz concurred with its findings, but added that his associate's mistakes "were errors of judgment committed under stress of war operations and stemming from a commendable desire to meet military requirements."[14] Nimitz, cognizant of Halsey's compassion toward the men he commanded, believed that Halsey had suffered enough knowing he had led his fleet into a typhoon, and he had no desire to add to the man's embarrassment. Besides, no matter what anyone might think, Halsey was still the nation's most recognizable naval hero, and he told an associate that in time of war you simply do not court-martial a hero.

Admiral King agreed. After taking a month to review the matter, on February 21, 1945 he issued a statement assessing blame to Halsey, but concluded that the commander was not guilty of negligence. Neither Nimitz nor King had any desire to go after a man who had done so much for the war effort.

Nimitz took advantage of the situation to issue a Fleet Letter about typhoons. He stated that even in 1945, when recent advances in aerology made predictions more scientific, a commander could not ignore common sense and personal weather estimates. Commanders should not assume that the absence of a radio report indicating a typhoon did not mean that one did not exist, and emphasized that each ship's commander faced the ultimate duty to keep his ship and crew safe.

The incident mortified Halsey, a man who took pride in his navigational skills and in his concern for the welfare of his men. He rarely discussed the matter afterward, and mail from families who had lost a son or brother in the storm prolonged his agony. Though Halsey offered consolation to those families, he could offer little to himself.

"THE SOUTH CHINA SEA HAD CHANGED OWNERSHIP"

He rebounded with a January raid into the South China Sea that was more reminiscent of the old-time Halsey. He had pestered Nimitz since November 18 for permission to strike Japanese airfields and bases along the Indochina coast and to locate any remnants of the Combined Fleet that had avoided destruction at Leyte Gulf. Nimitz, however, deferring to MacArthur's need for air support, withheld approval until he met with Halsey aboard the *New Jersey* at Ulithi in December. With an improving situation in the Philippines, and possibly as an attempt to bolster his friend's morale, on the same day Halsey appeared before the Court of Inquiry, Nimitz gave him the thumbs-up on the raid.

On January 9 Halsey turned his three task groups toward the South China Sea. While offering benefits, the raid featured risks from the numerous Japanese airfields that lay within easy reach of his ships. He had to strike before they spotted him, both for his own safety and to prevent any navy units in Cam Ranh Bay from fleeing south to Singapore. Halsey intended to take his three groups, with Bogan and Halsey in the van, to the Indochina coast. While his carrier planes bombed shipping inside Cam Ranh Bay, his cruisers and battleships would bombard the bay and counter any resistance from Japanese surface units.

Vintage Halsey reappeared during the next ten days as he transformed the South China Sea into his own domain, steaming 3,800 miles and puncturing a swath of destruction against shoreline targets along 600 miles of the Indochina and Chinese coastlines. Halsey executed a triumphant series of raids—striking one target before withdrawing farther out to sea, then reappearing at a second location to repeat the process. The thrill of an offensive mission replaced the disappointments of Leyte Gulf and the typhoon, medicine for what ailed the old warhorse. For ten days the South China Sea mutated into Halsey's Sea.

He once again returned to what a staff member called "The cavalry tactics of our carrier operations—deception, hit them where we couldn't possibly be, etc." One operations officer, frazzled by the demands of scheduling missions for aircraft that answered Halsey's lightning pace, said "it was a pretty razzle-dazzle outfit. It was kind of like Carlson's Raiders, I guess, and understandably because we were really raiders. We were operating on the spur of the moment, which was certainly good."[15]

It was no coincidence that Spruance received command of most of the major amphibious assaults throughout the Central Pacific, complex operations that suited the more intellectual, methodical admiral. Halsey performed better as a free spirit, much as Stonewall Jackson and his cavalry had in the Civil War, instead of being tied down by orchestrating vast forces.

With Halsey's task group in the lead, Halsey launched dawn strikes on January 12 from only fifty miles out of Cam Ranh Bay. The aircraft pounded shipping convoys and land targets along a 400-mile stretch of the Indochina coast between Saigon and Qui Nhon while the night fighter groups assaulted airfields to keep opposition to a minimum and to prevent suicide planes from lifting off. In almost 1,500 sorties, Halsey's aviators sank 44 ships, including two large convoys totaling 26 ships, and destroyed 15 combatants and 100 aircraft. They demolished docks, airfield installations, and oil storage tanks in what Halsey called one of the most devastating strikes against Japanese shipping in the war. While he lost 23 aircraft, most of the pilots were rescued. "This was an excellent day's work," Halsey declared of the day's efforts, "and was a very strongly worded notice to the Nips that the South China Sea had changed ownership from Japan to the United States of America."[16]

Halsey swerved northward for his next objective—a January 15–16 strike against Formosa and China. On January 15 aviators struck Formosa, destroying or seriously damaging a large factory, ten locomotives, a magnesium plant, railroad yards, warehouses, barracks, and drydocks. The next day they targeted Hong Kong, Canton, Amoy, and the coastal areas in between, as part of what Halsey called "our social call on the China coast," damaging a Texaco oil dump, the Royal Navy Yard, power plants, refineries, and hangars. The air groups scoured every mile of the Indochina coast to find the elusive battleships and cruisers that, according to intelligence, were there, but they found nothing.

Hong Kong's heavy antiaircraft fire, which Halsey described as "a hornet's nest," shot down twenty-two of his airplanes, but the raids proved so effective that "worthwhile targets had become very scarce and I decided to move out of the South China Sea."[17] He informed Nimitz that the situation no longer warranted keeping the Third Fleet in the South China Sea.

Halsey intended to leave via the Balintang Channel between Luzon and Formosa in order to be in a position to hit Formosa and Okinawa, but he worried whether, with Japanese forces on alert now that he had already raided Indochina, the Japanese might be waiting for him to execute precisely that move. Tokyo Rose had already promised dire events for the man the Japanese considered their most infamous villain. "We don't know how you got in," Tokyo Rose boasted of Halsey's entrance into the South China Sea, "but how the hell are you going to get out?"[18] Halsey's worries ceased on January 20 when the Third Fleet entered the Balintang Channel and left the South China Sea without incident.

The next day Halsey veered north and mounted his planned air strikes against Formosa, where pilots sank ten vessels. Okinawa followed on January 22, when aviators destroyed twenty-eight Japanese aircraft and mounted air reconnaissance missions for the upcoming assault on the island.

These strikes terminated Halsey's South China Sea raid and concluded his first tenure as Commander Third Fleet on a triumphant note. Halsey claimed that air opposition in Indochina "appeared as wide open and defenseless from an air and naval standpoint as the Mindanao and Visayas appeared in October." After conducting his raids, Halsey boasted, "The outer defenses of the Japanese Empire no longer include Burma and the Netherlands East Indies; those countries are now isolated outposts, and their products are no longer available to the Japanese war machine except with staggering and prohibitive losses en route."[19]

On January 25 the ships steamed into Ulithi. At midnight on January 27, Halsey turned over command to Admiral Spruance. While Halsey and his staff headed to Pearl Harbor and the United States to rest and plan future operations, Admiral Spruance would lead the ships and crews—now called the Fifth Fleet rather than the Third Fleet—to sea.

"I'LL KEEP HIM. HE FIGHTS"

On January 27 Halsey, accompanied by Rear Admiral Carney and other staff members, departed Ulithi in a Coronado seaplane for Pearl Harbor. He spent the next two weeks working on various reports before flying to the United States and a reunion with family in mid-February.

For the next nine weeks Halsey relaxed, hunted, and inspected various military installations. On March 3 he visited the White House, where President Roosevelt awarded him a Gold Star in lieu of a third Distinguished Service Medal. A proud Fan pinned the medal on her husband as the president watched; the award was given for the accomplishments with the Third Fleet and for administering "a crushing defeat on the Japanese carrier force in the battle off Cape Engano on October 25."[20] Halsey and the president then retired to an upstairs office, where Roosevelt informed him of Russia's pledge to enter the war against Japan and other top secrets. Nothing was said, however, of any new weapon then in the planning stages.

While in Washington a reporter asked Halsey if the emperor's palace had been marked as a target for bombers or carrier aircraft. Halsey answered it was not. "If by chance the B–29's or somebody came over there in an undercast, they might hit it by mistake, but it would have been a mistake," Halsey explained. He then added facetiously, "I'd hate to have them kill Hirohito's white horse, because I want to ride it."[21]

Navy public relations personnel shuddered at the comment. Once the United States had defeated Japan, they were likely to need the emperor's assistance in convincing his people to surrender, and officials feared this remark might stiffen resolve in Tokyo. Their concerns intensified when the American public welcomed Halsey's statement, which received widespread coverage in every major newspaper. The Reno, Nevada, chamber of commerce even sent Halsey a saddle for the postwar ride, and other organizations mailed him a blanket, bridle, lariat, and spurs.

In early April, Halsey returned to Pearl Harbor, where, over the coming weeks, he and his staff polished plans for the Third Fleet. News that Germany had surrendered interrupted his work on May 8. Though delighted that the war against Hitler was over, Halsey saw hard times still remaining for his forces. "Eisenhower's job was finished; ours was not."[22]

With the *New Jersey* in a navy yard for repairs, Halsey asked to be given her sister ship, *Missouri,* as his flagship. As Halsey hoisted his flag aboard the vessel at Guam on May 18, he fondly recalled the service he had performed aboard another *Missouri* in starting his career thirty years earlier. Three days later, the battleship steamed out of Guam and adopted a course northwest for Okinawa, where Halsey would relieve Spruance.

As his ship arrived off Okinawa's coast, Halsey ordered the gunners to fire a few rounds at Japanese positions ashore, explaining, "I wanted him to know I was back." At midnight on May 27 Halsey officially relieved Spruance and once again commanded the Third Fleet. "I was delighted, as we were raring to go."[23]

Though anxious to break free and strike Japan, Halsey had to remain off Okinawa and provide air support for the forces ashore, who were still facing stiff opposition from the Japanese. Any doubts that his aircraft were needed dissolved that first night when the enemy launched one of the most violent kamikaze attacks of the campaign. More than

150 aircraft, which the Third Fleet War Diary called "suiciders,"[24] attacked over a twenty-four-hour period and sank or damaged fourteen American ships. Halsey watched as his ships and aircraft splashed over one hundred of the kamikazes.

When Halsey met with Spruance, his longtime friend explained that the Army's delay in installing radar, which could give his ships more time to prepare for approaching kamikaze attacks, was hampering his operations at sea. That same day Halsey headed to shore to confer with Army and Marine commanders. Though he brought quarts of whiskey as peace offerings, Halsey also informed his hosts that he could not provide air cover to the degree needed until the radar stations were activated.

Always in his sights, lying temptingly close to the northeast, stood Japan. A *New York Times* reporter mentioned this in an article written after Halsey met with reporters that first week in June. "An offensive mood hangs over the Third Fleet with the return of Admiral Halsey to the wars. There is a general feeling that his return will mean more trouble and more surprises for Japan just as it always has."[25]

Though occupied with Okinawa operations for the next two weeks, Halsey was also able to hit the Home Islands. He sent aircraft northward to strike airfields on the southern island of Kyushu on three of June's first eight days, but his elation over finally striking Japan proper came to a dramatic end. Nature had returned.

"On 3 June 1945 a tropical disturbance was reported East of the Philippines and there began a most unfortunate series of events which culminated in extensive storm damage to many ships of the Third Fleet,"[26] said Halsey of once again being trapped by a typhoon. Early indications that a threat brewed occurred on June 1, when Weather Central at Guam issued a warning that a storm had formed north of the Palaus. Two days later a pilot reported the storm 360 miles east of Manila and tracking to the north, which if true placed Halsey's ships in jeopardy.

Based on incorrect estimates that plotted the storm farther to the west and on a northerly course, Halsey steamed east-southeast to avoid the turbulence. When he learned a few hours later that the typhoon stood farther south than he expected and was barreling directly toward the Third Fleet, he consulted his aerologist, who recommended a second course change to the northwest. Halsey issued the order at 1:34 on June 5, believing the new course would, at worst, take them safely into the navigable portion of the storm.

At 4:01 A.M. Rear Admiral J. J. "Jocko" Clark, commander of Task Group 38.1, informed McCain that if they maintained a northerly course, they would run directly into the worst of the typhoon. He asked permission to change course to south-southeast, but McCain lingered for twenty minutes, asking Halsey for advice and checking his own charts. Finally, at 4:35, McCain granted Clark, then twenty miles south, permission to change his course, but by then the typhoon had already started rocking Clark's ships. Two of Halsey's three task forces steamed through the roughest portion of the typhoon, while twenty miles to the north McCain's group, containing Halsey and the flagship, churned through relatively calm waters.

Seventy-foot waves and gusts up to 127 knots buffeted the fleet, but no ship succumbed to the storm. Many suffered damage, more than fifty aircraft were swept overboard or damaged beyond repair, and six men were killed, but the losses paled compared to December's debacle.

Halsey turned back to Leyte on June 10, arriving three days later. He knew he would have to account for his actions in taking the Third Fleet into a second typhoon in six months. He immediately defended his actions, first in a message to Nimitz in which he again, as he had in December, blamed incorrect estimates, delayed messages, and a lack of sufficient weather information.

For eight days commencing on June 15 the court, again headed by Admiral Hoover, listened to testimony. The court issued its opinion that Halsey had ignored the lessons of the first typhoon, that his course change to the northwest at 1:34 A.M. caused most of the damage suffered, and that McCain had erred in delaying his approval to Jocko Clark. The court urged that serious thought be given to transferring both Halsey and McCain from their current posts.

Secretary of the Navy Forrestal agreed with the harsh censure and wanted to remove Halsey. Admiral King concurred, but as in December he argued that he could hardly remove a hero of Halsey's stature without causing irreparable harm to morale. He added that a removal was unjust punishment for a man who had given so much to the war effort, and that it would create negative publicity for the Navy just as the war entered its final stages. Though reluctant, Forrestal followed King's counsel to retain Halsey.

Though furious with Halsey for again blundering at sea, Nimitz counseled patience with his commander. How could he justify the removal of the popular Halsey, especially in light of the fact that Halsey's image then graced the July 23 issue of *Time* magazine, perched significantly above his slogan, "Kill Japs, kill Japs, and then kill more Japs"?[27]

McCain became the scapegoat. In mid-July Nimitz informed the admiral that he would be relieved of duty and reassigned as deputy head of the Veterans Administration. By the slimmest of margins, Halsey had escaped censure and been given the opportunity to make amends.

He would have only two months in which to atone for his mishaps.

CHAPTER 11

"VICTORY HAS CROWNED YOUR EFFORTS"

For the next two months, Halsey's three task groups steamed at will off Japan's coast, strafing and bombing airfields and installations and bombarding industrial targets. "Our planes would strike inland; our big guns would bombard coastal targets," stated Halsey, and "together they would literally bring the war home to the average Japanese citizen." Each bomb was Halsey's payback for those ships he saw smoking on Pearl Harbor's bottom on December 7, 1941. As Carney recalled, Halsey "set about the business of completely destroying every vestige of major naval power in Japan. Call this what you will, it was a deep-seated feeling in the minds of all of us that the ignominy of Pearl Harbor would never be wiped off the slate until they had been repaid in full, and until they were utterly destroyed."[1]

"INTO THE ENEMY'S JAWS"

Halsey selected Japan's most important center for his first raids. On July 10 he launched 1,160 sorties against airfields in the Tokyo region. Though he lost thirteen men and eighteen aircraft, Halsey was surprised at the ineffective opposition he found protecting such an important center.

Four days later Halsey veered north to hit a major concentration of kamikaze aircraft in Hokkaido and northern Honshu, areas that rested beyond range of the Army's B–29 bombers and had until then escaped American attacks. Halsey's Dirty Tricks Department fooled the Japanese by broadcasting messages indicating Halsey would hit southern Honshu. When the Japanese strengthened their defenses in that area, Halsey sent in his air groups to ravage airfields to the north containing neatly aligned aircraft that became sitting ducks for their bombs and machine guns.

While his aviators handily demolished the kamikazes, Halsey and fourteen ships nestled daringly close to the Japanese shore in broad daylight to conduct a bombardment against a steel plant on Honshu. Expecting to be either attacked by air or bombarded by large coastal guns for much of the three hours required to maneuver into a position landlocked on three sides, Halsey "had my first sight of the hated enemy shores since the cruise around the world in 1908." When he had drawn within 28,000 yards, Halsey issued the order to fire, and for the next hour the *Missouri*'s mammoth guns and two other battleships hurled 1,000 tons of shells at their targets. Halsey called the event "a magnificent spectacle,"[2] but he kept a wary eye skyward for incoming Japanese planes. He could not believe that this offshore bombardment would not provoke some reaction from the Japanese.

After completing the bombardment, Halsey turned his ships seaward for the three-hour exit, again expecting squadrons of Japanese aircraft to appear. He safely extracted his ships, but Halsey later called the moment "the longest 7 hours I spent in my life"[3] because of the constant anticipation of an enemy attack.

Halsey enjoyed staging a bombardment that "showed the enemy that we made no bones about playing in his front yard." He claimed that the event "brought the war intimately to the Jap on the home islands. They could not convince a man an American ship had been sunk when his home had just been bombarded by it, and he had seen both the American ships and the effects of the bombardment."[4]

On July 15 Halsey hit the Nihon Steel Works, the Kanishi Iron Works, and a coal liquefaction plant at Hokkaido while also launching air strikes against airfields, shipping, and transportation in both northern Honshu and Hokkaido. Two days later he materialized to the south and commenced two days of strikes against six major factories near Tokyo and against the Yokosuka Naval Yard in Tokyo Bay.

Once again the home front welcomed news of Halsey's strikes. "For the first time, Japan's home islands saw a U.S. fleet and felt the lightning strokes of its big guns," bragged *Time* magazine in an issue bearing Halsey's image on its cover. "The blow was delivered in the Halsey manner that they had learned to expect. It was daring, powerful, crushing. The Third Fleet's battleships could have run into serious trouble, standing off Japan for a shore bombardment. Halsey took the chance."[5]

These strikes again convinced Halsey that Japan "was little more than a hollow shell. We were operating outside their front door at will, hitting them with bombs and shells, and meeting only light opposition from antiaircraft and a few planes." Sensing a wounded opponent, Halsey intensified his raids. "We stepped up our sweeps and bombardments by light forces"[6] so that the Japanese would not enjoy a chance to breathe.

This led to a series of raids occupying the remainder of the month. Though the Japanese cleverly concealed their aircraft in graveyards, fields, and outside small villages, Third Fleet aviators steadily reduced their numbers.

On July 23 Halsey's destroyers attacked a four-ship convoy near the coast, sinking two and damaging the other pair. The next day aircraft demolished airfields from Northern Kyushu to Nagoya, after which Halsey moved westward to conduct the first strike against shipping in the Inland Sea, a body of water lying between the three southernmost Home Islands of Kyushu, Shikoku, and Honshu. Though Halsey viewed any vessel as a target, he was most interested in locating undamaged combatant ships.

He found them on July 28 at the Kure Naval Base along the Inland Sea's northern shoreline. His aviators forced the battleship *Haruna* to beach, sank the commander in chief of the Combined Fleet's flagship, the cruiser *Oyodo,* and so damaged the battleships *Ise* and *Hyuga,* two vessels Halsey had missed in the South China Sea, that they settled on the bottom. "By sunset that evening," recalled a satisfied Halsey, "the Japanese Navy had ceased to exist."[7]

"WE ALL LET OUT A CHEER"

One event loomed over every proceeding—the prospect that Halsey and most Americans then in the Pacific would have to invade the Home Islands. Halsey understood the necessity for such a bloody campaign and had even been waging a battle in the press to ensure that the United States did not let the enemy off the hook. In a February radio interview with NBC and in an April 28, 1945, article in *Collier's* magazine, Halsey argued that Japan, which was "not fit to live in a civilized world," be reduced to a fourth-rate country so it could no longer threaten the peace, that traces of Japanese militarism be eradicated, and that a Japanese officer be executed for every American prisoner of war killed. "If we go easy on these rats now," he said to the NBC audience, "they'll use the next twenty years just like the Nazis used the last twenty-five."[8]

Halsey's part had already been decided for the November 1 operation. While the Fifth Fleet under Spruance supported the landings on Kyushu, Halsey's Third Fleet would support the Eighth U.S. Army in its assault on the region near Tokyo. Massive kamikaze strikes against both fleets would undoubtedly accompany the bitter land fighting. Carney stated that in late July "it was pretty apparent that we were flogging a dead horse. . ." with the offshore bombardments, "and the only thing that remained, that unnerved people, was the prospect of having to land in Japan, and probably killing every man, woman, child and dog, to overcome their fanatical resistance." As August approached, "I thought that this terrible experience was still ahead of us, before we could truthfully say that Japan had been suppressed."[9]

Halsey could not understand the only restriction Nimitz placed on his operations—he was to avoid bombing a handful of cities, including Hiroshima. He thought little of it, as he had a multitude of targets, but wondered why those cities were off limits.

He learned the answer on July 22 when Rear Admiral William R. Purnell arrived with information of a new weapon, a single bomb that alone could destroy a large city. Carney dismissed the development as another wild idea that came straight from science fiction, but Halsey was intrigued. He wrote Nimitz in early August that he was "most anxious to hear what you can tell me about this appalling new weapon and about future developments."[10]

Until then, he had missions to conduct. On August 9, the same day an atom bomb ravaged Nagasaki and three days after a similar bomb destroyed Hiroshima, he struck a reported concentration of 200 kamikaze aircraft in northern Honshu as well as industrial targets in the area, destroying hangars, locomotives, freight cars, and a refining company. The Third Fleet blasted airfields and installations on Honshu and near Tokyo on August 10 and August 13, but the War Diary noted the scarcity of viable targets.

On August 12 Halsey learned that the Japanese had agreed to surrender, but as he received no official confirmation, he continued to apply pressure on the enemy. Individual kamikaze attacks led him to believe that even if the report of the impending surrender were true, many Japanese had either not received word to lay down their arms or had refused to follow orders.

Halsey prepared for the surrender. By August 10 he organized landing parties consisting of 2,000 Marines and 1,200 sailors culled from various Third Fleet ships to secure surrendered military installations. He also assembled specialists to repair or operate shore facilities, created a plan to liberate Allied prisoners of war under the guidance of Commodore R. W. Simpson, and assigned Rear Admiral Oscar C. Badger to command the force to occupy the Yokosuka Navy Base, man enemy ships, and demilitarize other military objectives. Four days later Nimitz issued his occupation plan, calling for Halsey to land Army units in Honshu, and told Halsey to be ready to implement the orders on short notice.

At 4:15 A.M. on August 15, with rumors of war's end compounding, Halsey launched the first of three scheduled air strikes against Tokyo. The aircrafts were already attacking and a second strike was in the air when, at 6:14, a message from Nimitz arrived. "Suspend attack air operations. Acknowledge."[11] Halsey canceled the third strike and recalled the first two, but not before seven pilots had been killed in the raid. Aviators in the second wave, hesitant to believe that the war had finally ended, twice demanded that the recall order be authenticated before they pulled back.

Official word arrived at 8:04 A.M. that President Harry Truman, who had succeeded Roosevelt after his death on April 12, had accepted surrender terms. Halsey's air operations officer, Doug Moulton, the same man who had given Halsey the news on December 7, 1941, that the Japanese had attacked Pearl Harbor, ran down from the bridge clutching a dispatch. "Admiral, here she is" he said breathlessly. Halsey sat still for a few seconds, savoring the realization that the war was finally over. "We all let out a cheer," recalled Halsey. "My first reaction, of course, was great joy that the war that had started for us so badly had ended up so successfully. . . . My next thought was, 'Thank God I don't have to send any more men out to die.'" Halsey walked around slapping everyone's shoulders and yelling, "Yippee!"[12]

The brief jubilation over, Halsey ordered additional fighters placed in combat air patrols over the Third Fleet, cleared torpedo planes and bombers from the flight deck to make room for the fighters, and maintained condition one, the top defensive stance, on all antiaircraft batteries. He told his fighter directors to instruct every pilot that they were to "Investigate and shoot down all snoopers—not vindictively, but in a friendly sort of way."[13]

At 11:00, with Halsey watching and listening from the bridge, the *Missouri* and surrounding ships "blew the whistles of the fleet like school boys" for one minute to mark the war's end. Two hours later Halsey broadcast a fifteen-minute victory message to his fleet, relayed by the battleship *Iowa* to a waiting audience back home, in which he declared, "You have brought an implacable, treacherous, and barbaric foe to his knees in abject surrender. This is the first time in the recorded history of the misbegotten Japanese race that they as a nation have been forced to submit to this humiliation." Then, thinking of all the officers and enlisted who had served under him, many of whom had perished, he continued, "Your names are writ in golden letters on the pages of history—your fame is and shall be immortal. . . . Whether in the early days, when fighting with a very frayed shoestring, or at the finish, when fighting with the mightiest combined fleet the world has ever seen, the results have been the same—victory has crowned your efforts. The forces of righteousness and decency have triumphed."[14]

The Third Fleet Log summed up the moment. "So closes the watch we have been looking forward to. Unconditional surrender of Japan—with Admiral Halsey at sea in command of the greatest combined fighting fleet of all history! There is a gleam in his eye that is unmistakable!"[15]

"WHAT A GREAT DAY THIS IS"

With the cessation of hostilities, Halsey's focus switched to another group of men. Allied prisoners of war languished in camps throughout the Home Islands, some in the Omori prison camp only a few miles inside Tokyo Bay. On August 14 Halsey ordered Commodore Simpson to prepare to evacuate those men but, as arranged with the Army, to wait for MacArthur's arrival so the Army commander could direct the operation.

Plans changed when Halsey learned from two escaped British prisoners of the atrocious conditions that existed in the camps. Halsey ordered the hospital ship *Benevolence* into Tokyo Bay, directed Simpson to step up his preparations, and sent photo reconnaissance planes to locate and identify camps so that other aircraft could parachute food and medical supplies.

On August 29 Halsey dropped anchor inside Tokyo Bay in the shadow of Mount Fuji. When Nimitz arrived later that day, Halsey informed him of the squalor amidst which the prisoners were living. Nimitz authorized an immediate rescue mission, stating that MacArthur would understand why they took the initiative on this matter. Halsey contacted Simpson with the simple command, "Those are our boys! Go get them!"[16]

Within twenty-four hours almost 800 men had been evacuated from Omori. They were taken to the *Benevolence* for thorough examinations, at which time those requiring further care were kept aboard the hospital ship while the healthier ex-prisoners were issued clean clothing and sent to other ships in Tokyo Bay.

In the next two weeks, rescue missions freed 19,000 prisoners of war throughout Japan. Upon being liberated one captive gleefully shouted, "I knew it! I told those Jap bastards that Admiral Halsey would be here after us!"[17]

TWO DAYS LATER the Japanese destroyer *Hatsuzakura* pulled alongside to conduct the *Missouri* and other American combatants safely to berths inside Tokyo Bay. Halsey ordered all crews to quarters, guns manned, and air patrols to guard against any treachery, but one look at the aging destroyer eased Halsey's concerns. Her guns depressed according to instructions, the filthy ship maneuvered close as Halsey and Carney watched from the bridge. "You wanted the Jap Navy, Admiral," said Carney. "Well, there it is." Halsey stared at the *Hatsuzakura* for a few seconds and wondered, "Why in hell did it take us four years to lick these people?"[18]

Halsey and the *Missouri* arrived safely at the ship's berth, a time Halsey called "the supreme moment of my career."[19] With his carriers remaining outside the bay where they had the necessary room to launch aircraft for combat air patrols, Halsey eased the conditions aboard the ships inside Tokyo Bay, including the approval for showing movies topside. He told each captain, however, to maintain his vigilance and ordered that destroyers and smaller armed boats patrol around the clock.

That night, as Halsey's Third Fleet rested at anchor inside Tokyo Bay, the setting sun chose an apt location for its descent. From the *Missouri* it appeared as if it were plunging directly into Mount Fuji's crater. Halsey ordered photographers to catch the image, filled with irony as it was. "The Rising Sun of Japan," Halsey wrote, "had now set."[20]

Halsey felt honored when President Truman, a native of Missouri, selected his flagship to host the surrender ceremony. He sent a request to the Naval Academy Museum to send the American flag that Commodore Matthew C. Perry had flown when he entered Tokyo Bay in 1853, then had it mounted on a bulkhead overlooking the deck where Japan would sign the documents officially terminating the war. Admiral Sir Bruce Fraser sent over a beautiful mahogany table that had been aboard a ship during the World War I Battle of Jutland for the ceremony, but at the last moment officials realized it was too small to hold all the documents, and crew scattered to locate a replacement. A mess table from the crew's mess was rushed to the deck and covered with a green cloth.

September 2 began calmly. Halsey posted Marine guards throughout the battleship while boats patrolled the harbor waters to prevent suicide attacks. A few hours before the scheduled 9:00 A.M. ceremony, 225 correspondents, 75 photographers, and government dignitaries began arriving alongside the *Missouri.* Spectators marveled at the array of American might. Not only were aircraft flying above, but 258 warships of Halsey's Third Fleet and Allied Nations were spread out in majestic fashion.

At 8:43 MacArthur boarded the *Missouri* and bounded over to Halsey and his staff, offering handshakes and proclaiming that "it was grand to see so many of Bill Halsey's old South Pacific fighting scoundrels in at the kill." Halsey led MacArthur to his cabin for coffee and conversation and told his Army friend, "God what a great day this is. We have fought a long long time for it."[21]

A few minutes before 9:00 the Japanese delegation arrived. Foreign Minister Mamoru Shigemitsu boarded first, followed by the chief of the Army General Staff, General Yoshijiro Umezu, and eight other officials.

MacArthur opened the proceedings with a few words expressing his hopes for a lasting peace. Halsey noticed that the general's hands trembled from the emotion of the moment. At 9:04 Shigemitsu slowly stepped to the table, but he fumbled with his pen and stared at the document when he was uncertain where to sign. Halsey, who misinterpreted the action as a stalling technique, wanted to slap him and shout, "Sign you bastard, sign,"[22] but he concealed his emotions while MacArthur asked his chief of staff to show Shigemitsu where to sign.

With Halsey observing from a few paces away, MacArthur and Nimitz affixed their signatures. MacArthur closed the brief ceremony at 9:25, walked to Halsey and put his arm around his Navy companion, and said, "Start 'em now!"[23] At his signal almost 500 carrier aircraft and Army bombers flew overhead in a display of might that awed onlookers.

That the surrender documents rested on a crew's mess table was fitting. The United States won the war in part because expert leadership as exemplified by Halsey merged with the commitment to duty exhibited by the forces. That powerful combination propelled a drive across the Pacific that started at Pearl Harbor, continued through the early island and Doolittle raids, swerved into the South Pacific, and then north beyond the Philippines to Japan.

A poem written during the war expressed those sentiments. Written from the viewpoint of a sailor, the poem concluded that Halsey and his Third Fleet floated in Tokyo Bay that September 2 due to the combined efforts of admiral and sailors.[24]

"IT BECOMES JUST ANOTHER DAMNED OCEAN"

Halsey's brief role in the occupation of Japan started August 30 when Rear Admiral Badger, accompanied by Carney, led the landing team ashore to take control of the Yokosuka Naval Base near Tokyo. After Yokosuka had been secured, Halsey and Nimitz went ashore for the raising of the American flag. The pair then toured the shipyard, dry dock, officer's club, and other facilities at Yokosuka.

The most fascinating stop occurred when he visited the Yokohama jail that housed Japan's most influential military and government officials. With images of abused prisoners of war fresh in his mind, Halsey walked toward the cell containing the former commandant of Omori prison camp. "I was so infuriated with this man, whose name I do not remember, but whose deeds will never die in my brain, that I would have liked to kill him," wrote Halsey. He stepped directly into the man's cell, drew within feet of the officer, and stared without uttering a sound, hoping to make the Japanese think he was about to slap him. For a few moments victor and vanquished gazed at one another, the emotions of wartime simmering just beneath the surface before Halsey turned away. "He stood there, his hands shook a little. Neither one of us said a word."[25]

Lighthearted moments cut through the gravity. Admiral Sir Bruce Fraser awarded Halsey the Knight's Insignia of the Order of the British Empire, and as thanks Halsey recorded an address to be broadcast to the British Empire.

BEFORE LEAVING JAPAN, Halsey looked after the welfare of his men. He ordered his staff to check action reports and ensure that every individual deserving of a medal received one. Halsey also stipulated that the men who had been sent to the Pacific most recently should be transferred to ships remaining in Japan so that others who had been in combat a long time could be berthed aboard a homeward-bound vessel.

Halsey even arranged air travel back home for members of his staff so they could reach the West Coast before the troop-laden ships and make arrangements with naval authorities and railroad officials for the speedy transportation of these men to their separation centers. "We took great pride in this particular operation because we were determined that our men were going to be looked out for up to the last minute."[26]

On September 5, after President Truman ordered the *Missouri* to New York for a Navy Day celebration, Halsey switched his flag from the *Missouri* to the *South Dakota*. The admiral mused that, not counting the *South Dakota*, he had begun his naval career on the USS *Missouri* (BB 11) and ended it aboard the same-named battleship, USS *Missouri* (BB 63). Upon relief by Admiral Spruance, Halsey would command the ships steaming from Japan to the West Coast.

General MacArthur expressed the prevailing sentiment about Halsey's departure. "When you leave the Pacific, Bill, it becomes just another damned ocean!" his message stated. In another dispatch MacArthur added, "Your departure leaves all your old comrades of the Pacific war lonesome indeed. You carry with you the admiration and affection of every officer and man. May your shadow never decrease."[27]

One final detail remained. With his World War II command at an end and claiming it was time to give younger officers a chance to make their mark, the sixty-two-year-old admiral sent Nimitz and King a request that he be placed on the retired list upon completion of his duty with the Third Fleet. He then boarded an aircraft for the thirty-six-hour flight to Pearl Harbor, where he would rest in Oahu before returning to the United States and a life in peacetime. On October 9, in command of Task Force 30 comprising all the vessels then leaving the Pacific, Halsey boarded the *South Dakota* and said farewell to Hawaii.

Six days later, with whistles blowing, bells ringing, and a band playing "There'll Be a Hot Time in the Old Town Tonight," Halsey steamed underneath the Golden Gate Bridge for a warm California welcome headed by Governor Earl Warren and San Francisco Mayor Roger Lapham. "All hell broke loose," wrote Carney, and Halsey battled tears as he observed the affair. "Oh, he ate it up. He ate it up."[28] Thirteen ships passed by for review, and legendary entertainer Bob Hope aired his popular radio show from aboard the *South Dakota,* with Halsey as his guest.

The next day Halsey led the returnees in a military parade that ended at City Hall, where he delivered a speech that was broadcast throughout the nation by radio. On October 17 he departed for Los Angeles in the first of his stops along a five-week speaking tour in major cities across the country. Crowds lined Los Angeles streets ten deep to get a glimpse of the hero. When police detained one man who had leaped onto the running board of Halsey's car, he explained, "I just wanted to shake the hand of the man who shook the foundations from under Japan." One of Halsey's aides, astonished at the wild reception Halsey seemed to incite among young females, suggested tongue-in-cheek that he rivaled the nation's most famous crooner. "Bobby-soxers just go crazy over the admiral. We're going to put him on a circuit with Frank Sinatra."[29]

Following a trip to Boston, where Halsey was reunited with Fan, Halsey returned to Elizabeth, New Jersey, for the second "Halsey Day" celebration hosted by his hometown. The current student body at his old elementary school, joined by a large number of Halsey's classmates, hosted a reception for the local conqueror, who told the students he would love being in their shoes. "I haven't much to say to you, except that I envy you. I would give anything I have today to change places with you—to be starting out instead of ending up."[30] As a motorcade took him through city streets for the official ceremony, church bells rang, fire sirens blared, and thousands of admirers littered Halsey and Fan with confetti.

On November 20 Halsey completed his speaking tour and returned to the *South Dakota,* where he was relieved of his duties as commander of the Third Fleet. "I am terminating a seagoing career of slightly over 45 years," he told assembled officers and crew. "This is far from a pleasure, but I deem it necessary for men of my age to step aside so that younger men can take over the greatest Navy in the world."[31] He added a "Well done" to the men and wished them long and rewarding careers. Later, in chatting with reporters, Halsey said that leaving his beloved navy was like cutting off his right arm.

Halsey requested retirement, but the Navy instead promoted him to fleet admiral and retained him on active duty until 1947. He received full pay in the largely ceremonial post, which the Navy awarded him as recognition for his splendid war record. Some thought Spruance should have received the honor—the last of four such titles authorized by Congress—but the Navy gave the final fleet admiral post to Halsey and gave full pay for life to Spruance as consolation.

"I WANT TO FIGHT"

One triumph—peace of mind over his role at Leyte Gulf—eluded Halsey. The dispute about whether he had erred in racing after Ozawa's carriers remained out of public view until the war's aftermath, when Vice Admiral Ozawa admitted to U.S. interrogators that he had served as the bait to attract Halsey from his post off San Bernardino Strait. Two 1947 books repeated Ozawa's testimony, although neither harshly censured Halsey. The first open criticism occurred in a 1947 review of those two books in the *Virginia Quarterly Review* in which the reviewer, Bernard Brodie, claimed that Halsey had blundered because he lacked judgment and intellect.

Later that year Halsey published his account, first in a series of articles appearing in the *Saturday Evening Post,* and then in his autobiography, written with Lieutenant Commander J. Bryan. Halsey hoped the stories would yield what he considered an accurate assessment of his actions as well as present the real Admiral Halsey rather than the public-relations version created by the press.

Instead, he fanned the flames. The articles and subsequent book rankled few until Halsey came to the section pertaining to Leyte Gulf, where he repeated his contention that his main mission was to seek the enemy's fleet. He blamed divided command for the attending confusion and said he wondered how Kinkaid could have allowed Clifton Sprague's escort carriers to be caught flat-footed by Kurita.

The accounts created a maelstrom in the Navy. Admiral King rebuked Halsey and asked his friend to rewrite the sections. Raymond Spruance wrote Kinkaid, "I suspect you had to loosen your collar when reading Bill's account of the battle," and a stung Kinkaid broke his silence to defend himself. "I had kept quiet on the subject for nearly three years," he wrote Arleigh Burke, "because I believed a controversy would do the Navy no good and I declined . . . until Halsey's seventh installment appeared in the *Saturday Evening Post.*"[32]

Kinkaid teamed with a *Life* magazine writer to print a rebuttal to Halsey's charges. While admitting Halsey's talents as a leader, Kinkaid questioned his judgment and argued that his desire to destroy the Japanese carriers had caused him to leave fellow Americans in the lurch.

The debate intensified in 1958 when historian Samuel Eliot Morison published the volume dealing with Leyte in his monumental fourteen-volume history of the U.S. Navy in World War II. He called Halsey's rush to the north a mistake, stated that Halsey had ignored crucial intelligence in forming his decision, and rubbed salt in the wound by dedicating the volume to Clifton Sprague, the commander of the escort carriers abandoned by Halsey.

Halsey reacted vigorously to what he saw as an attack on his character. "My idea is to get the son-of-a-bitches cajones [sic] in a vise and set up on them," he wrote Doug Moulton of Morison. Halsey aired his laments to Carney, his trusted former chief of staff, whose advice Halsey had often followed. Halsey mentioned that while some staff members urged caution, that if he did not respond, "I and my staff are going down in history as dubs. I'm not willing to do this without showing my claws." Halsey added, "I want to fight Morison on every point."[33]

Carney's wisdom prevailed. He reminded Halsey that Morison's stature as a Pulitzer Prize–winning historian would weather any comments Halsey aired, and that all Halsey should do was emphasize that, as a result of the battle, Japanese naval power ended. Though it pained him to keep quiet, Halsey heeded Carney's advice.

The following year, historian E. B. Potter teamed with Admiral Nimitz to publish a naval history textbook to be used by midshipmen at the Naval Academy. In an early draft dealing with Leyte Gulf, Potter concluded, "Halsey had made the wrong decision. In the light of what we now know, there can be no question about that." When Potter sent Halsey a copy of that early draft, Halsey argued that the only mistake he had made was to turn away from Ozawa and that divided command had hampered operations. Halsey cautioned Potter, "I do not intend to allow grossly wrong statements about my thoughts to go into a book which will be used to teach Midshipmen, without making trouble for you."[34] The last thing Nimitz wanted was to contribute to another Sampson-Schley controversy or to offend his friend, so on Nimitz's advice the historian eliminated the offending remarks.

Riding his wartime popularity, Halsey cashed in on lucrative business opportunities that offered attractive salaries in stress-free posts. He represented Pan American World Airways and the Carlisle Tire and Rubber Company in 1946 and appeared on the lecture circuit for $500–$750 per speech. In 1947 he chaired a funding drive for his alma mater, the University of Virginia, which gave Fan and him the luxury of residing in a beautiful home in the Blue Ridge Mountains, his first lengthy domestic stint since his Academy days.

A favorite topic in his speeches was national security. Though the war had ended, he advocated the necessity of maintaining a strong military, especially in light of actions by America's former ally, the communist Soviet Union. Halsey sided with his old friend Douglas MacArthur when the Army general openly disagreed with President Truman over proper strategy in the Korean War. When Truman eventually relieved MacArthur of command in 1951, Halsey planned to join in a New York parade arranged in the general's behalf, but illness forced him to cancel his appearance.

Lighthearted moments made his retirement more rewarding. In 1957 the aging admiral attended a celebration at the Naval Academy to honor the wartime naval commanders. As the senior officer present, Halsey reviewed the midshipmen's parade and proudly beamed as he, Nimitz, and the other Pacific officers gained recognition from the Academy for their exploits. In 1960 director-producer Robert Montgomery, who had briefly served on Halsey's Pacific staff, premiered *The Gallant Hours,* a movie depicting Halsey's time as South Pacific commander. Starring Jimmy Cagney in the role of Admiral Halsey, the film garnered excellent reviews.

Cagney was both honored to be playing the role of such a national hero and touched that he had the chance to meet the admiral, who visited Camp Pendleton when Montgomery filmed some of the scenes at the California Marine base. Cagney, who closely resembled Halsey, claimed, "This film is a labor of love and gratitude to a man who, when the chips were down, performed for us."[35]

"A SEAGOING GENERAL PATTON"

Declining health hampered Halsey in his final two years. A mild stroke in 1957 left him with a slight speech impediment, and when Carl Solberg, the former lieutenant on Halsey's staff, visited Halsey two years later, "his eyes were dimmed by double-cataract surgery, his wide shoulders bent, his gait unsteady." However, when Solberg recalled the desperate October–November 1942 days at Guadalcanal, a time when Halsey's repeated order to attack turned the situation, "his face lit up."[36]

On August 16, 1959, while vacationing on Fisher's Island off Connecticut's shore, Halsey died of a heart attack. His body was taken by helicopter to New York, where Bill Junior and Mick Carney made the preparations for a Washington funeral and burial at Arlington.

Tributes immediately poured in. Eleanor Roosevelt, who had grown fond of the man who so graciously hosted her in the South Pacific, wrote in her syndicated newspaper column, "To me, as to many other people, Admiral William F. Halsey's death seems a real personal loss. He was a courageous, able and fine leader in the Navy, particularly in the Pacific during World War II, and after his retirement he served the cause of peace in the United Nations with great devotion."[37]

Halsey's casket was flown to Washington, D.C., where his body lay in state in the National Cathedral. On August 20, with Nimitz and a host of military and government officials in attendance, the funeral service was conducted. Military personnel gently lifted Halsey's casket onto a horse-drawn caisson, which slowly passed through the muted throngs that had assembled along the route to Arlington National Cemetery. At his gravesite an honor guard conducted the second of two nineteen-gun salutes before a sailor played taps.

The Navy honored Halsey's accomplishments by naming two ships for him. In 1963 the USS *Halsey* (CG–23), a *Leahy*-class guided missile cruiser, was commissioned, and in 2004 Halsey family members christened the second ship, the USS *Halsey* (DDG–97), an *Arleigh Burke*–class guided missile destroyer, fitting for a man who built a naval career from destroyers. The University of Virginia opened Halsey Hall, and the Naval Academy named its fieldhouse after the admiral.

WHAT OF HALSEY'S legacy? He participated nonstop from the war's opening day, when he prowled the Hawaiian coast in search of the Japanese, to the final moment, when he hosted the surrender ceremony aboard his *Missouri,* but he is overshadowed by MacArthur, Eisenhower, and Patton. His accomplishments against the Japanese cultivated a passionate following in wartime United States, yet few citizens today recognize his name. Historians all too often focus on his actions at Leyte Gulf and in the typhoons while ignoring his victories before and after those events. In 2007 alone, three separate books appeared about Halsey's catastrophes with nature, while no decent work cataloging his feats has appeared in a quarter century.

He deserves better. In 1947 *Time* magazine compared Halsey to George Patton, his illustrious Army colleague who favored fast action with armored divisions, much as Halsey delivered speedy thrusts with carrier air arms or destroyers. "Admiral Halsey was a kind of seagoing General Patton," stated the magazine article. "Both Halsey and Patton took long, unorthodox chances and won brilliant victories. Both were profane and histrionic commanders. Each stubbed his well-polished boot when he stepped outside his own field of fire."[38] Despite the recognition during and immediately after the war, while Patton is generally recognized today, few, unless they served with him, could list any of Halsey's achievements.

In evaluating an individual, one must look at the importance of the person to his times and view him the way his contemporaries did. In that light, with the possible exception of MacArthur, the Pacific War enjoyed no bigger hero than Halsey. People during the war waited for his words and expected his victories. He was their answer to the calamitous events that beset the nation early in the war; he was the one who would gain vengeance for Pearl Harbor. Halsey was the leader who, when the nation learned of Japanese atrocities, would make the enemy pay for their crimes, the commander who prisoners of war contended would one day liberate them, and the victor who would ride the white horse to the emperor's palace. From 1941 to 1945 Halsey amassed a reputation that equaled or surpassed that of his European counterpart, George Patton.

Despite his disappointment at never engaging the Japanese Fleet in a major surface action, particularly one involving carriers, Halsey's accomplishments stand at least on par with Chester Nimitz's and dwarf those of his other naval colleagues in the Pacific. He mounted the first response to Pearl Harbor with his 1942 island raids and the Doolittle mission; he recommended that Spruance command the forces at Midway and urged the bypassing of Mindanao for a strike directly against Leyte; he wrested the South China Sea from Japanese control; he brought the war to Japan's shores with thunderous coastal bombardments and aerial assaults of Kyushu and Honshu. Halsey stumbled at Leyte Gulf, but the mistakes were made from a desire to strike the enemy and were executed with the blessing of Admiral Nimitz, upon whose shoulders much of the blame must rest. Only with the typhoons can Halsey be charged.

Even without those impressive accomplishments, Halsey's performance at Guadalcanal and in the Solomons alone, where he single-handedly transformed a disastrous situation into an offensive thrust to match those of Patton, would be sufficient to gain him recognition as one of the great naval commanders in the nation's history. Halsey thought as much, as he showed during the 1959 visit from Solberg when he grinned broadly and displayed his pride in running the South Pacific.

During World War II Halsey stood as the nation's response to Japanese might and power. In diverse ways he "found that fight" he so badly sought, and as such he deserves a spot alongside John Paul Jones and the other naval greats in U.S. history.

NOTES

INTRODUCTION

1. Admiral Halsey's Victory Speech as Broadcast to Third Fleet During Kamikaze Attack—August 15, 1945, "Speeches 1939–45," in the William F. Halsey Collection, Library of Congress.
2. Owen Cedarburg letter to Admiral Halsey, January 25, 1944, in "General Correspondence, November 1943–March 1944," in the William F. Halsey Collection, Library of Congress.

CHAPTER 1

1. William F. Halsey, *Life of Admiral W. F. Halsey,* undated typewritten memoirs dictated by Halsey after the war, p. 11 (hereafter cited as Halsey, *Memoirs*); Fleet Admiral William F. Halsey and Lieutenant Commander J. Bryan III, *Admiral Halsey's Story* (New York: McGraw-Hill, Inc., 1947), p. 2.
2. Halsey and Bryan, *Admiral Halsey's Story,* p. 2.
3. *The History of the Lives and Bloody Exploits of the Most Noted Pirates; Their Trials and Executions* (New York: Empire State Book Company, 1926), p. 102.
4. Halsey, *Memoirs,* p. 9.
5. Halsey, *Memoirs,* p. 3.
6. Halsey, *Memoirs,* p. 6.
7. Halsey, *Memoirs,* p. 7.
8. Halsey and Bryan, *Admiral Halsey's Story,* pp. 3–4.
9. Halsey, *Memoirs,* p. 16; in E. B. Potter, *Bull Halsey* (Annapolis, Md.: Naval Institute Press, 1985), p. 27.
10. Halsey and Bryan, *Admiral Halsey's Story,* p. 5.
11. Halsey and Bryan, *Admiral Halsey's Story,* p. x.
12. Halsey and Bryan, *Admiral Halsey's Story,* p. 7.
13. Halsey and Bryan, *Admiral Halsey's Story,* p. 7.
14. Halsey and Bryan, *Admiral Halsey's Story,* p. 8.
15. Halsey, *Memoirs,* p. 9.
16. Halsey, *Memoirs,* p. 38.
17. Halsey, *Memoirs,* p. 43.
18. Halsey and Bryan, *Admiral Halsey's Story,* p. 9.
19. Halsey and Bryan, *Admiral Halsey's Story,* p. 10.
20. Halsey, *Memoirs,* p. 56.
21. Potter, *Bull Halsey,* p. 89.
22. Halsey, *Memoirs,* pp. 66–67.
23. Halsey, *Memoirs,* p. 79.
24. Halsey, *Memoirs,* p. 71.
25. Halsey, *Memoirs,* p. 86.

26. Robert A. Hart, *The Great White Fleet* (Boston: Little, Brown, 1965), p. 295.
27. Hart, *The Great White Fleet,* pp. 295–296.
28. Hart, *The Great White Fleet,* p. 299.
29. Halsey and Bryan, *Admiral Halsey's Story,* p. 15.
30. Halsey, *Memoirs,* p. 123.
31. Halsey, *Memoirs,* p. 3-X.
32. Halsey, *Memoirs,* pp. 154–155.
33. Halsey's World War I diary, found in Halsey, *Memoirs,* p. 162, hereafter cited as Halsey, *Wartime Diary.*
34. Halsey, *Wartime Diary,* p. 165.
35. Halsey, *Wartime Diary,* p. 168.
36. Potter, *Bull Halsey,* p. 111.
37. Halsey, *Wartime Diary,* p. 171.
38. Halsey, *Wartime Diary,* p. 178.
39. Halsey, *Wartime Diary,* p. 173.
40. Halsey, *Wartime Diary,* p. 174.

CHAPTER 2

1. Fleet Admiral William F. Halsey and Lieutenant Commander J. Bryan III, *Admiral Halsey's Story* (New York: McGraw-Hill, 1947), p. 41; William F. Halsey, *Life of Admiral W. F. Halsey,* undated typewritten memoirs dictated by Halsey after the war, p. 218 (hereafter cited as Halsey, *Memoirs*).
2. The Reminiscences of Robert Bostwick Carney, 1964, pp. 342–343, in the Oral History Collection of Columbia University.
3. E. P. Forrestel, *Admiral Raymond A. Spruance, USN: A Study in Command* (Washington, D.C.: U.S. Government Printing Office, 1966), p. 9.
4. Halsey, *Memoirs,* p. 222; Drew Pearson, "The Washington Merry-Go-Round," *Washington Post,* November 6, 1942, p. 12.
5. Halsey, *Memoirs,* p. 241.
6. Halsey and Bryan, *Admiral Halsey's Story,* pp. 50, 52.
7. Halsey, *Memoirs,* p. 253.
8. Captain W. F. Halsey, U.S. Navy, "The Relationship in War of Naval Strategy, Tactics, and Command," Senior Class of 1933, Naval War College, May 16, 1933 (hereafter cited as Halsey, "Thesis"), pp. 6, 11.
9. Halsey, "Thesis," p. 4.
10. Halsey, "Thesis," p. 6.
11. Halsey, "Thesis," p. 2.
12. Halsey, "Thesis," pp. 6–7.
13. Halsey, "Thesis," p. 7.
14. Halsey and Bryan, *Admiral Halsey's Story,* pp. 54–55.
15. E. B. Potter, *Bull Halsey* (Annapolis, Md.: Naval Institute Press, 1985), p. 130.
16. Reminiscences of Rear Admiral Francis D. Foley, U.S. Navy (Ret.), U.S. Naval Institute, Annapolis, Maryland, p. 163.
17. Halsey and Bryan, *Admiral Halsey's Story,* p. 60.
18. Reminiscences of Admiral Thomas M. Moorer, U.S. Navy (Ret.), U.S. Naval Institute, Annapolis, Maryland, p. 76.
19. William H. Ashford Oral History, East Carolina Manuscript Collection, J. Y. Joyner Library, East Carolina University, Greenville, N.C., January 16, 1979 through May 25, 1983, p. 36 (hereafter cited as Ashford Oral History).
20. Reminiscences of Vice Admiral Gerald F. Bogan, U.S. Navy (Ret.), 1970–1986, Naval War College, Newport, Rhode Island, pp. 66–67.
21. James M. Merrill, *A Sailor's Admiral: A Biography of William F. Halsey* (New York: Crowell, 1976), p. 13.

22. Halsey, *Memoirs*, p. 290.
23. Halsey, *Memoirs*, p. 302.
24. Hiroyuki Agawa, *The Reluctant Admiral: Yamamoto and the Imperial Navy* (Tokyo: Kodansha International Ltd., 1979), p. 189.
25. Halsey, *Memoirs*, pp. 307–308.
26. "Battle Order Number One—41," November 28, 1941, found at the USS *Enterprise* (CV–6) Association's web site, www.cv6.org; in Eugene Burns, *Then There Was One* (New York: Harcourt, Brace, 1944), pp. 7–8.
27. Lieutenant Clarence E. Dickinson with Boyden Sparkes, *The Flying Guns* (New York: Charles Scribner's Sons, 1943), p. 5.
28. Halsey, *Memoirs*, pp. 309–310.
29. Halsey and Bryan, *Admiral Halsey's Story*, p. 76.
30. "Battle Stations," *Time*, December 8, 1941, p. 15.

CHAPTER 3

1. William F. Halsey, *Life of Admiral W. F. Halsey*, undated typewritten memoirs dictated by Halsey after the war, p. 312 (hereafter cited as Halsey, *Memoirs*); Fleet Admiral William F. Halsey and Lieutenant Commander J. Bryan III, *Admiral Halsey's Story* (New York: McGraw-Hill, 1947), p. 77.
2. Halsey and Bryan, *Admiral Halsey's Story*, p. 77.
3. Halsey and Bryan, *Admiral Halsey's Story*, p. 80.
4. Halsey, *Memoirs*, p. 316; Halsey and Bryan, *Admiral Halsey's Story*, p. 79.
5. Halsey, *Memoirs*, p. 317; Halsey and Bryan, *Admiral Halsey's Story*, p. 80.
6. Halsey, *Memoirs*, pp. 314–315.
7. Halsey and Bryan, *Admiral Halsey's Story*, p. 81.
8. Eugene Burns, *Then There Was One* (New York: Harcourt, Brace, 1944), p. 17; Edward P. Stafford, *The Big E: The Story of the USS Enterprise* (New York: Random House, 1962), p. 24.
9. Robert J. Casey, *Torpedo Junction: With the Pacific Fleet from Pearl Harbor to Midway* (Indianapolis: Bobbs-Merrill, 1942), pp. 24–25.
10. Burns, *Then There Was One*, p. 18.
11. "National Ordeal," *Time*, December 15, 1941, p. 18; "Tragedy at Honolulu," *Time*, December 15, 1941, p. 19.
12. "Lifeline Cut," *Time*, December 15, 1941, pp. 24–25.
13. Daniel Rush, "John Doherty and Bombing Six," p. 4, posted on the USS *Enterprise* (CV–6) Association web site, www.cv6.org; Stafford, *The Big E: The Story of the USS Enterprise*, p. 2.
14. Peter Andrews, "The Defense of Wake," *American Heritage*, July-August 1987, p. 78; John Toland, *But Not in Shame: The Six Months after Pearl Harbor* (New York: Random House, 1961), p. 103.
15. Halsey and Bryan, *Admiral Halsey's Story*, p. 84.
16. John Lardner, *Southwest Passage: The Yanks in the Pacific* (Philadelphia: J. B. Lippincott, 1943), pp. 11–12.
17. "Where Is the Fleet?" *Time*, January 12, 1942, p. 10; Lardner, *Southwest Passage*, p. 14.
18. Edwin P. Hoyt, *How They Won the War in the Pacific: Nimitz and His Admirals* (New York: Lyons Press, 2000), pp. 50.
19. E. B. Potter, *Bull Halsey* (Annapolis, Md.: Naval Institute Press, 1985), p. 37.
20. John B. Lundstrom, *Black Shoe Carrier Admiral: Frank Jack Fletcher at Coral Sea, Midway, and Guadalcanal* (Annapolis, Md.: Naval Institute Press, 2006), p. 56.
21. Casey, *Torpedo Junction*, p. 124.
22. Halsey and Bryan, *Admiral Halsey's Story*, p. 89.
23. Dickinson with Sparkes, *The Flying Guns*, p. 113.
24. John B. Lundstrom, *The First Team: Pacific Naval Air Combat from Pearl Harbor to Midway* (Annapolis, Md.: Naval Institute Press, 1984), p. 78.

25. Halsey, *Memoirs*, p. 332.
26. Halsey and Bryan, *Admiral Halsey's Story*, p. 90; Halsey, *Memoirs*, pp. 333–334.
27. Matome Ugaki, *Fading Victory: The Diary of Admiral Matome Ugaki 1941–1945.* Translated by Masataka Chihaya (Pittsburgh: University of Pittsburgh Press, 1991), p. 82.
28. Halsey, *Memoirs*, pp. 337–338.
29. Captain G. D. Murray to Commander in Chief, U.S. Pacific Fleet, "Report of Action on February 1, 1942 against Marshall Island Group," 7 February 1942, p. 3, found at the USS *Enterprise* (CV–6) Association's web site, www.cv6.org; Casey, *Torpedo Junction: With the Pacific Fleet from Pearl Harbor to Midway*, pp. 154–155.
30. Halsey, *Memoirs*, pp. 338–339.
31. Halsey and Bryan, *Admiral Halsey's Story*, p. 94.
32. Halsey, *Memoirs*, p. 342.
33. Halsey, *Memoirs*, p. 343; Halsey and Bryan, *Admiral Halsey's Story*, pp. 96–97.
34. Halsey, *Memoirs*, p. 343; in Halsey and Bryan, *Admiral Halsey's Story*, p. 96.
35. Halsey, *Memoirs*, p. 343.
36. C. P. Trussell, "U.S. Fleet Batters Japanese Bases in Marshalls and Gilbert Islands," *New York Times*, dateline February 2, 1942, pp. 1, 3.
37. *New York Times*, February 14, 1942, p. 2; Fletcher Pratt, "Americans in Battle—No. 3: Campaign in the Coral Sea," *Harper's* Magazine, March 1943, p. 359.
38. Halsey, *Memoirs*, p. 346.
39. Dickinson with Sparkes, *The Flying Guns*, p. 123.
40. Casey, *Torpedo Junction*, pp. 16, 35–36, 184.
41. Casey, *Torpedo Junction*, p. 184; Clark Lee, *They Call It Pacific: An Eye-Witness Story of Our War against Japan from Bataan to the Solomons* (New York: Viking Press, 1943), p. 358.
42. "Seamen at Work," *Time*, April 6, 1942, p. 25.
43. Ugaki, *Fading Victory*, pp. 83–84.

CHAPTER 4

1. Joseph P. Lash, *Roosevelt and Churchill, 1939–1941* (New York: W. W. Norton, 1976), p. 488.
2. Fleet Admiral William F. Halsey and Commander J. Bryan III, *Admiral Halsey's Story* (New York: McGraw-Hill, 1947), p. 101.
3. William Tuohy, *America's Fighting Admirals* (St. Paul, Minn.: Zenith Press, 2007), p. 14.
4. General James H. Doolittle with Carroll V. Glines, *I Could Never Be So Lucky Again* (New York: Bantam, 1991), p. 262.
5. James C. Barnhill, *Tell Us, Daddy* (New York: Vantage, 1980), p. 66.
6. William F. Halsey, *Life of Admiral W. F. Halsey*, undated typewritten memoirs dictated by Halsey after the war, p. 352 (hereafter cited as Halsey, *Memoirs*).
7. Eugene Burns, *Then There Was One* (New York: Harcourt, Brace, 1944), p. 41.
8. Halsey, *Memoirs*, p. 90; John Toland, *The Rising Sun: The Decline and Fall of the Japanese Empire, 1936–1945* (New York: Random House, 1970), p. 382.
9. Carroll Glines, *The Doolittle Raid: America's Daring First Strike against Japan* (New York: Orion, 1988), p. 72.
10. Casey, *Torpedo Junction*, p. 426.
11. Halsey and Bryan, *Admiral Halsey's Story*, p. 102; W. F. Halsey to Commander-in-Chief, U.S. Pacific Fleet Task Force 16 Action Report, "Report of Action in Connection with the Bombing of Tokyo on April 18, 1942," at sea, April 24, 1942; Halsey, *Memoirs*, pp. 353–354; Lieutenant Colonel James H. Doolittle to the Commanding General, Army Air Forces, "Report on Japanese Raid, April 18, 1942," July 9, 1942.
12. Toland, *The Rising Sun*, p. 383.
13. Halsey, *Memoirs*, p. 355; Halsey and Bryan, *Admiral Halsey's Story*, p. 103.
14. Casey, *Torpedo Junction*, p. 431.
15. Casey, *Torpedo Junction*, pp. 306–308, 312, 429.

16. Lisle A. Rose, *The Ship That Held the Line* (Annapolis, Md.: Naval Institute Press, 1995), p. 74.
17. John Costello, *The Pacific War, 1941–1945* (New York: Quill, 1982), p. 235; "President Puts Raiders of Tokyo at '*Shangri-La*,'" *New York Times*, April 22, 1942; Clark Lee, *They Call It Pacific: An Eye-Witness Story of Our War against Japan from Bataan to the Solomons.* (New York: Viking, 1943), p. 289.
18. Ugaki, *Fading Victory*, p. 113.
19. "Text of War Department's Account of Raid on Tokyo April 18, 1942," *New York Times*, April 21, 1943.
20. Sidney Shalett, "The *Hornet* Was '*Shangri-la*' For Doolittle's Tokyo Raid," *New York Times*, April 21, 1943, pp. 1, 3.
21. "Big Raids on Tokyo Promised by Knox," *New York Times*, August 31, 1943; Halsey, *Memoirs*, p. 356; Halsey and Bryan, *Admiral Halsey's Story*, p. 104.
22. Halsey, *Memoirs*, pp. 356–357.
23. Ashford Oral History, p. 61.
24. "In the Coral Sea," *Time*, May 18, 1942, pp. 18–20.
25. Lieutenant Clarence E. Dickinson with Boyden Sparkes, *The Flying Guns* (New York: Charles Scribner's Sons, 1943), p. 135–136.
26. Halsey, *Memoirs*, p. 363; Dickinson with Sparkes, *The Flying Guns*, p. 136; Casey, *Torpedo Junction*, pp. 351, 354.
27. Halsey, *Memoirs*, p. 363.
28. Thomas B. Buell, *The Quiet Warrior: A Biography of Admiral Raymond A. Spruance* (Boston: Little, Brown, 1974), p. 122.
29. Ashford Oral History, p. 63.
30. Fleet Admiral C. W. Nimitz, "Command Summary," June 3, 1942 (hereafter cited as Greybook).
31. Halsey and Bryan, *Admiral Halsey's Story*, p. 107.
32. Casey, *Torpedo Junction*, pp. 14, 396.
33. Halsey, *Memoirs*, p. 363.
34. Halsey, *Memoirs*, p. 364.
35. Author's interview with Halsey Spruance, December 11, 2008; Halsey and Bryan, *Admiral Halsey's Story*, p. 108.
36. "The First Six Months." *Time*, June 8, 1942, pp. 19–22.
37. Potter, *Bull Halsey*, p. 150.
38. Halsey, *Memoirs*, p. 365; Halsey and Bryan, *Admiral Halsey's Story*, p. 108.
39. James M. Merrill, *A Sailor's Admiral: A Biography of William F. Halsey* (New York: Crowell, 1976), pp. 48–49.

CHAPTER 5

1. Fleet Admiral C. W. Nimitz, "Command Summary," October 15, 1942 (hereafter cited as Greybook).
2. John Costello, *The Pacific War, 1941–1945* (New York: Quill, 1982), p. 326; Jon T. Hoffman, *Chesty: The Story of Lieutenant General Lewis B. Puller, USMC* (New York: Random House, 2001), p. 181.
3. Ronald H. Spector, *Eagle Against the Sun* (New York: Free Press, 1985), p. 207.
4. A. A. Vandegrift, *Once A Marine* (New York: W. W. Norton, 1964), pp. 177, 180.
5. Vandegrift, *Once A Marine*, pp. 177–178.
6. Reminiscences of Hanson W. Baldwin, U.S. Naval Institute, Annapolis, Maryland, p. 349; Hanson W. Baldwin, "Lessons of the Solomons Campaign," *New York Times*, October 24, 1942, p. 3.
7. Clark Lee, *They Call It Pacific: An Eye-Witness Story of Our War against Japan from Bataan to the Solomons* (New York: Viking, 1943), p. 324.
8. Potter, *Nimitz*, p. 193.

9. H. H. Arnold, *Global Mission* (New York: Harper & Brothers, 1949), p. 342.
10. Potter, *Nimitz,* pp. 206–208.
11. William F. Halsey, *Life of Admiral W. F. Halsey,* undated typewritten memoirs dictated by Halsey after the war, (hereafter cited as Halsey, *Memoirs*), p. 367; Fleet Admiral William F. Halsey and Lieutenant Commander J. Bryan III, *Admiral Halsey's Story* (New York: McGraw-Hill, 1947), p. 109.
12. Halsey, *Memoirs,* p. 368.
13. Halsey and Bryan, *Admiral Halsey's Story,* p. 116.
14. Gilbert Cant, *America's Navy in World War II* (New York: John Day, 1943), p. 359.
15. Douglas MacArthur, *Reminiscences* (New York: McGraw-Hill, 1964), pp. 173–174.
16. *Los Angeles Times,* October 26, 1942; *New York Times,* October 25, 1942; *Washington Post,* November 1, 1942.
17. Foster Hailey, "Halsey Is Known as a Fighting Man," *New York Times,* October 25, 1942, p. 41.
18. James M. Merrill, *A Sailor's Admiral: A Biography of William F. Halsey* (New York: Crowell, 1976), p. 54.
19. Robert E. Sherwood, *Roosevelt and Hopkins: An Intimate History* (New York: Harper & Brothers, 1948), p. 622.
20. Donald F. Crosby, S.J., *Battlefield Chaplains: Catholic Priests in World War II* (Lawrence: University Press of Kansas, 1994), p. 47; William H. Ashford Oral History, East Carolina Manuscript Collection, J. Y. Joyner Library, East Carolina University, Greenville, N.C., January 16, 1979, through May 25, 1983, p. 77 (hereafter cited as Ashford Oral History).
21. Ashford Oral History, p. 72.
22. Vandegrift, *Once A Marine,* p. 184; Halsey and Bryan, *Admiral Halsey's Story,* p. 117.
23. Halsey, *Memoirs,* p. 403.
24. Matome Ugaki, *Fading Victory: The Diary of Admiral Matome Ugaki 1941–1945.* Translated by Masataka Chihaya (Pittsburgh: University of Pittsburgh Press, 1991), p. 245.
25. Lundstrom, *The First Team and the Guadalcanal Campaign,* p. 353; Halsey, *Memoirs,* pp. 379–380.
26. Greybook, "Estimate of Enemy Capabilities," November 1, 1942.
27. Gerald Wheeler, *Kinkaid of the Seventh Fleet* (Annapolis, Md.: Naval Institute Press, 1996), p. 288.
28. Halsey, *Memoirs,* p. 384.
29. Vandegrift, *Once A Marine,* p. 196.
30. Foster Hailey, "Halsey Defends Battleship's Role," *New York Times,* November 19, 1942, pp. 1, 8.
31. Lieutenant D. C. Rubb, ComSoPac Staff, "Operational History of the South Pacific," Compiled 1945, World War II Command File, South Pacific Naval Force, Air Combat Intelligence Report, National Archives and Records Administration, College Park, Md., p. 3.
32. Hailey, "Halsey Defends Battleship's Role," p. 8.
33. Message from Nimitz to Halsey, November 9, 1942, 2107; Greybook, November 9, 1942; Dan Kurzman, *Left to Die: The Tragedy of the USS* Juneau (New York: Pocket Books, 1994), p. 91.
34. Halsey, *Memoirs,* p. 389.
35. Halsey, *Memoirs,* pp. 382–383; Halsey and Bryan, *Admiral Halsey's Story,* p. 125.
36. Vandegrift, *Once A Marine,* p. 198.
37. Halsey, *Memoirs,* pp. 386–388.
38. South Pacific War Diary, November 13, 1942; Greybook, November 13, 1942.
39. Lundstrom, *The First Team and the Guadalcanal Campaign,* p. 487.
40. Halsey, *Memoirs,* p. 390; South Pacific War Diary, November 13, 1942.
41. Halsey, *Memoirs,* pp. 391–392, 394.
42. South Pacific War Diary, November 15, 1942; Halsey, *Memoirs,* p. 394.

43. Halsey, *Memoirs,* p. 392; W. F. Halsey, The Commander Third Fleet to The Commander in Chief, United States Fleet, "South Pacific Campaign—Narrative Account," September 3, 1944, p. 5 (hereafter cited as Halsey, "Narrative Account").
44. Halsey and Bryan, *Admiral Halsey's Story,* pp. 131–132.
45. Halsey and Bryan, *Admiral Halsey's Story,* p. 132.
46. Halsey, *Memoirs,* p. 396.
47. Merrill, *A Sailor's Admiral: A Biography of William F. Halsey,* p. 64; Samuel Eliot Morison, *History of United States Naval Operations in World War II, Volume V: The Struggle for Guadalcanal, August 1942–February 1943* (Boston: Little, Brown and Co., 1960), p. 287.
48. Message from General Alexander Vandegrift to Admiral William Halsey, November 16, 1942, in "General Correspondence, November 1943-March 1944," in the William F. Halsey Collection, Library of Congress.
49. "Hit Hard, Hit Fast, Hit Often," *Time,* November 30, 1942, pp. 28–31.
50. "Admiral Takes Big Chances to Gain Big Victories," *Washington Post,* November 17, 1942, pp. 1, 8; John G. Norris, "Battleship, 10 Other War Vessels Sunk," *Washington Post,* November 17, 1942, pp. 1–2; "Halsey's Triumph," *Washington Post,* November 18, 1942, p. 12; "Aggressive Spirit," *Washington Post,* November 22, 1942, p. B6; John G. Norris, "Victory Over Japs in Pacific May Be 'Turning Point,'" *Washington Post,* November 22, 1942, pp. B1-B2; Ernest K. Lindley, "Solomon Victory," *Washington Post,* November 23, 1942, p. 13.
51. "Leader of Battle at Solomons Refuses to Fight by Rule Book," *Los Angeles Times,* November 17, 1942, p. 2.
52. Halsey, *Memoirs,* p. 399.
53. John B. Polhemus letter to Vice Admiral Admiral William F. Halsey, Jr., November 18, 1942, in "Halsey Letters, 1942," in the William F. Halsey Collection, Library of Congress.
54. Captain Rufus F. Zogbaum letter to Admiral William Halsey, November 27, 1942; Admiral William Halsey letter to Rufus Zogbaum, December 14, 1942, in "Halsey Letters, 1942–1943," in the William F. Halsey Collection, Library of Congress.
55. "Halsey Promoted to Admiral's Rank," *New York Times,* November 21, 1942, p. 3; Halsey, *Memoirs,* p. 398.
56. W. L. Calhoun letter to Commanding Officer, U.S.S. *Argonne,* November 21, 1942, in "Halsey Letters, 1942," in the William F. Halsey Collection, Library of Congress; Halsey and Bryan, *Admiral Halsey's Story,* p. 132.

CHAPTER 6

1. William F. Halsey letter to Chester Nimitz, November 29, 1942, "Halsey-Nimitz Letters, 1942–1943," in the William F. Halsey Collection, Library of Congress (hereafter Halsey-Nimitz correspondence).
2. Halsey-Nimitz correspondence, January 1, 1943.
3. "Die, But Do Not Retreat," *Time,* January 4, 1943, pp. 21–22.
4. Samuel Eliot Morison, *History of United States Naval Operations in World War II: Volume V, The Struggle for Guadalcanal, August 1942–February 1943* (Boston: Little, Brown and Co., 1960), p. 317.
5. Fleet Admiral William F. Halsey and Lieutenant Commander J. Bryan III, *Admiral Halsey's Story* (New York: McGraw-Hill, 1947), p. 143.
6. J. Norman Lodge, "Halsey Predicts Victory This Year," *New York Times,* January 3, 1943, p. 14; "Halsey Minimizes Foe," *New York Times,* January 7, 1943, p. 4.
7. Halsey and Bryan, *Admiral Halsey's Story,* p. 144.
8. "That Man Halsey," *Seattle Daily Journal,* January 5, 1943, enclosed in M. D. Haire letter to Admiral William Halsey, January 5, 1943, in "Halsey Letters, 1942–1943," in the William F. Halsey Collection, Library of Congress.

9. J. I. Faynes letter to Admiral Halsey, January 4, 1943; Bertram Jay Gumpert letter to Admiral Halsey, January 3, 1943, in "Halsey Letters, 1942–1943," in the William F. Halsey Collection, Library of Congress.
10. Haire letter to Halsey, January 5, 1943.
11. Halsey and Bryan, *Admiral Halsey's Story,* pp. 141–142.
12. Fleet Admiral C. W. Nimitz, "Command Summary," December 24, 1942 (hereafter cited as Greybook); Halsey-Nimitz correspondence, January 26, 1943.
13. Halsey-Nimitz correspondence, January 11, 1943.
14. Halsey-Nimitz correspondence, December 11, 1942, December 20, 1942, July 16, 1943.
15. Samuel Eliot Morison, *History of United States Naval Operations in World War II, Volume V: The Struggle for Guadalcanal, August 1942–February 1943* (Boston: Little, Brown and Co., 1960), p. 371; William F. Halsey, *Life of Admiral W. F. Halsey,* undated typewritten memoirs dictated by Halsey after the war, p. 413 (hereafter cited as Halsey, *Memoirs*).
16. Clark Lee, *They Call It Pacific: An Eye-Witness Story of Our War against Japan from Bataan to the Solomons* (New York: Viking, 1943), p. 358.
17. Richard B. Frank, *Guadalcanal* (New York: Random House, 1990), pp. 605, 614.
18. Halsey, *Memoirs,* pp. 393, 397.
19. Halsey, "Narrative Account," p. 4.
20. Admiral Arleigh Burke, "Unforgettable 'Bull' Halsey," *Reader's Digest,* September 1973, p. 120.
21. Halsey-Nimitz correspondence, July 16, 1943.
22. William H. Ashford Oral History, East Carolina Manuscript Collection, J. Y. Joyner Library, East Carolina University, Greenville, N.C., January 16, 1979 through May 25, 1983, p. 104 (hereafter cited as Ashford Oral History).
23. Halsey *Memoirs,* p. 372.
24. Admiral Halsey letter to Charles Belnap, October 8, 1943, in "Halsey Letters, 1943," in the William F. Halsey Collection, Library of Congress.
25. Edwin P. Hoyt, *How They Won the War in the Pacific: Nimitz and His Admirals* (New York: Lyons Press, 2000), p. 169.
26. Halsey and Bryan, *Admiral Halsey's Story,* p. 139.
27. Halsey and Bryan, *Admiral Halsey's Story,* p. 165.
28. Halsey, "Narrative Account," p. 2.
29. Mrs. Bainbridge letter to William F. Halsey, July 1, 1943; W. F. Halsey letter to Mrs. Bainbridge, July 14, 1943, "Missing Persons," William F. Halsey Collection, Library of Congress.
30. Halsey, *Memoirs,* p. 369.
31. Halsey, *Memoirs,* p. 371.
32. Reminiscences of Vice Admiral William R. Smedberg, III, U.S. Naval Institute, Annapolis, Md., pp. 236–237.
33. Betty Carney Taussig, *A Warrior for Freedom* (Manhattan, Kan.: Sunflower University Press, 1995), pp. 82, 92.
34. James J. Fahey, *Pacific War Diary, 1942–1945* (Boston: Houghton Mifflin, 1963), p. 71.
35. Burke, "Unforgettable 'Bull' Halsey," pp. 117–119.

CHAPTER 7

1. E. B. Potter, *Bull Halsey* (Annapolis, Md.: Naval Institute Press, 1985), p. 206.
2. William F. Halsey letter to Chester Nimitz, January 11, 1943, "Halsey-Nimitz Letters, 1942–1943," in the William F. Halsey Collection, Library of Congress (hereafter Halsey-Nimitz correspondence.
3. Halsey-Nimitz correspondence, February 13, 1943.
4. Fleet Admiral Halsey and Lieutenant Commander J. Bryan III, *Admiral Halsey's Story* (New York: McGraw-Hill, 1947), pp. 154–155.
5. William F. Halsey, *Life of Admiral W. F. Halsey,* undated typewritten memoirs dictated by Halsey after the war, pp. 451–452 (hereafter cited as Halsey, *Memoirs;* Benis Frank, *Halsey* (New York: Ballantine, 1947), p. 49.
6. Halsey and Bryan, *Admiral Halsey's Story,* p. 166; Halsey, *Memoirs,* pp. 441–442.

7. Halsey and Bryan, *Admiral Halsey's Story,* p. 167; Halsey, *Memoirs,* p. 442.
8. Halsey and Bryan, *Admiral Halsey's Story,* pp. 167–168; Eleanor Roosevelt, "My Day," January 13, 1944, The Eleanor Roosevelt Papers included at the Franklin D. Roosevelt Library, Hyde Park, New York, available for downloading at http://www.gwu.edu/~erpapers/myday/.
9. "War's End," *Time,* August 16, 1943.
10. Potter, *Halsey,* p. 246.
11. William H. Ashford Oral History, East Carolina Manuscript Collection, J. Y. Joyner Library, East Carolina University, Greenville, N.C., January 16, 1979 through May 25, 1983, p. 83 (hereafter cited as Ashford Oral History).
12. Halsey and Bryan, *Admiral Halsey's Story,* p. 136; James M. Merrill, *A Sailor's Admiral: A Biography of William F. Halsey* (New York: Crowell, 1976), p. 69.
13. Potter, *Halsey,* p. 245.
14. Halsey and Bryan, *Admiral Halsey's Story,* p. xiii.
15. Betty Carney Taussig, *A Warrior for Freedom* (Manhattan, Kan.: Sunflower University Press, 1995), p. 84.
16. Halsey and Bryan, *Admiral Halsey's Story,* p. xv.
17. E. B. Potter, *Nimitz* (Annapolis, Md.: Naval Institute Press, 1976), p. 233.
18. Halsey and Bryan, *Admiral Halsey's Story,* p. 157.
19. E. B. Potter, *Admiral Arleigh Burke: A Biography* (New York: Random House, 1990), p. 114.
20. Gregory Boyington, *Baa Baa Black Sheep* (New York: G. P. Putnam's Sons, 1958), p. 131.
21. United States Strategic Bombing Survey, *Interrogations of Japanese Officials,* Volume II, p. 474; Masatake Okumiya, Jiro Horikoshi, and Martin Caidon, *Zero* (New York: Simon & Schuster, 2002), p. 213.
22. Halsey-Nimitz correspondence, December 11, 1942.
23. South Pacific War Diary, July 15, 1943; Halsey-Nimitz correspondence, July 16, 1943, August 19, 1943.
24. Halsey-Nimitz correspondence, July 13, 1943.
25. Halsey, *Memoirs,* p. 425; South Pacific War Diary, August 15, 1943.
26. Halsey and Bryan, *Admiral Halsey's Story,* pp. 180–181.
27. Halsey, *Memoirs,* p. 434.
28. South Pacific War Diary, November 5, 1943; Taussig, *Warrior for Freedom,* p. 93; Halsey and Bryan, *Admiral Halsey's Story,* p. 181.
29. Clark G. Reynolds, *The Fast Carriers* (McGraw-Hill, 1968), p. 100.
30. South Pacific War Diary, November 11, 1943; Halsey, "Narrative Account," p. 10; Potter, *Halsey,* p. 257.
31. Okumiya, Horikoshi, and Caidon, *Zero,* p. 214.
32. "Toward a Jap Defeat?" *Time,* February 28, 1944, p. 25.
33. Halsey and Bryan, *Admiral Halsey's Story,* p. 191.
34. William F. Halsey letter to Eleanor Roosevelt, April 20, 1944, in the Eleanor Roosevelt Papers, "Letters from Servicemen, 1944: Ha," Box 836, Franklin D. Roosevelt Library, Hyde Park, New York; Halsey, *Memoirs,* p. 446.
35. Halsey and Bryan, *Admiral Halsey's Story,* p. 197.
36. Halsey and Bryan, *Admiral Halsey's Story,* p. 192.
37. Douglas MacArthur, *Reminiscences* (New York: McGraw-Hill, 1964), p. 192.
38. South Pacific War Diary, June 15, 1944; Merrill, *A Sailor's Admiral,* p. 120.
39. Halsey and Bryan, *Admiral Halsey's Story,* p. 193; Halsey, *Memoirs,* p. 459; "The Admiral Shoves Off," *Time,* June 26, 1944, p. 64.
40. "The Admiral Shoves Off," *Time,* June 26, 1944, p. 64.
41. Ashford Oral History, p. 112.

CHAPTER 8

1. Fleet Admiral William F. Halsey and Lietutenant Commander J. Bryan, *Admiral Halsey's Story* (New York: McGraw-Hill, 1947), p. 198.

2. William F. Halsey letter to Chester Nimitz, June 29, 1943, "Halsey-Nimitz Letters, 1942–1943," in the William F. Halsey Collection, Library of Congress (hereafter Halsey-Nimitz correspondence).
3. Ronald H. Spector, *Eagle against the Sun* (New York: Free Press, 1985), p. 423; Eric Larrabee, *Commander in Chief: Franklin Delano Roosevelt, His Lieutenants, and Their War* (New York: Harper & Row, 1987), p. 391.
4. William F. Halsey, *Life of Admiral W. F. Halsey,* undated typewritten memoirs dictated by Halsey after the war, pp. 464, 469 (hereafter cited as Halsey, *Memoirs*)
5. Halsey-Nimitz correspondence, September 9, 1944.
6. Halsey, *Memoirs,* p. 33-X; The Reminiscences of Robert Bostwick Carney, 1964, p. 422, in the Oral History Collection of Columbia University.
7. Third Fleet War Diary, September 12, 1944.
8. Halsey, *Memoirs,* p. 464.
9. Halsey and Bryan, *Admiral Halsey's Story,* pp. 199–200.
10. William F. Halsey, "Comments on By-passing of Rabaul," notes included the folder, "By-passing Rabaul," Box 35, in the William F. Halsey Collection, Library of Congress.
11. Text of Roosevelt's 1945 State of the Nation address is found at http://www.jewishvirtuallibrary.org/jsource/ww2/fdr010645.html.
12. Halsey-Nimitz correspondence, October 6, 1944.
13. Halsey, *Memoirs,* p. 466; Halsey, "Comments on By-passing of Rabaul."
14. Third Fleet War Diary, September 21, 1944.
15. Halsey and Bryan, *Admiral Halsey's Story,* p. 209.
16. E. B. Potter, *Nimitz* (Annapolis, Md.: Naval Institute Press, 1976), p. 325.
17. Halsey-Nimitz correspondence, September 28, 1944.
18. Halsey and Bryan, *Admiral Halsey's Story,* p. 205.
19. Halsey, *Memoirs,* p. 496.
20. Halsey and Bryan, *Admiral Halsey's Story,* pp. 207–208.
21. Halsey, *Memoirs,* p. 500; Halsey and Bryan, *Admiral Halsey's Story,* p. 208.
22. Halsey and Bryan, *Admiral Halsey's Story,* p. 211; William Tuohy, *America's Fighting Admirals* (St. Paul, Minn.: Zenith Press, 2007), p. 296.
23. Halsey and Bryan, *Admiral Halsey's Story,* p. 214.
24. David C. Evans, ed. and trans., *The Japanese Navy in World War II: In the Words of Former Japanese Naval Officers.* Annapolis, Md.: Naval Institute Press, 1986, p. 366.
25. Evans, *Japanese Navy in World War II,* p. 365.
26. Halsey and Bryan, *Admiral Halsey's Story,* p. 214.
27. Halsey, *Memoirs,* p. 505.
28. Halsey, *Memoirs,* p. 510.

CHAPTER 9

1. Fleet Admiral William F. Halsey and Lieutenant Commander J. Bryan III, *Admiral Halsey's Story* (New York: McGraw-Hill, 1947), p. 216.
2. Halsey and Bryan, *Admiral Halsey's Story,* p. 217.
3. Halsey and Bryan, *Admiral Halsey's Story,* p. 217.
4. Reminiscences of Vice Admiral Gerald F. Bogan, p. 109.
5. Author's interview with Admiral James Russell, April 21, 1992.
6. Gilbert Cant, "Bull's Run: Was Halsey Right at Leyte Gulf?" *Life,* November 14, 1947, p. 75; E. B. Potter, *Halsey* (Annapolis, Md.: Naval Institute Press, 1985), pp. 297–98.
7. Author's interview with Captain Henry Burt Bassett, February 2, 1994.
8. Author's interview with Vernon D. Hipchings, Jr., January 31, 1994; Rear Admiral C. A. F. Sprague, as told to Lieutenant (jg) Philip H. Gustafson, "The Japs Had Us on the Ropes," *American Magazine,* April 1945; Lieutenant Verling Pierson, "The Battle off Samar," p. 2.

9. Halsey and Bryan, *Admiral Halsey's Story,* p. 218.
10. Halsey, "Action Report," November 13, 1944, p. 39.
11. Solberg, *Decision and Dissent,* p. 151.
12. Solberg, *Decision and Dissent,* p. 151.
13. Third Fleet War Diary, October 25, 1944; T. G. Kinkaid, Commander Task Force Seventy-Seven to Commander-in-Chief, United States Fleet. "Preliminary Action Report of Engagements in Leyte Gulf and off Samar Island on 25 October, 1944," November 18, 1944, p. 10.
14. Solberg, *Decision and Dissent,* pp. 135, 152–153.
15. Halsey, "Action Report," November 13, 1944, p. 44; Third Fleet War Diary, October 25, 1944.
16. Halsey, "Action Report," November 13, 1944; Third Fleet War Diary, October 25, 1944.
17. Admiral James Russell interview.
18. Lieutenant Robb White, USNR, Public Relations, CinCPac, Confidential Report on board *Natoma Bay,* 25 October 1944, Aviation History Files, Naval Historical Center, p. C3.
19. Halsey, "Action Report," November 13, 1944, p. 42; Third Fleet War Diary, October 25, 1944.
20. Halsey and Bryan, *Admiral Halsey's Story,* p. 220.
21. Halsey and Bryan, *Admiral Halsey's Story,* p. 220; Cant, "Bull's Run: Was Halsey Right at Leyte Gulf?" p. 76.
22. Halsey, "Action Report," November 13, 1944, p. 44.
23. Potter, *Halsey,* p. 303.
24. Halsey and Bryan, *Admiral Halsey's Story,* p. 220; Solberg, *Decision and Dissent,* p. 154.
25. Halsey and Bryan, *Admiral Halsey's Story,* p. 220; William Halsey letter to Vice Admiral Ralph E. Wilson, February 5, 1959, in "Leyte Correspondence," in the William F. Halsey Collection, Library of Congress; Halsey, *Memoirs,* p. 514.
26. Halsey and Bryan, *Admiral Halsey's Story,* p. 221.
27. Halsey and Bryan, *Admiral Halsey's Story,* p. 224.
28. Halsey, *Memoirs,* p. 518.
29. Halsey, "Action Report," November 13, 1944, p. 8.
30. Third Fleet War Diary, October 26, 1944.
31. Third Fleet War Diary, October 25, 1944.
32. Halsey, *Memoirs,* p. 521; Halsey and Bryan, *Admiral Halsey's Story,* pp. 226–227; "Main Fleet Broken," *New York Times,* October 27, 1944, p. 1.
33. Solberg, *Decision and Dissent,* p. 170; Gerald Wheeler, *Kinkaid of the Seventh Fleet* (Annapolis, Md.: Naval Institute Press, 1996), p. 405.
34. W. F. Halsey, the Commander Third Fleet to the Commander in Chief, United States Fleet. "Report on Seizure of Southern Palau Islands and Ulithi, and Concurrent Operations in Support of the Seizure of Morotai," November 14, 1944, p. 7.
35. Halsey-Nimitz correspondence, November 4 and November 9, 1944; W. F. Halsey, The Commander Third Fleet to the Commander in Chief, United States Fleet. "Action Report—Period 23–26 October 1944, both dates inclusive," November 13, 1944, p. 10.
36. Halsey, "Action Report," November 13, 1944, p. 10.
37. E. B. Potter, *Nimitz* (Annapolis, Md.: Naval Institute Press, 1976), p. 344.
38. Potter, *Nimitz,* p. 344.
39. Potter, *Halsey,* p. 307.
40. Thomas B. Buell, *Master of Sea Power: A Biography of Fleet Admiral Ernest J. King* (Boston: Little, Brown and Co., 1980), p. 479; Reminiscences of Robert Bostwick Carney, 1964, pp. 400–401, in the Oral History Collection of Columbia University.
41. Potter, *Halsey,* p. 39.
42. Halsey, "Action Report," November 13, 1944, p. 10.
43. Potter, *Nimitz,* p. 343.
44. C. A. F. Sprague letter to Annabel Sprague, May 15, 1945, in the Clifton Sprague Collection.

CHAPTER 10

1. James J. Fahey, *Pacific War Diary, 1942–1945* (Boston: Houghton Mifflin, 1963), p. 250.
2. Fleet Admiral William F. Halsey and Lieutenant Commander J. Bryan III, *Admiral Halsey's Story* (New York: McGraw-Hill, 1947), p. 229; William F. Halsey, *Life of Admiral W. F. Halsey,* undated typewritten memoirs dictated by Halsey after the war, p. 524 (hereafter cited as Halsey, *Memoirs*).
3. Cato D. Glover, The Commanding Officer to the Commander in Chief, United States Fleet. "Action Report—Fleet Action and Operations Against the Philippine Islands Area, from 22 to 31 October 1944," November 3, 1944, p. 6, found at the USS *Enterprise* (CV–6) Association's web site, www.cv6.org.
4. Carl Solberg, *Decision and Dissent: With Halsey at Leyte Gulf* (Annapolis, Md.: Naval Institute Press, 1995), p. 66.
5. Reminiscences of Vice Admiral Jerome H. King, Jr., U.S. Naval Institute, Annapolis Maryland, p. 111; Evan Thomas, *Sea of Thunder: Four Commanders and the Last Great Naval Campaign, 1941–1945* (New York: Simon & Schuster, 2006), p. 326; Author's interview with Carnes Weeks Jr., August 24, 2009.
6. Halsey and Bryan, *Admiral Halsey's Story,* p. 236.
7. Third Fleet War Diary, December 18, 1944.
8. Halsey and Bryan, *Admiral Halsey's Story,* p. 239.
9. Samuel Eliot Morison, *History of United States Naval Operations in World War II, Volume 13: The Liberation of the Philippines, 1944–1945* (Boston: Little, Brown, 1959), pp. 79–80.
10. The descriptions from the action reports of the USS *Hull,* USS *Dewey,* USS *Independence,* and USS *San Jacinto* are taken from Commander in Chief, U.S. Pacific Fleet and Pacific Ocean Areas, "Operations in the Pacific Ocean Areas During the Month of December 1944," pp. 12–13, and 72–86. World War II Command File, Operational Archives Branch, Naval Historical Center, Washington, DC Found at: http://www.history.navy.mil/faqs/faq 102–4f.htm
11. Halsey and Bryan, *Admiral Halsey's Story,* p. 236; W. F. Halsey, "Third Fleet Operations, 1 November 1944 to 19 September 1945." Undated report found in "3rd Fleet Operations 1943–1945," in the William F. Halsey Collection, Library of Congress, p. 3; Solberg, *Decision and Dissent: With Halsey at Leyte Gulf,* p. 25.
12. Record of Proceedings of a Court of Inquiry convened on board the USS *Cascade* by order of the Commander-in-Chief, U.S. Pacific Fleet, United States Fleet, to inquire into all the circumstances connected with the loss of the USS *Hull* (DD 350), USS *Monaghan* (DD 354), and the USS *Spence* (DD 512), and damage sustained by the USS *Monterey* (CVL 26) and the USS *Cowpens* (CVL 28), and other damage sustained by ships of the Third Fleet as the result of adverse weather on or around December 18, 1944, submitted December 28, 1944, p. 74 (hereafter cited as December Court of Inquiry).
13. December Court of Inquiry, p. 75.
14. E. B. Potter, *Nimitz* (Annapolis, Md.: Naval Institute Press, 1976), p. 350.
15. Memorandum for Lieutenant Commander Hughes, found in "3rd Fleet Operations 1943–45," William F. Halsey Collection, Library of Congress; Reminiscences of Vice Admiral Andrew McBurney Jackson, Jr., U.S. Naval Institute, Annapolis, Maryland, p. 123.
16. Halsey, *Memoirs,* p. 552; W. F. Halsey, The Commander Third Fleet to the Commander in Chief, United States Fleet. "Report on the Operations of the Third Fleet, 30 December 1944 to 23 January 1945," January 23, 1945, p. 6.
17. Halsey, *Memoirs,* p. 554.
18. Morison, *The Liberation of the Philippines, 1944–1945,* p. 172.
19. Halsey, "Action Report," January 23, 1945, pp. 6, 8.
20. Halsey and Bryan, *Admiral Halsey's Story,* p. 249.
21. Halsey and Bryan, *Admiral Halsey's Story,* p. 290.
22. Halsey and Bryan, *Admiral Halsey's Story,* p. 251.

23. Halsey and Bryan, *Admiral Halsey's Story,* p. 251; Halsey, *Memoirs,* p. 561.
24. Third Fleet War Diary, May 28, 1945.
25. James M. Merrill, *A Sailor's Admiral: A Biography of William F. Halsey* (New York: Thomas Y. Crowell, 1976), p. 215.
26. W. F. Halsey, The Commander Third Fleet to the Commander in Chief, United States Fleet. "Report on the Operations of the Third Fleet, 26 January 1945 to 1 July 1945," July 14, 1945, p. 6.
27. *Time,* July 23, 1945.

CHAPTER 11

1. Fleet Admiral William F. Halsey and Lieutenant Commander J. Bryan III, *Admiral Halsey's Story* (New York: McGraw-Hill, 1947), p. 257; The Reminiscences of Robert Bostwick Carney, 1964, p. 465, in the Oral History Collection of Columbia University.
2. Halsey and Bryan, *Admiral Halsey's Story,* p. 260; William F. Halsey, *Life of Admiral W. F. Halsey,* undated typewritten memoirs dictated by Halsey after the war, p. 575 (hereafter cited as Halsey, *Memoirs*). .3. Halsey, *Memoirs,* p. 575.
4. Halsey and Bryan, *Admiral Halsey's Story,* p. 263; Halsey, *Memoirs,* p. 575.
5. "Bull's Eye," *Time,* July 23, 1945, pp. 27–28.
6. Halsey, *Memoirs,* p. 581.
7. Halsey and Bryan, *Admiral Halsey's Story,* p. 264.
8. Admiral William F. Halsey, as told to Frank D. Morris, "A Plan for Japan," *Collier's,* April 28, 1945, p. 18; Transcript of NBC Radio Interview, February 19, 1945, found in "Speeches 1939–45," William F. Halsey Collection, Library of Congress.
9. The Reminiscences of Robert Bostwick Carney, 1964, p. 442, in the Oral History Collection of Columbia University.
10. William F. Halsey letter to Chester Nimitz, August 9, 1945, "Halsey-Nimitz Letters, 1942–1943," in the William F. Halsey Collection, Library of Congress (hereafter Halsey-Nimitz correspondence.
11. Third Fleet War Diary, August 15, 1945.
12. Halsey, *Memoirs,* p. 592; Potter, *Nimitz,* p. 389.
13. Halsey and Bryan, *Admiral Halsey's Story,* p. 272.
14. Admiral Halsey's Victory Speech, as broadcast to the Third Fleet, August 15, 1945, found in "Speeches 1939–45," William F. Halsey Collection, Library of Congress; Halsey, *Memoirs,* p. 592–593; Halsey and Bryan, *Admiral Halsey's Story,* p. 272; E. B. Potter, *Bull Halsey* (Annapolis, Md.: Naval Institute Press, 1985), p. 348.
15. Halsey, *Memoirs,* p. 591.
16. Halsey and Bryan, *Admiral Halsey's Story,* p. 278.
17. Halsey and Bryan, *Admiral Halsey's Story,* p. 279.
18. Halsey and Bryan, *Admiral Halsey's Story,* p. 275; Halsey, *Memoirs,* p. 598.
19. Halsey and Bryan, *Admiral Halsey's Story,* p. 277.
20. Halsey, *Memoirs,* p. 599.
21. Halsey, *Memoirs,* pp. 608–609.
22. Halsey, *Memoirs,* p. 610.
23. Halsey and Bryan, *Admiral Halsey's Story,* p. 283.
24. "Plug," *Time,* October 22, 1945; "By Nimitz and Halsey and Me," *The Raider Patch,* May 1986.
25. Halsey, *Memoirs,* p. 621.
26. Halsey, *Memoirs,* p. 614.
27. Halsey and Bryan, *Admiral Halsey's Story,* p. 290.
28. The Reminiscences of Robert Bostwick Carney, 1964, p. 478, in the Oral History Collection of Columbia University.
29. James M. Merrill, *A Sailor's Admiral: A Biography of William F. Halsey* (New York: Crowell, 1976), p. 247.

30. Potter, *Halsey,* p. 365.
31. Halsey and Bryan, *Admiral Halsey's Story,* p. 292.
32. Admiral Raymond A. Spruance letter to Admiral T. C. Kinkaid, August 21, 1947, in the Personal Papers of Thomas C. Kinkaid, Naval Historical Center, Washington, D. C., Box 19B, Folder 21; Admiral Thomas C. Kinkaid letter to Captain Arleigh Burke, December 4, 1947, in the Personal Papers of Thomas C. Kinkaid, Naval Historical Center, Washington, D. C., Box 19B, Folder 14.
33. W. F. Halsey letter to Captain H. D. Moulton, November 14, 1958; W. F. Halsey letter to Admiral Robert B. Carney, November 10, 1958, "Leyte Correspondence," William F. Halsey Collection, Library of Congress.
34. Potter, *Halsey,* p. 380; Gerald Wheeler, *Kinkaid of the Seventh Fleet* (Annapolis, Md.: Naval Institute Press, 1996), p. 483.
35. "People," *Time,* June 1, 1959, p. 1.
36. Carl Solberg, *Decision and Dissent: With Halsey at Leyte Gulf* (Annapolis, Md.: Naval Institute Press, 1995), p. 177.
37. Eleanor Roosevelt, "My Day," August 19, 1959.
38. "The General and the Admiral," *Time,* November 10, 1947, p. 1.

SOURCES

PRIMARY SOURCES—COLLECTIONS

William F. Halsey Papers, Library of Congress, contains Halsey's professional papers, letters, and incidental items.

The Eleanor Roosevelt Papers included at the Franklin D. Roosevelt Library, Hyde Park, New York, contains valuable material pertaining to Mrs. Roosevelt's activities and views on the war and personalities. Helpful for this biography were:

—Eleanor Roosevelt Papers, "Letters from Servicemen, 1944: Ha," Box 836

—Eleanor Roosevelt Papers, "Speech and Article File, 1943: Trip to the South Pacific, August–September 1943," Box 1414.

—Roosevelt, Eleanor. "My Day," a newspaper column written during the war. The articles provided Mrs. Roosevelt's thoughts about her trip to the South Pacific while Halsey was commander. Issues consulted were dated August 30, 1943 to February 23, 1960.

Naval Historical Center, Washington, D. C., contains various collections, such as the Clifton A. F. Sprague Collection and the Personal Papers of Thomas C. Kinkaid.

U. S. Naval Institute Oral History Collection, U. S. Naval Academy, the U. S. Naval Institute in Annapolis, Maryland, has a large collection of oral histories. The ones consulted were the reminiscences of:

Adm. George W. Anderson, Jr.
Comdr. Paul H. Backus
Michael J. Bak, Jr.
Hanson W. Baldwin
Roger L. Bond
Adm. Arleigh A. Burke
Rear Adm. Julian T. Burke, Jr.
Vice Adm. John B. Colwell, U.S. Navy (Ret.)
Rear Adm. George van Deurs, U.S. Navy (Ret.)
Capt. Slade D. Cutter
Rear Adm. John F. Davidson
Capt. Robert E. Dornin
Adm. Charles K. Duncan
Vice Adm. George C. Dyer
Rear Adm. Ernest M. Eller
Rear Adm. Francis D. Foley
Rear Adm. Thomas J. Hamilton
LComdr. Richard A. Harralson
Vice Adm. Truman J. Hedding
Vice Adm. Edwin B. Hooper

Vice Adm. Olaf M. Hustvedt
Vice Adm. Andrew McBurney Jackson, Jr.
Adm. Roy L. Johnson
Capt. Stephen Jurika, Jr.
Rear Adm. Draper L. Kauffman
Vice Adm. Jerome H. King, Jr.
Rear Adm. Edwin T. Layton
Vice Adm. Fitzhugh Lee
Vice Adm. Kent L. Lee
Vice Adm. Ruthven E. Libby
Rear Adm. Charles Elliott Loughlin
Vice Adm. William P. Mack
Comdr. Charles M. Melhorn
Vice Adm. Charles S. Minter, Jr.
Adm. Thomas M. Moorer
Rear Adm. Albert G. Mumma
Comdr. Albert K. Murray
Adm. Stuart S. Murray
Vice Adm. Lloyd M. Mustin
Capt. John V. Noel
Vice Adm. Robert B. Pirie
Vice Adm. Herbert D. Riley
Vice Adm. Murrey L. Royar
Adm. James S. Russell
Rear Adm. Malcolm F. Schoeffel
Ambassador William J. Sebald
Adm. Harold E. Shear
Vice Adm. William R. Smedberg, III
Vice Adm. J. Victor Smith
Vice Adm. Roland N. Smoot
Vice Adm. Paul D. Stroop
Rear Adm. Raymond D. Tarbuck
Adm. John S. Thach
Rear Adm. Kemp Tolley
Capt. Daniel W. Tomlinson
Rear Adm. George van Deurs
Adm. Alfred G. Ward
Vice Adm. Charles Wellborn, Jr.
Rear Adm. Joseph M. Worthington

The Naval War College in Newport, Rhode Island contains some helpful oral histories. The one used in this book is: Reminiscences of Vice Admiral Gerald F. Bogan, U.S. Navy (Ret.), 1970–1986, Naval War College, Newport, Rhode Island.

The Oral History Research Office, Columbia University, holds the oral history of Halsey's chief of staff, Robert B. Carney: The Reminiscences of Robert Bostwick Carney, Naval History Project, Oral History Research Office, Columbia University, 1964.

William H. Ashford Oral History, East Carolina Manuscript Collection, J.Y. Joyner Library, East Carolina University, Greenville, N.C., is a series of ten interviews dated January 16, 1979 through May 25, 1983.

United States Strategic Bombing Survey. *Interrogations of Japanese Officials, Volumes I and II.* Washington, D.C.: Naval Analysis Division. Interrogations used:

—Interrogation No. 11: Interrogation of Captain Susumu Kawaguchi, Air Officer on the *Hiryu,* pp. 4–6.

—Interrogation No. 65: Interrogation of Captain Y. Watanabe Kawaguchi, Gunnery Officer on Admiral Yamamoto's staff, pp. 65–70.
—Interrogation No. 60: Interrogation of Captain Yasumi Toyama, Chief of Staff Second Destroyer Squadron, pp. 249–254.
—Interrogation No. 75: Interrogation of Comdr. Masatake Okumiya, on Air Staff and Commander Rabaul Air Group, pp. 77–82.
—Interrogation No. 195: Interrogation of Lieut. Comdr. S. Yunoki, fire control director on *Hiei*, pp. 191–193.
—Interrogation No. 224: Interrogation of Comdr. Yasumi Doi, gunnery officer on staff of South Eastern Fleet based at Rabaul, pp. 209–211.
—Interrogation No. 435: Interrogation of Comdr. Yasumi Doi, gunnery officer on staff of South Eastern Fleet based at Rabaul, pp. 397–398.
—Interrogation No. 446: Interrogation of Capt. Takashi Miyazaki, Commanding Officer of the Fourth Air Group, pp. 413–421.
—Interrogation No. 464: Interrogation of Rear Admiral Keizo Komura, IJN, Commanding Officer of *Chikuma*, pp. 456–462.
—Interrogation No. 467: Interrogation of Capt. Toshikazu Ohmae, Chief of Staff, Southeastern Fleet at Rabaul, pp. 468–484.
—Interrogation No. 503: Interrogation of Vice Adm. Shigeru Fukudome, IJN, Chief of Staff, Combined Fleet, 1940–1941, 1943–1944, pp. 501–530.

PRIMARY SOURCES—ACTION REPORTS

FOR EVENTS SURROUNDING PEARL HARBOR:

Anderson, Lt. (jg) E. L. to Commander, Bombing Squadron Six, "Contact with Enemy Submarine, 10 December 1941," December 15, 1941 found at the USS *Enterprise* (CV-6) Association's web site, www.cv6.org.
Dickinson, Lt. C. E. to Commander, Scouting Squadron Six, "Report of Action with Japanese on Oahu on 7 December, 1941," December 12, 1941, found at the USS *Enterprise* (CV-6) Association's web site, www.cv6.org.
Gallaher, Lt. W. E. to Commander, Scouting Squadron Six, "Report ofAction with Japanese on Oahu on 7 December, 1941," December 13, 1941, found at the USS *Enterprise* (CV-6) Association's web site, www.cv6.org.
Hilton, Lt. (jg) H. D. to Commander, Scouting Squadron Six, "Report of Action with Japanese on Oahu on 7 December, 1941," December 13, 1941, found at the USS *Enterprise* (CV-6) Association's web site, www.cv6.org.
Hopping, LCDR. H. L. to Commanding Officer, USS *Enterprise* (CV-6), "Scouting Squadron Six Action Report, 7 December 1941," December 15, 1941, found at the USS *Enterprise* (CV-6) Association's web site, www.cv6.org.
Murray, Capt. G. D., "Battle Order Number 1," November 28, 1941, found at the USS *Enterprise* (CV-6) Association's web site, www.cv6.org.
Murray, Capt. G. D., "Battle Order Number 2," November 28, 1941, found at the USS *Enterprise* (CV-6) Association's web site, www.cv6.org.
Patriarca, Ens. F. A. to Commanding Officer, USS *Enterprise* (CV-6), "Report of Action with Japanese on Oahu on 7 December, 1941," December 20, 1941, found at the USS *Enterprise* (CV-6) Association's web site, www.cv6.org.
Roberts, Ens. W. E. to Commander, Bombing Squadron Six, "Air Attack on Oahu Observed Sunday Morning, 7 December 1941," December 13, 1941, found at the USS *Enterprise* (CV-6) Association's web site, www.cv6.org.
Walters, Ens. C. R. to Commander, Bombing Squadron Six, "Contacts For War Diary," December 13, 1941, found at the USS *Enterprise* (CV-6) Association's web site, www.cv6.org.

Young, LCDR H. L. to Commanding Officer, USS *Enterprise* (CV-6), "*Enterprise* Air Group Action Report, 7 December 1941," December 15, 1941, found at the USS *Enterprise* (CV-6) Association's web site, www.cv6.org.

FOR THE MARSHALL ISLAND RAID:

Best, Lt. R. H., "Action Report of Attack on Taroa Island, Maloelap Atoll, 1 February 1942 by Nine Bomber Land Planes," February 2, 1942, found at the USS *Enterprise* (CV-6) Association's web site, www.cv6.org.
"Damage Reports, Marshall Islands," February 2, 1942, found at theUSS *Enterprise* (CV-6) Association's web site, www.cv6.org.
Hollingsworth, LCDR W. R. to Commanding Officer, USS *Enterprise* (CV-6), "FlightLeader's Report of Dawn Attack on Kwajalein Atoll, 1 February, 1942," February 2, 1942, found at the USS *Enterprise* (CV-6) Association's web site, www.cv6.org.
Hollingsworth, LCDR W. R. to Commanding Officer, USS *Enterprise* (CV-6), "Flight Leader's Report of Dawn Attack on Maloelap at 1030, 1 February, 1942, by Nine SBD's" February 2, 1942, found at the USS *Enterprise* (CV-6) Association's web site, www.cv6.org.
Murray, Capt. G. D. to Commander in Chief, U.S. Pacific Fleet, "Report of Action on February 1, 1942 against Marshall Island Group," 7 Feb. 1942,found at the USS *Enterprise* (CV-6) Association's web site, www.cv6.org.
Rush, Daniel, "John Doherty and Bombing Six," pp. 1–4, found at the USS *Enterprise* (CV-6) Association's web site, www.cv6.org.

FOR THE WAKE AND MARCUS RAIDS

Hollingsworth, LCDR W. R. to Commander *Enterprise* Air Group, "Attack on Wake Island, February 24, 1942," February 25, 1942,found at the USS *Enterprise* (CV-6) Association's web site, www.cv6.org.
Hollingsworth, LCDR W. R. to Commander *Enterprise* Air Group, "Attack on Marcus Island, March 4, 1942," March 4, 1942,found at the USS *Enterprise* (CV-6) Association's web site, www.cv6.org.

FOR THE DOOLITTLE RAID

Biard, Capt. Forrest "Tex." Speech delivered to the National Cryptologic Museum Foundation, July 12, 2002, found in http://www.usspennsylvania.com/TheDungeon.htm, pp. 1–9.
Doolittle, Lt. Col. James H. to the Commanding General, Army Air Forces, "Report on Japanese Raid, April 18, 1942," July 9, 1942.
Halsey, W. F. to Commander-in-Chief, U. S. Pacific Fleet, Task Force 16 Action Report, "Report of action in connection with the bombing of Tokyo on April 18, 1942," at sea, April 24, 1942, found at the USS *Enterprise* (CV-6) Association's web site, www.cv6.org.
Mitscher, Capt. Marc A. to Commander-in-Chief, U. S. Pacific Fleet, USS *Hornet* (CV-8) Action Report, "Report of Action, 18 April 1942," April 28, 1942.
Murray, G. D. to Commander-in-Chief, U. S. Pacific Fleet, USS *Enterprise* (CV-6)Action Report, "Report of action in connection with the bombing of Tokyo on April 18, 1942," April 23, 1942, found at the USS *Enterprise* (CV-6) Association's web site, www.cv6.org.

FOR MIDWAY:

USS *Enterprise,* "War Diary, April 1942 to June 1942."
Mitscher, Capt. Marc A. to Commander-in-Chief, U. S. Pacific Fleet, USS *Hornet* (CV-8) Action Report, "Report of Action, 4–6 June 1942," June 13, 1942.
Spruance, R. A., to Commander-in-Chief, U. S. Pacific Fleet, Task Force 16 ActionReport, "Battle of Midway," June 16, 1942.

FOR THE SOUTH PACIFIC:

Combat Narrative, "Kolombangara and Vella Lavella, 6 August–7 October 1943."

USS *Enterprise,* "War Diary, November 1942 to January 1943."

Halsey, W. F., The Commander South Pacific Area and South Pacific Force to the Commander-in-Chief, U. S. Pacific Fleet, "Loss of *Juneau,* circumstances of," November 22, 1942.

———. The Commander Third Fleet to the Commander in Chief, United States Fleet, "South Pacific Campaign—Narrative account," September 3, 1944.

Hamberger, D. C. The Commanding Officer USS *Converse* to the Commander in Chief,United States Fleet, "Report of action 24–25 November 1943 off Cape Saint George," November 27, 1943.

Hardison, O. B. Commanding Officer, USS *Enterprise* to the Commander in Chief,United States Fleet, "Action against Japanese Air Forces Attacking Task Force Eighteen off Rennell Island," February 6, 1943.

Hill, A. J. The Commanding Officer, USS *Nicholas* to the Commander-in-Chief, U. S. Pacific Fleet, "Action Report," July 7, 1943.

Hoover, Captain Gilbert C., U.S.N., Commanding Officer to Commander-in-Chief, U. S. Pacific Fleet, "Submarine Torpedo Attack on Task Unit and Sinking of U.S.S. *Juneau,* report of," At sea, November 14, 1942.

Hoover, Captain Gilbert C., U.S.N., ex-Commanding Officer, U.S.S. *Helena* to Commander-in-Chief, U. S. Pacific Fleet, "Loss of *Juneau,* circumstances of," November 28, 1942.

McCleary, Lt. (jg) E. E. "History US Naval Advanced Base Guadalcanal, 1942–1945," Naval History Division, October 31, 1945, National Archives and Records Administration, College Park, Maryland.

Moosbrugger, Frederick. Commander Destroyer Division Twelve to the Commander in Chief, U.S. Pacific Fleet, "Action Report for Night of August 6–7, 1943—Battle of Vella Gulf," August 16, 1943.

Nimitz, Adm. Chester W., Commander-in-Chief, U. S. Pacific Fleet to Commander-in-Chief, United States Fleet, "Loss of *Juneau,* circumstances of," December 4, 1942.

Rubb, Lt. D. C., ComSoPac Staff, "Operational History of the South Pacific," Compiled 1945, World War II Command File, South Pacific Naval Force, Air Combat Intelligence Report, in National Archives, College Park, Maryland.

THIRD FLEET:

Glover, Cato D. The Commanding Officer to The Commander in Chief, United States Fleet. "Action Report—Fleet Action and Operations Against the Philippine Islands Area, from 22 to 31 October 1944," November 3, 1944.

Halsey, W. F. The Commander Third Fleet to The Commander in Chief, United States Fleet. "Action Report—Period 23–26 October 1944, both dates inclusive," November 13, 1944.

———. The Commander Third Fleet to The Commander in Chief, United States Fleet. "Report on Seizure of Southern Palau Islands and Ulithi, and Concurrent Operations in Support of the Seizure of Morotai," November 14, 1944.

———. The Commander Third Fleet to The Commander in Chief, United States Fleet. "Action Reports—forwarding of (in regards to Baitdiv)," November 26, 1944.

———. The Commander Third Fleet to The Commander in Chief, United States Fleet. "Report on operations preliminary to and in support of the Leyte-Samar Operations, October 1944," November 28, 1944.

———. The Commander Third Fleet to The Commander in Chief, United States Fleet. "Report on Operations in Support of the Leyte-Samar Operations for period 27 October–30 November 1944," December 9, 1944.

———. The Commander Third Fleet to The Commander in Chief, United States Fleet. "Typhoon in Philippine Sea, 17–22 December 1944," December 25, 1944.

———. The Commander Third Fleet to The Commander in Chief, United States Fleet. "Report on the Operations of the Third Fleet, 1–29 December 1944," January 10, 1945.
———. The Commander Third Fleet to The Commander in Chief, United States Fleet. "Report on the Operations of the Third Fleet, 30 December 1944 to 23 January 1945," January 23, 1945.
———. The Commander Third Fleet to The Commander in Chief, United States Fleet. "Third Fleet experience with typhoon, 3–6 June 1945," June 18, 1945.
———. The Commander Third Fleet to The Commander in Chief, United States Fleet. "Report on the Operations of the Third Fleet, 26 January 1945 to 1 July 1945," July 14, 1945.
———. The Commander Third Fleet to The Commander in Chief, United States Fleet. "Report on the Operations of the Third Fleet 1 July 1945 to 15 August 1945," August 1945.
———. The Commander Third Fleet to The Commander in Chief, United States Fleet. "Report on the Operations of the Third Fleet 16 August 1945 to 19 September 1945," October 6, 1945.
Kinkaid, T. G. Commander Task Force Seventy-Seven to Commander-in-Chief, United States Fleet. "Preliminary Action Report of Engagements in Leyte Gulf and off Samar Island on 25 October, 1944," November 18, 1944.
Lee, W. A. Commander Task Force Thirty-Four to Commander in Chief, United States Fleet. "Report of Operations of Task Force Thirty-Four During the Period 6 October 1944 to 3 December 1944," December 14, 1944.
Nimitz, Chester W. Commander in Chief, U.S. Pacific Fleet and Pacific Ocean Areas, "Operations in the Pacific Ocean Areas During the Month of December 1944," pp.12–13, and 72–86. World War II Command File, Operational Archives Branch, Naval Historical Center, Washington, DC. Found at: http://www.history.navy.mil/faqs/faq102–4f.htm
Office of Naval Air Combat Intelligence, South Pacific Force. "The Reduction of Rabaul, 19 February to 15 May 1944," June 8, 1944.
Record of Proceedings of a Court of Inquiry convened on board the U.S.S.*Cascade* by order of the Commander-in-Chief, U.S. Pacific Fleet, United States Fleet, To inquire into all the circumstances connected with the loss of the U.S.S. *Hull* (DD 350), U.S.S. *Monaghan* (DD 354), and the U.S.S. *Spence* (DD 512), and damage sustained by the U.S.S. *Monterey* (CVL 26) and the U.S.S. *Cowpens* (CVL 28), and other damage sustained by ships of the Third Fleet as the result of adverse weather on or about December 18, 1944, submitted December 28, 1944.
Sprague, Rear Adm. Clifton to The Commander in Chief, United States Fleet. "Action against the Japanese Main Body off Samar Island, 25 October 1944, Special Report of," October 29, 1944.
Third Fleet War Diary, August 1944 to November 1945.
Turner, R. K. Commander Amphibious Force, South Pacific to Commander South Pacific Force. "Report of Occupation of Russell Islands February 12 to April 17, 1943," April 21, 1943.
White, Lt. Robb, USNR, Public Relations, CinCPac. Confidential Report on board *Natoma Bay,* 25 October 1944, Aviation History Files, Naval Historical Center.

SURRENDER OF JAPAN:

Halsey, W. F. "Third Fleet Operations, 1 November 1944 to 19 September 1945." Undated report found in "3rd Fleet Operations 1943–1945," in the William F. Halsey Collection, Library of Congress.
"Memorandum for Lt. Comdr. Hughes," a handwritten set of notes found in the Folder, "3rd Fleet Operations 1943–45," in the William F. Halsey Collection, Library of Congress.
"Summary of Damage to Enemy Inflicted by Third Fleet Forces, 28 May thru Aug. 1945," in the Folder, "3rd Fleet Operations 1943–45," in the William F. Halsey Collection, Library of Congress.

INTERVIEWS

CAPT. HENRY BURT BASSETT
Torpedo plane pilot, USS *Gambier Bay*
Personal interview, October 4, 2007
Telephone interview, February 2, 1994

JOSEPH GOICOECHEA
Prisoner of War, Omori Prison Camp
Personal interviews, April 10, 2002; April 12, 2002
Telephone interviews, February 26, 2002; March 5, 2002
RAYMOND "HAP" HALLORAN
Prisoner of War, Omori Prison Camp
Telephone interview, September 26, 2007
VICE ADM. TRUMAN HEDDING
Deputy Chief of Staff for Adm. Marc A. Mitscher
Telephone interview, September 30, 1993
VERNON D. HIPCHINGS, JR.
Visual fighter-director, USS *Fanshaw Bay*
Telephone interview, January 31, 1994
JOHN DUDLEY MOYLAN
Sonar officer, USS *Samuel B. Roberts*
Telephone interview, February 7, 1994
ADM. JAMES RAMAGE
Aviator, USS *Enterprise*
Telephone interview, January 15, 2009
ADM. JAMES S. RUSSELL
Chief of Staff for Rear Adm. Ralph E. Davison
Telephone interviews, April 14, 1992 and April 21, 1992
COURTNEY SPRAGUE VAUGHAN
Daughter of Vice Adm. Clifton A. F. Sprague
Personal interview, August 16, 1991
THOMAS STEVENSON
Communications officer, USS *Samuel B. Roberts*
Telephone interview, February 7, 1994
CARNES WEEKS JR.
Son of Dr. Carnes Weeks
Telephone interview, August 24, 2009.

BOOKS

Abend, Hallett. *Ramparts of the Pacific.* Garden City, New York: Doubleday, Doran, 1942.
Adamson, Hans Christian and George Francis Kosco. *Halsey's Typhoons.* New York: Crown, 1967.
Agawa, Hiroyuki. *The Reluctant Admiral: Yamamoto and the Imperial Navy.* Tokyo: Kodansha International Ltd., 1979.
Arnold, H. H. *Global Mission.* New York: Harper & Brothers, 1949.
Arpee, Edward. *From Frigates to Flat-Tops.* Chicago: Lakeside Press, 1953.
Barnhill, James C. *Tell Us, Daddy.* New York: Vantage Press, 1980.
Belote, James H. and William M. *Titans of the Seas.* New York: Harper & Row, 1975.
Bergerud, Eric M. *Fire in the Sky: The Air War in the South Pacific.* Boulder, Colo.: Westview Press, 2000.
Bix, Herbert P. *Hirohito and the Making of Modern Japan.* New York: HarperCollins, 2000.
Boyington, Col. Gregory. *Baa Baa Black Sheep.* New York: G. P. Putnam's Sons, 1958.
Buell, Thomas B. *Master of Sea Power: A Biography of Fleet Admiral Ernest J. King.* Boston: Little, Brown, 1980.
———. *The Quiet Warrior: A Biography of Admiral Raymond A. Spruance.* Boston: Little, Brown, 1974.
Burns, James MacGregor. *Roosevelt: The Soldier of Freedom.* New York: Harcourt Brace Jovanovich, Inc., 1970.
Calhoun, Captain C. Raymond. *Typhoon: The Other Enemy.* Annapolis, Md.: Naval Institute Press, 1981.

Cant, Gilbert. *America's Navy in World War II.* New York: John Day, 1943.
Casey, Robert J. *Torpedo Junction: With the Pacific Fleet from Pearl Harbor to Midway.* Indianapolis: Bobbs-Merrill, 1942.
Clark, J. J. and Clark G. Reynolds. *Carrier Admiral.* New York: David McKay, 1967.
Clayton, James, D. *The Years of MacArthur.* Boston: Houghton Mifflin, 1975.
Coffey, Thomas, M. *Hap.* New York: Viking, 1982.
Costello, John. *The Pacific War, 1941–1945.* New York: Quill, 1982.
Cressman, Robert J. and J. Michael Wenger. *Steady Nerves and Stout Hearts.* Missoula, Mont.: Pictorial Histories Publishing Company, 1989.
Crosby, Donald F., S.J. *Battlefield Chaplains: Catholic Priests in World War II.* Lawrence: University Press of Kansas, 1994.
Cutler, Thomas J. *The Battle of Leyte Gulf.* New York: HarperCollins, 1994.
Davis, Burke. *The Billy Mitchell Affair.* New York: Random House, 1967.
Dickinson, Lieut. Clarence E. with Boyden Sparkes. *The Flying Guns.* New York: Charles Scribner's Sons, 1943.
Dillard, Nancy R. "Operational Leadership: A Case Study of Two Extremes During Operation *Watchtower.*" Newport, R.I.: Naval War College, 1997.
Doolittle, General James H., with Carroll V. Glines. *I Could Never Be So Lucky Again.* New York: Bantam, 1991.
Dower, John W. *War Without Mercy: Race and Power in the Pacific War.* New York: Pantheon, 1986.
Drury, Bob and Tom Clavin. *Halsey's Typhoon.* New York: Atlantic Monthly Press, 2007.
Dull, Paul S. *A Battle History of the Imperial Japanese Navy (1941–1945).* Annapolis, Md.: Naval Institute Press, 1978.
Dyer, Vice Admiral George Carroll, USN (Ret.). *The Amphibians Came to Conquer: The Story of Admiral Richmond Kelly Turner.* 2 Volumes. Washington, D.C.: U.S. Government Printing Office, 1971.
Evans, Dr. David C., Editor and Translator. *The Japanese Navy in World War II: In the Words of Former Japanese Naval Officers.* Annapolis, Md.: Naval Institute Press, 1986.
Fahey, James J. *Pacific War Diary, 1942–1945.* Boston: Houghton Mifflin, 1963.
Field, James A., Jr. *The Japanese at Leyte Gulf: The Sho Operation.* Princeton, N. J.: Princeton University Press, 1947.
Forrestel, E. P. *Admiral Raymond A. Spruance, USN: A Study in Command.* Washington, D.C.: U.S. Government Printing Office, 1966.
Frank, Benis. *Halsey.* New York: Ballantine Books, 1947.
Frank, Richard B. *Guadalcanal.* New York: Random House, 1990.
Fuchida, Mitsuo and Masatake Okumiya. *Midway: The Battle That Doomed Japan.* Annapolis, Md.: Naval Institute Press, 1955.
Gailey, Harry A. *Bougainville, 1943–1945: The Forgotten Campaign.* Lexington: University Press of Kentucky, 1991.
Gilbert, Alton Keith. *A Leader Born: The Life of Admiral John Sidney McCain, Pacific Carrier Commander.* Philadelphia: Casemate, 2006.
Glines, Carroll. *Doolittle's Tokyo Raiders.* Princeton, N. J.: D. Van Nostrand, 1964.
———. *The Doolittle Raid.* New York: Orion Books, 1988.
Halsey, Fleet Admiral William F. and Lieutenant Commander J. Bryan III. *Admiral Halsey's Story.* New York: McGraw-Hill, 1947.
———. *Life of Admiral W. F. Halsey,* undated typewritten memoirs dictated by Halsey after the war.
Hammel, Eric. *Munda Trail.* New York: Orion, 1989.
Hara, Captain Tameichi, Fred Saito and Roger Pineau. *Japanese Destroyer Captain.* New York: Ballantine, 1961.
Hart, Robert A. *The Great White Fleet.* Boston: Little, Brown, 1965.
Heefner, Wilson Allen, M.D. *Twentieth Century Warrior: The Life and Service of Major General Edwin D. Patrick.* Shippensburg, Pa.: White Mane Publishing, 1995.

Henderson, Bruce. *Down to the Sea.* New York: Smithsonian Books, 2007. *The History of the Lives and Bloody Exploits of the Most Noted Pirates; Their Trials and Executions.* New York: Empire State Book Company, 1926.

Hoffman, Lt. Col. Jon T. USMCR. *Chesty: The Story of Lieutenant General Lewis B. Puller, USMC.* New York: Random House, 2001.

Holmes, W.J. *Double-Edged Secrets: U.S. Naval Intelligence Operations in the Pacific during World War II.* Annapolis, Md.: Naval Institute Press, 1979.

Hough, Lt. Col. Frank O., Major Verle E. Ludwig, and Henry I. Shaw. *History of U. S. Marine Corps Operations in World War II: Volume I: Pearl Harbor to Guadalcanal.* Washington, D.C.: Historical Branch, Headquarters, U. S. Marine Corps, 1958.

Hoyt, Edwin P. *Yamamoto: The Man Who Planned Pearl Harbor.* New York: McGraw-Hill, 1990.

———. *How They Won the War in the Pacific: Nimitz and His Admirals.* New York: Lyons Press, 2000.

James, D. Clayton. *The Years of MacArthur, Volume II: 1941–1945.* Boston: Houghton Mifflin Company, 1975.

Jordan, Ralph. *Born to Fight: The Life of Admiral Halsey.* Philadelphia: David McKay, 1946.

Karig, Capt. Walter, Lt. Comdr. Russell L. Harris, and Lt. Comdr. Frank A. Manson. *Battle Report: The End of An Empire.* New York: Rinehart, 1948.

Kenney, George C. *General Kenney Reports.* New York: Duell, Sloan and Pearce, 1949.

King, Ernest J. and Walter Muir Whitehill. *Fleet Admiral King: A Naval Record.* New York: W. W. Norton, 1952.

Kurzman, Dan. *Left to Die: The Tragedy of the USS* Juneau. New York: Pocket Books, 1994.

Lardner, John. *Southwest Passage: The Yanks in the Pacific.* Philadelphia: J. B. Lippincott, 1943.

Larrabee, Eric. *Commander in Chief: Franklin Delano Roosevelt, His Lieutenants, and Their War.* New York: Harper & Row, 1987.

Lash, Joseph P. *Eleanor and Franklin.* New York: W. W. Norton, 1971.

———. *Roosevelt and Churchill, 1939–1941.* New York: W. W. Norton, 1976.

Lee, Clark. *They Call It Pacific: An Eye-Witness Story of Our War Against Japan from Bataan to the Solomons.* New York: Viking, 1943.

Lingeman, Richard R. *Don't You Know There's A War On?* New York: G. P. Putnam's Sons, 1970.

Lord, Walter. *Incredible Victory.* New York: Harper & Row, 1967.

Lundstrom, John B. *The First South Pacific Campaign: Pacific Fleet Strategy, December 1941-June 1942.* Annapolis, Md.: Naval Institute Press, 1976.

———. *The First Team: Pacific Naval Air Combat from Pearl Harbor to Midway.* Annapolis, Md.: Naval Institute Press, 1984.

———. *The First Team and the Guadalcanal Campaign.* Annapolis, Md.: Naval Institute Press, 1994.

———. *Black Shoe Carrier Admiral: Frank Jack Fletcher at Coral Sea, Midway, and Guadalcanal.* Annapolis, Md.: Naval Institute Press, 2006.

MacArthur, Douglas. *Reminiscences.* New York: McGraw-Hill, 1964.

Manchester, William. *American Caesar.* Boston: Little, Brown, 1978.

———. *Goodbye, Darkness.* Boston: Little, Brown, 1979.

Manning, Paul. *Hirohito: The War Years.* New York: Dodd, Mead, 1986.

Mason, John T., Jr., Editor. *The Pacific War Remembered.* Annapolis, Md.: Naval Institute Press, 1986.

McClurg, Lieut. Col. Robert W. *On Boyington's Wing.* Westminster, Md.: Eagle Editions, 2006.

Melton, Buckner F., Jr. *Sea Cobra.* Guilford, Conn.: Lyons Press, 2007.

Merrill, James M. *A Sailor's Admiral: A Biography of William F. Halsey.* New York: Crowell, 1976.

Mersky, Peter B. *U.S. Marine Corps Aviation: 1912 to the Present.* Annapolis, Md.: The Nautical & Aviation Publishing Company of America, 1983.

Miller, John Jr. *The United States Army in World War II: The War in the Pacific: Guadalcanal: The First Offensive.* Washington, D.C.: Center of Military History, 1989.

Miller, Nathan. *War at Sea: A Naval History of World War II.* New York: Oxford University Press, 1995.

Morella, Joe, Edward Z. Epstein, and John Griggs. *The Films of World War II.* Secaucus, N.J.: Citadel Press, 1973.

Morison, Samuel Eliot. *History of United States Naval Operations in World War II, Volume III: The Rising Sun in the Pacific, 1931–April 1942.* Boston: Little, Brown, 1948.

———. *History of United States Naval Operations in World War II, Volume IV: Coral Sea, Midway and Submarine Actions, May 1942–August 1942.* Boston: Little, Brown, 1949.

———. *History of United States Naval Operations in World War II, Volume V: The Struggle for Guadalcanal, August 1942–February 1943.* Boston: Little, Brown, 1949.

———. *History of United States Naval Operations in World War II, Volume VI: Breaking the Bismarcks Barrier, 22 July 1942–1 May 1944.* Boston: Little, Brown, 1950.

———. *History of United States Naval Operations in World War II, Volume XII: Leyte, June 1944-January 1945.* Boston: Little, Brown, 1958.

———. *History of United States Naval Operations in World War II, Volume XIII: The Liberation of the Philippines, 1944–1945.* Boston: Little, Brown, 1959.

———. *History of United States Naval Operations in World War II, Volume XIV: Victory in the Pacific, 1945.* Boston: Little, Brown, 1960.

———. *The Two-Ocean War.* Boston: Little, Brown, 1963.

Murphy, Francis X. *Fighting Admiral: The Story of Dan Callaghan.* New York: Vantage Press, 1952.

Okumiya, Masatake, Jiro Horikoshi, and Martin Caidon. *Zero.* New York: Simon & Schuster, 2002.

Parshall, Jonathan B. and Anthony P. Tully. *Shattered Sword: The Untold Story of The Battle of Midway.* Washington, D.C.: Potomac Books, 2005.

Perret, Geoffrey. *Old Soldiers Never Die: The Life of Douglas MacArthur.* Holbrook, Mass.: Adams Media Corporation, 1996.

Pierson, Lt. Verling. "The Battle off Samar." Personal recollections.

Pogue, Forrest C. *George C. Marshall: Ordeal and Hope, 1939–1942.* New York: Viking, 1966.

———. *George C. Marshall: Organizer of Victory, 1943–1945.* New York: Viking, 1973.

Potter. E. B. *Nimitz.* Annapolis, Md.: Naval Institute Press, 1976.

———. *Bull Halsey.* Annapolis, Md.: Naval Institute Press, 1985.

———. *Admiral Arleigh Burke: A Biography.* New York: Random House, 1990.

Potter, E. B. and Fleet Admiral Chester W. Nimitz, U.S.N., Editors. *Triumph in the Pacific: The Navy's Struggle Against Japan.* Englewood Cliffs, N.J.: Prentice-Hall, 1963.

Prados, John. *Combined Fleet Decoded.* New York: Random House, 1995.

Prange, Gordon W. with Donald M. Goldstein and Katherine V. Dillon. *Miracle at Midway.* New York: Penguin, 1982.

Pyle, Ernie. *Last Chapter.* New York: Henry Holt, 1945.

Reckner, James R. *Teddy Roosevelt's Great White Fleet.* Annapolis, Md.: Naval Institute Press, 1988.

Reynolds, Clark G. *The Fast Carriers.* McGraw-Hill, 1968.

———. *The Carrier War.* Alexandria, Virginia: Time-Life Books, 1982.

———. *On the Warpath in the Pacific: Admiral Jocko Clark and the Fast Carriers.* Annapolis, Md.: Naval Institute Press, 2005.

Rose, Lisle A. *The Ship That Held the Line.* Annapolis, Md.: Naval Institute Press, 1995.

———. *Power at Sea, Volume 2: The Breaking Storm, 1919–1945.* Columbia: University of Missouri Press, 2007.

Satterfield, John R. *We Band of Brothers: The Sullivans and World War II.* Parkersburg, Iowa: Mid-Prairie Books, 1995.

Schom, Alan. *The Eagle and the Rising Sun: The Japanese-American War, 1941–1943.* New York: W. W. Norton, 2004.

Sherman, Frederick C., Admiral (USN, Ret.). *Combat Command.* New York: E. P. Dutton, 1950.

Sherrod, Robert. *History of Marine Corps Aviation in World War II.* Baltimore, Md.: The Nautical & Aviation Publishing Company of America, 1987.

Sherwood, Robert E. *Roosevelt and Hopkins: An Intimate History.* New York: Harper & Brothers, 1948.

Shindler, Colin. *Hollywood Goes to War.* London: Routledge & Kegan Paul, 1979.

Smith, S. E., Editor. *The United States Navy in World War II.* New York: Quill, 1966.

Solberg, Carl. *Decision and Dissent: With Halsey at Leyte Gulf.* Annapolis, Md.: Naval Institute Press, 1995.
Spector, Ronald H. *Eagle Against the Sun.* New York: Free Press, 1985.
Stafford, Edward P. *The Big E: The Story of the USS Enterprise.* New York: Random House, 1962.
Styling, Mark. *Corsair Aces of World War 2.* London: Osprey Publishing, 1995.
Taussig, Betty Carney. *A Warrior for Freedom.* Manhattan, Kans.: Sunflower University Press, 1995.
Taylor, Theodore. *The Magnificent Mitscher.* New York: W. W. Norton, 1954.
Thomas Evan. *Sea of Thunder: Four Commanders and the Last Great Naval Campaign, 1941–1945.* New York: Simon & Schuster, 2006.
Toland, John. *But Not In Shame: The Six Months After Pearl Harbor.* New York: Random House, 1961.
———. *The Rising Sun: The Decline and Fall of the Japanese Empire, 1936–1945.* New York: Random House, 1970.
Tuohy, William. *America's Fighting Admirals.* St. Paul, Minn.: Zenith Press, 2007.
Ugaki, Matome. *Fading Victory: The Diary of Admiral Matome Ugaki 1941–1945.* Translated by Masataka Chihaya. Pittsburgh: University of Pittsburgh Press, 1991.
Vandegrift, A. A. *Once A Marine.* New York: W. W. Norton, 1964.
Walton, Frank. *Once They Were Eagles.* Lexington: University Press of Kentucky, 1986.
Wheeler, Gerald. *Kinkaid of the Seventh Fleet.* Annapolis, Md.: Naval Institute Press, 1996.
Wheeler, Richard. *A Special Valor: The U.S. Marines and the Pacific War.* New York: New American Library, 1983.
Wilhelm, Major Karen S. "The Image of Military Leadership: To Be or Not to Be a Hero." Newport, R.I.: Naval War College, 1994.
Willoughby, Major General Charles A. and John Chamberlain. *MacArthur, 1941–1945.* New York: McGraw-Hill, 1054.
Woodward, C. Vann. *The Battle for Leyte Gulf.* New York: Macmillan, 1947.
Wooldridge, E. T., Editor. *Carrier Warfare in the Pacific: An Oral History Collection.* Washington, D.C.: Smithsonian Institution Press, 1993.
Wukovits, John F. *Devotion to Duty.* Annapolis, Md.: Naval Institute Press, 1995.
Y'Blood, William T. *Red Sun Setting: The Battle of the Philippine Sea.* Annapolis, Md.: Naval Institute Press, 1981.

ARTICLES

"Adm. Halsey, Hero of Marshalls, Addresses Senior Midshipmen." *Washington Post,* September 6, 1942, p. S4.
"Admiral Halsey vs. Gen. Yahagi—Two Predictions." *Los Angeles Times,* January 5, 1943, p. A4.
"The Admiral Shoves Off." *Time,* June 26, 1944, p. 64.
"Admiral Takes Big Chances to Gain Big Victories." *Washington Post,* November 17, 1942, pp. 1, 8.
"The Admirals." *Time,* December 6, 1943, pp. 72–75.
"Against the Periphery." *Time,* July 12, 1943.
"Aggressive Spirit." *Washington Post* Editorial, November 22, 1942, p. B6.
"A Letter to Tojo." *Time,* March 29, 1943, pp. 16–17.
Andidora, Ronald. "Pacific Fleet Commanders in Contrast." *World War II,* November 1994, pp. 46–50, 87–88.
Andrews, Marshall. "Halsey Replaces Ghormley." *Washington Post,* October 25, 1942, pp. 1–2.
———. "Yanks Make New Guadalcanal Gains." *Washington Post,* November 22, 1942, p.5.
Andrews, Peter. "The Defense of Wake." *American Heritage,* July-August 1987, pp. 65–80.
"Another Coral Sea?" *Time,* November 9, 1942, pp. 27–28.
"Attack on the U.S." *Time,* March 2, 1942, p. 9.
Baldwin, Hanson W. "They Provide Enemy with a Fortified Screen and Points For Attack Against United Nations in Southwest Pacific." *New York Times,* February 9, 1942, p. 4.
———. "Lessons of the Solomons Campaign." *New York Times,* October 24, 1942, p. 3.
———. "Most Dramatic Sea Battle of History." *New York Times Magazine,* October 24, 1954, pp. 14, 61–67.

"Battle Lost." *Time,* September 28, 1942, p. 57.
"Battle Stations." *Time,* December 8, 1941, pp. 15–16.
Bernstein, Marc D. "He Predicted Leyte Gulf." *Naval History,* October 2001, pp. 26–29.
Bradsher, Greg. "The 'Z Plan' Story: Japan's 1944 Naval Battle Strategy Drifts into U.S. Hands." *Prologue,* Fall 2005, found at www.archives.gov/publications/prologue/2005/fall/z-plan–1.html
"Bull's-Eye." *Time,* July 23, 1945, pp. 27–29.
Burke, Adm. Arleigh. "Unforgettable 'Bull' Halsey." *Reader's Digest,* September 1973, pp. 117–121.
"By Nimitz and Halsey and Me." *Raider Patch,* May 1986.
"Calhoun of Serfor." *Time,* September 14, 1942, pp. 55–56.
Cant, Gilbert. "Bull's Run: Was Halsey Right at Leyte Gulf?" *Life,* November 14, 1947, pp. 73–80.
"C. E. Dickinson Jr. Honored by Navy." *New York Times,* September 14, 1942, p. 10.
Clausen, Walter B. "Jap Air Raids Menace Knox, Nimitz, Halsey on Pacific Tour." *Washington Post,* February 1, 1943, pp. 1, 3.
"Colonel Blunt." *Time,* March 9, 1942, p. 10.
"Come Out and Fight." *Time,* November 8, 1943, pp. 26–30.
Crowther, Bosley. "With Halsey in the Pacific." *New York Times,* June 23, 1960, p. 19.
"Die, But Do Not Retreat." *Time,* January 4, 1943, pp. 21–24.
Drury, Robert and Tom Clavin. "How Lieutenant Ford Saved His Ship." *New York Times,* December 28, 2006.
"Dulling of the Thorns." *Time,* February 9, 1942, pp. 19–20.
Eliot, Maj. George Fielding. "New South Pacific Chief Aggressive Commander." *Los Angeles Times,* October 26, 1942, p. 2.
"Elizabeth Honors Halsey, Native Son." *New York Times,* November 31, 1942, p. 3.
"Face to Face." *Time,* November 9, 1942, pp. 17–18.
"Facts." *Time,* January 17, 1944, pp. 11–12.
"Fall of Java." *Time,* March 16, 1942, p. 21.
"Fight Coming Up?" *Time,* January 18, 1943, pp. 26–29.
"Fine Fettle." *Time,* June 15, 1942, p. 59.
"First Jitters." *Time,* December 22, 1941, pp. 11–12.
"The First Six Months." *Time,* June 8, 1942, pp. 19–22.
"The Five Battles of the Solomons." *Time,* November 30, 1942, p. 30.
Foley, Rear Admiral Francis D., U.S. Navy (Ret.). "Every Good Ship Has A Heart." *Naval History,* Winter 1992, pp. 22–26.
Frank, Richard B. ". . . Nailed the Colors to the Mast." *Naval History,* Winter 1992, pp. 6–12.
Glines, C. V. "First Strike Against Japan." *World War II Presents 1942,* 2002, pp. 26–29, 93–95.
"Great Change." *Time,* December 22, 1941, pp. 10–11.
Hailey, Foster. "Toll of U.S. Raids Detailed by Navy." *New York Times,* February 14, 1942, p. 4.
———. "Halsey, New Commander in South Pacific, Known to Navy as Rough, Tough Fighter." *Los Angeles Times,* October 25, 1942, p. 6.
———. "Halsey Is Known as a Fighting Man." *New York Times,* October 25, 1942, p. 41.
———. "Halsey Defends Battleship's Role." *New York Times.* November 19, 1942, pp. 1, 8.
"Halsey and Eisenhower Clash Over Army-Navy Merger Plan." *Washington Times-Herald,* May 8, 1947.
"Halsey Finds War in Pacific 'Rolling.'" *New York Times,* May 31, 1944.
"Halsey Gets His Wish—He Leads Fighting Fleet." *Chicago Tribune,* June 18, 1944, p. 7.
"Halsey Insists He'll Have Unity." *Washington Post,* December 7, 1942, p. 2.
"Halsey Minimizes Foe." *New York Times,* January 7, 1943, p. 4.
"Halsey Named Full Admiral by Roosevelt." *Washington Post,* November 21, 1942, p. 2.
"Halsey Promoted to Admiral's Rank." *New York Times,* November 21, 1942, p. 3.
"Halsey Takes Command." *New York Times* Editorial, October 26, 1942, p. 14.
"Halsey Told *Hornet*'s Escort to Expect Death." *Los Angeles Times,* April 22, 1943, p. 5.
"Halsey's Daughter Will Christen Aircraft Carrier." *Washington Post,* January 15, 1943, p. B5.
"Halsey's Triumph." *Washington Post* Editorial, November 18, 1942, p. 12.
Halsey, Admiral William F. as told to Frank D. Morris. "A Plan for Japan." *Collier's,* April 28, 1945, pp. 18–19, 28.

Hayes, Richard L. "Scout Squadron 6 at Pearl Harbor." *WWII History,* November 2005, pp. 60–65.
Heaton, Colin D. "Jimmy Doolittle: The Man Behind the Legend." *World War II,* March 2003, pp. 30–42.
Heinl, Lt. Col. R. D. Jr. "We're Headed for Wake." *Marine Corps Gazette,* June 1946, pp. 35–38.
Heyn, Allen Clifton. "One Who Survived." *American Heritage,* June 1956, found at AmericanHeritage.com, pp. 1–9.
"Hit Hard, Hit Fast, Hit Often." *Time,* November 30, 1942, pp. 28–31.
Hurd, Charles. "Pacific Command Shake-Up Is Laid to Guadalcanal Crisis." *New York Times,* October 25, 1942, pp. 1, 41.
"The Incident Becomes A Crisis." *Time,* June 1, 1942, pp. 18–21.
"In the Coral Sea." *Time,* May 18, 1942, pp. 18–20.
"Intoxication Deplored." *Time,* December 22, 1941, p. 28.
"Jimmy Did It." *Time,* June 1, 1942, p. 17.
Johnson, David Alan. "Action Off Santa Cruz." *WWII History,* May 2009, pp. 30–39.
Jones, John E. "Stassen's Full Part in Rescues of Captives in Japan Revealed." *Pittsburgh Post-Gazette,* January 22, 1946.
Jones, Captain William, U.S. Navy (Ret.). "The *Helena* at Guadalcanal." *Naval History,* Winter 1992, pp. 30–31.
Kettering, Charles F. "There Is Only One Mistake: To Do Nothing." *Saturday Evening Post,* March 28, 1942, pp. 13, 48–52.
"Leader of Battle at Solomons Refuses to Fight by Rule Book." *Los Angeles Times,* November 17, 1942, p. 2.
"Let's Begin to Strike." *Time,* March 9, 1942, pp. 9–10.
"Lifeline Cut." *Time,* December 15, 1941, pp. 24–25.
Lindley, Ernest K. "Solomon Victory." *Washington Post,* November 23, 1942, p.13.
———. "Needs in the Pacific." *Washington Post,* March 19, 1943, p. 13.
Lippmann, Walter. "Today and Tomorrow." *Los Angeles Times,* April 16, 1943, p. A4.
Lodge, J. Norman. "Halsey Predicts Victory This Year." *New York Times,* January 3, 1943, p. 14.
"Maas Attack." *Time,* November 23, 1942, pp. 77–78.
"Macnimsey's Show." *Time,* July 12, 1943.
"Main Fleet Broken." *New York Times,* October 27, 1944.
Maurer, David A. "Naval Hero's Last Days at UV were Less Than Smooth Sailing." Charlottesville (VA) *Daily Progress,* March 14, 1999, in www.stat.virginia.edu/maurer1.html, pp. 1–3, accessed August 2, 2008.
McCain, Vice Admiral John Sidney. "So We Hit Them in the Belly." *Saturday Evening Post,* Part I: July 14, 1945, pp. 12–14, 40–44; Part II: July 21, 1945, pp. 22–23, 37–39.
McMurtry, Charles. "Jap Fleet Defeat Rated Heaviest Modern Blow." *Los Angeles Times,* November 30, 1942, p. 6.
McSherry, Patrick. "'Wallowin' in a Typhoon Before Morning." *Naval History,* October 2008, pp. 26–31.
"My Day in the South Pacific." *Time,* September 13, 1943.
"National Ordeal." *Time,* December 15, 1941, pp. 18–19.
Norris, John G. "Admiral Halsey, Unorthodox Fighter, Takes Over Navy's Toughest Command." *Washington Post,* November 1, 1942, p. B2.
———. "Battleship, 10 Other War Vessels Sunk." *Washington Post,* November 17, 1942, pp. 1–2.
———. "Victory Over Japs In Pacific May Be 'Turning Point'." *Washington Post,* November 22, 1942, pp. B1-B2.
———. "Pacific Counter Drives Begin to Show Results." *Washington Post,* January 3, 1943, p. B5.
———. "What Comes Next in the South Pacific?" *Washington Post,* January 10, 1943, p. B5.
———. "Guadalcanal Seen as Base of New Push." *Washington Post,* February 11, 1943, pp. 1, 6.
———. "Stage Set, Pledge Made for Action in Pacific." *Washington Post,* February 14, 1943, pp. B1, B4.
"Only One Answer?" *Time,* November 2, 1942, p. 19.
"Patch of Destiny." *Time,* November 2, 1942, pp. 28–32.

Pearson, Drew. "The Washington Merry-Go-Round." *Washington Post,* November 6, 1942, p. 12.
———. "The Washington Merry-Go-Round." *Washington Post,* December 16, 1942, p. 16.
Pratt, Fletcher. "Americans in Battle—No. 3: Campaign in the Coral Sea." *Harper's* Magazine, March 1943, pp. 356–368.
———. "Nimitz and His Admirals." *Harper's,* February 1945, pp. 209–217.
———. "Spruance: Picture of the Admiral." *Harper's,* August 1946, pp. 144–157.
"The Road to Rabaul." *Time,* November 15, 1943, pp. 27–28.
"3 Separate U.S. Fleets Busy in Pacific." *Chicago Tribune,* October 26, 1944, p. 3.
"Safety Razor." *Time,* November 3, 1941, p. 23.
Schubert, Paul. "Pacific Plans." *Washington Post,* February 17, 1943, p. 10.
"Seamen at Work." *Time,* April 6, 1942, p. 25.
Shinnick, William. "Casey Sees Midway Battle as Turning Point of War." *Chicago Tribune,* November 29, 1942, p. H24.
Slonim, Captain Gilven M. "A Flagship View of Command Decision." *U.S. Naval Institute Proceedings,* April 1958, pp. 80–89.
Smith, Harold. "Halsey—Hero of the Seas." *Chicago Tribune,* July 23, 1944, pp. F1, F4.
Sprague, Rear Adm. C.A.F., as told to Lt. (jg) Philip H. Gustafson. "The Japs Had Us on the Ropes." *American Magazine,* April 1945.
"Stark Honors Hero of Dive-Bomb Attack." *New York Times,* February 23, 1942, p. 4.
"Strongest Jap Attempt Frustrated, Nimitz Says." *Washington Post,* November 17, 1942, p. 2.
"Sub Rescues Missionaries." *Los Angeles Times,* January 6, 1943, pp. 1, 6.
Sullivan, Mark. "Public Optimism." *Washington Post,* January 11, 1943, p. 6.
"That Heavy Rumbling." *Time,* January 11, 1943, p. 28.
"The Way to Win A War." *Time,* February 23, 1942, p. 22.
Thomas, Evan. "Understanding Kurita's 'Mysterious Retreat,'" *Naval History,* October 2004, pp. 22–26.
Tillman, Barrett. "Into the Rising Sun: The Doolittle Raid." *Naval Institute Proceedings,* April 2007, pp. 60–65.
———. "Was Halsey Out of His Depth?" *WWII History,* July/August 2007, pp. 54–59.
"Time of Hirohito Short, Says Halsey." *Los Angeles Times,* January 3, 1943, p. 1.
"Tokyo Loss Heavy." *New York Times,* February 13, 1942, pp. 1, 8.
"Toward a Jap Defeat?" *Time,* February 28, 1944, p. 25.
"Tragedy at Honolulu." *Time,* December 15, 1941, pp. 19–23.
"Travelers From Guadalcanal." *Time,* February 15, 1943, p. 86.
Tregaskis, Richard. "Halsey Sees 'Absolute Defeat' For Axis Forces This Year." *Washington Post,* January 3, 1943, pp. 1–2.
Trumbull, Robert. "Nimitz Confident After Pacific Trip." *New York Times* October 15, 1942, p. 6.
Trussell, C. P. "U.S. Pacific Fleet Batters Japanese Bases in Marshall and Gilbert Isles." *New York Times,* February 2, 1942, pp. 1, 3.
"United States." *New York Times,* February 2, 1942, p. 2.
"United States." *New York Times,* February 13, 1942, p. 2.
"United States." *New York Times,* February 14, 1942, p. 2.
"Victory in 194?" *Time,* August 2, 1943.
"Victory off Guadalcanal." *Time,* November 23, 1942, p. 28.
"Wanted . . . ." *Time,* April 17, 1944, p. 66.
"War's End." *Time,* August 16, 1943.
Webb, Thompson, Jr. "Battling the Pacific's Most Deadly Force." *Naval History,* October 2008, pp. 16–25.
"What the People Said." *Time,* December 15, 1941, pp. 17–18.
"What Then?" *Time,* March 9, 1942, pp. 16–17.
"Where Is the Fleet?" *Time,* January 12, 1942, pp. 9–10.
"World's Greatest." *Time,* October 18, 1943, p. 36.
"Worst Week." *Time,* February 23, 1942, p. 13.
Wukovits, John F. "Pearl Harbor Payback." *WWII History,* July 2002, pp. 34–43.

Wylie, Rear Admiral J. C., U.S. Navy (Ret.) "Captain Hoover: Right or Wrong?" *Naval History*, Winter 1992, pp. 28–29.

Time magazine has posted its past issues in an archive found at time.com/time. I used the following articles from this web site:

"A Horse on Halsey," September 3, 1945, p. 1.

"Bull," August 24, 1959, pp. 1–2.

"Closer to the Goal," February 5, 1945, p. 1.

"The Dirty Tricksters," November 20, 1944, pp. 1–2.

"Family Circles," April 30, 1945, pp. 1–4.

"The General and the Admiral," November 10, 1947, pp. 1–3.

"Halsey in the Empire," October 23. 1944, pp. 1–3.

"Insult & Injury," July 30, 1945, pp. 1–3.

"Merger: Religious Matter," December 17, 1945, p. 1.

"Mufti & Money," August 12, 1946, p. 1.

"People," February 26, 1945, pp. 1–4.

"Plug," October 22, 1945, pp. 1–2.

"Story of Victory," November 27, 1944, pp. 1–3.

"They Call Him Bull," September 10, 1945, p. 1.

"Two Teams, One Goal," June 11, 1945, pp. 1–2.

"The Uncovered Way," January 22, 1945, pp. 1–2.

"We Will Go Anywhere . . ." September 9, 1946, pp. 1–2.

INDEX